MEDIA PSYCHOLOGY

This book examines media psychology as a field of study and provides a fundamental understanding of its emergence and application. It covers various key themes such as consumer behavior, mass media and advertising, media and culture, media messages and their effects on individual and group behavior in the Indian context. It highlights the role of media psychology with reference to citizenship and pedagogy and studies the emerging concept of digital altruism. The author also discusses various research methods used in this field that help to objectively evaluate the impact of mass media messages on people and people's effect on the functioning of mass media.

This comprehensive book will be useful to students and researchers of psychology, media psychology, mass-communication, consumer behavior, digital marketing, corporate communication, and media studies.

Navin Kumar is Associate Professor in Psychology at Delhi University, India, with more than two decades of teaching experience. He is the author of *Criminal Psychology*, published in 2015. He is also the coordinator of the UGC e-P.G Pathshala project on the subject of criminal psychology. He is the executive editor of *Academia*, an international multidisciplinary bi-annual journal in social sciences, humanities and languages, and the joint secretary of the India Association of Positive Psychology. He is a member of the Board of Research Studies at Jind University, Haryana, and Amity University, India, and a member of the M.Phil. Committee IBHASH, Dilshad Garden, Delhi. He has supervised 16 PhD scholars as guide and co-guide from Delhi University, Amity University and Jamia Millia Islamia. He has published over 20 research papers in national and international journals and has also conducted counseling and training workshops for NTPC, Delhi Police, CRPF, Indian Woods Science Technology Institute, Indira Gandhi National Forest Academy and National Law University Delhi on wide-ranging topics. He also presented a research paper at ICAP, Paris. He has completed a major research project with ICSSR, UGC and an Innovative Research Project with the University of Delhi. His views are broadcast on national television at regular intervals.

MEDIA PSYCHOLOGY

Exploration and Application

Navin Kumar

LONDON AND NEW YORK

First published 2021
by Routledge
2 Park Square, Milton Park, Abingdon, Oxon OX14 4RN

and by Routledge
52 Vanderbilt Avenue, New York, NY 10017

Routledge is an imprint of the Taylor & Francis Group, an informa business

British Library Cataloguing-in-Publication Data
A catalogue record for this book is available from the British Library

Library of Congress Cataloging-in-Publication Data
A catalog record has been requested for this book

ISBN: 978-0-367-54233-7 (hbk)
ISBN: 978-0-367-67622-3 (pbk)
ISBN: 978-1-003-13205-9 (ebk)

Typeset in Bembo
by SPi Global, India

CONTENTS

FIGURES

PREFACE

One's destination is never a place, but a new way of seeing things. The struggle to be true to oneself is one of the most demanding characteristics of one's life in contemporary times. This project of media psychology was a result of care of the self in order to forge a realistic relationship to the emergent challenges of human behavior. This is an attempt of self-discovery self-expression of my interest in the field of media psychology.

My interactions with society made me realize that a major part of myself and others is influenced by media–mediated symbols and messages. I found to my surprise not a single book available on this title in India. I focused my attention on this field not to earn the distinction of being first; rather, it is felt necessary by every person in society. When they say my children are getting distracted due to over-indulgence in social media, students are not paying due attention to social and emotional aspects. In some places even riots were fueled due to social media and so forth. I certainly realized this urgent necessity during my close interaction with the best minds of print and electronic media. Initially I decided to explore this field during my numerous discussions on television channels, on topics related to psychological importance, and simultaneously guiding students towards their PhDs at Delhi University. Every time I see public opinion on topics of relevance mediated by media, a perceptible difference on the ground can be easily noticed. I also delivered dozens of keynote speeches in various institutions of eminence that people participating in it appreciated, which added to my motivation to come out with a textbook on media psychology. The mainstream academics of psychologists in India somehow could not pay much attention to it, though in recent years many universities and colleges have come up with papers on media psychology, and it is recognized as an established field in the discipline of psychology in the Indian context. At a reasonable standard, I presented my paper at the NAOP Conference, 2010, on the topic "Effects of Mass Media" in Bangalore. Subsequently, I did a major innovative research project as principal investigator on the topic of growing under the shadow of mass media in explorations into family lives and psycho–social well-being. I was chair of the symposium of NAOP in Bangalore in December 2012. My ten students—Durgesh Ojha, Mayank, Sanchita Johri, Ajay, Nikita Jain, Charvi Sharma, Prashansha, Kanchan, "Megha" and Sonali—presented their views at this symposium, a kind of first by students at the undergraduate level. On 13 April 2013, I organized a national seminar on "Media-mediated Realities and its Impact on Psycho-social Well-being" as organizing secretary. This seminar witnessed the presence of a galaxy of luminaries from various fields. The notable presence in this seminar included Sh. Tripurari Sharan (Direct-General DoorDarshan), Surendra Kumar (Joint Secretary Govt. of India) and Prof. Anand Prakash (Delhi University). This seminar was addressed by experienced persons as well.

Later students Sunil and Ravi Bhushan were awarded their PhD degrees in media psychology under my supervision from Delhi University. I also delivered talks at Indira Gandhi National Forest Academy in June 2012, and IWST Bangalore and Periyar Talks organized by the Government of Kerala in 2019. These talks, conferences, workshops and researches in the field of media psychology provided me the motivation and urge to come out with my own understanding of this field in the form of a textbook. Many of my lectures related to mass media at various institutions, some of them available on public domain. YouTube and Facebook allowed me the opportunity to discover new areas of media influence and on occasions like at S.P.M. College, Ramanujan College, my own college, Meerut University, I tried to uncover a diverse domain of mass media.

This decadal journey of mine in the field of mass media allowed me to grasp the why and how of its functioning. It is composed of series of interconnected experiences of people's interaction pattern with or without media.

Mass media and entertainment amuses people and influence them to feel things, forming an imagination of what they love and desire, who they want to be and how they would need to act. In fact people's pattern of life is largely governed by the messages of mass media.

In contemporary society, mass media plays a major role in shaping our perception, cognition and the worldview. People are influenced by media both negatively and positively with enormous malleability of mind and dynamically changing life circumstances. Media psychology deals with all forms of communication and its impact on human behavior. Media influence has an effect on micro and macro aspects of human behavior, which has increased drastically over the years and will continue to do so with an ever-changing field of mass media.

In large part, contemporary man's self-conscious view of himself rests upon the internalization of worldview through the communicative grammar of mass media. The public sphere of reason emerges through communicative exchanges between people and media messages. Our values, vocabularies of motive and styles of emotion are strongly guided by mass media-projected realities.

There are now many indigenous traditions which are losing relevance by the virtue of internalization of the standard and conformity constituted through media. Media creates dominant symbols and values in the society through influence and manipulation of the consent.

Production of scientific knowledge can't function in isolated and independent individual context but are enmeshed in a network of social-cultural relationships. The chapters in this textbook represent the state of the art knowledge about media psychology.

This book surveys a variety of perspectives for evaluating and assessing the realm of mass media and in its role in our daily lives. Mass media as a process of creating messages and transmitting it through a medium to the audience existed from pre-historic forms of art and writing and continued to evolve through print, radio, television, computers and internet, to name just a few.
Ever since the earliest civilizations came together, communication has been a staple element of society for different purposes.

Gutenberg's evolution of the printing press as a form of mass communication had lasting effects on society and culture. In an electronically saturated world like the one in which we live today there has been a great transformation the way we work, the way we get in touch with others, education, entertainment advertisement and culture as tools to reach wide audiences.

With the new forms of technology emerging rapidly, it is important to evaluate the corresponding changes in society and human behavior.

The first chapter on introduction to mass media offers readers an understanding of the field and a detailed analysis of mass media's growing importance in various sectors of life. This chapter also provides an unique description of early media psychology theories, early communication theories and contemporary media theories. This chapter reflects and encompasses some extremely critical insights for understanding unique aspects of Indian reality of mass media.

The second chapter on consumer behavior and psychology traces the trajectories of consumer behavior works and follows prominent concepts related to consumer culture and identity. Along with an emphasis on interactive and social media this, effort also attempts to unravel the implications of social media in our day-to-day life. The last section of this chapter is centered on critical concerns and issues in Indian context.

The third chapter on research methods provides a critical evaluation of research methods in mass media. The account offered in this chapter has deliberately captured the knowledge about qualitative and quantitative research methods. The complementarity of qualitative and quantitative methodologies in media and communication research has been suitably highlighted. At the concrete level of methodology, quantitative research instruments are considered to be more suitable, whereas qualitative approaches are a more desirable method to explore the singular occurrence of meaningful phenomena along with the full context. The research methods application suggests that choice of methods depends on which aspects of communication are to be examined and on the purpose of study. The 'how' of the study depends upon its what and why.

There is a growing appreciation of media's impact on society, for its potential plays a significant role in people's lives. There are diversity of views regarding its advantages and disadvantages. Technology's expansion has caused many good things, but it has also caused many problems in the society. Mass media is a powerful tool used to dictate our society in many ways, sometimes more often than we could imagine. In contemporary times, media and society are reciprocally influencing each other. In the fourth chapter, dominant paradigms of media sociology minutely describe the process of socialization carried out through media.

Media's effect on children deals with emotional aspects related to children as consumers. The trends related to media and family research indicate the changing dynamics of family relations. Media and youth subsection highlights various concepts, themes and researches reflecting significant developments in this field. It also addresses certain important questions pertaining to mass media and Indian society.

The fifth chapter reflects major conceptual models carefully crafted to articulate the relationship of media and culture. This chapter draws attention of its readers to the topics of mass society, mass culture and popular culture. A number of theoretical constructs related to entertainment media and its effects on audiences are well articulated. The differences in processing between narrative and rhetoric as well as persuasive influences are described in detail.

The sixth chapter deals with the psychological factors in advertising. The field of advertising has become extremely relevant for promotion of products and services. The rationale for use of emotions, desires, interests and dreams play a crucial role in advertising success. It also mentions the model for developing a successful advertisement program. Brand awareness concept and techniques related to developing positive attitude towards purchasing is adequately described.

The seventh chapter discusses the reinforcing ability of media messages to persuade and influence human behavior. Media message analysis from rhetorical and cultural perspective provides an understanding of decoding the meaning of media texts. The concepts of Saussure Ronald Barthes and other prominent thinkers related to media messages provide an in-depth understanding of the subject. The psychoanalytic perspective, represented by the theory of Sigmund Freud and its critical concepts of defense mechanism, is described in detail. Apparatus theory is a landmark concept which is also vividly described in this chapter, as is the concept of Male Gaze and Mulvey's theory of critical analysis of gendered conventions of cinema. Finally the queer perspective of media messages and Indian context is described with the help of examples.

The eighth chapter deals with the media effects on identity and interpersonal interaction. It further explores the media's effects on women and violence. Most of the relevant researchers and concepts have been included in this chapter. STEM identity concept and its implication for gender inequality through mass media is represented in a thoughtful way.

The ninth and final chapter of this book includes topics which are emergent and relevant in the present scenario. Media-mediated citizenship, media's role in pedagogy, meaning and myths of moving images and digital altruism are relevant from a contemporary point of view. The concept of alternative media representing the people's voice addresses empowering of citizen journalism. Digital altruism is also playing a crucial role in transforming the society to achieve prosocial objectives.

Digital pedagogy is a paradigm shift in the teaching-learning process which is well articulated in the Indian context.

This book attempts to provide a wide range of topics relevant and taught at various U.G. and P.G. students of media psychology, mass communication and advertisement students. This can also help professionals from various organizations gather understanding of media dynamics which is extremely relevant these days. This book can provide a meaningful insight to practicing journalists, who can apply these concepts to gain professional excellence. It can prove very useful for parents to understand the media behavior of their children. For a common citizen also, this book can provide an understanding as how to use media to their advantage.

Media psychology's unexplored realms have been anchored with the help of critical evaluation of its concept from an individual, social, cultural and contextual point of view. I am hopeful, of course, but regardless of my best efforts and academic insights, some possible issues will emerge only after its interaction with the enlightened readers and academia in general. My aim for this book is to provide a comprehensive understanding of contemporary condition of media psychology. My yearning for facts, meanings and search for coherence will be enriched through the valuable critical vocabularies of its readers.

ACKNOWLEDGEMENTS

I wish to express my deepest gratitude to a number of persons who contributed to the realization of the journey of this book.

I can't adequately acknowledge the long list of individuals who have contributed tremendous moral strength and persistence to complete this work. I would like to thank Prof. Girishwar Mishra, former Vice Chancellor Mahatma Gandhi International University, Wardha, for helping me at every stage of this work. I would like to express a profound sense of gratitude to Prof. Anand Prakash, Prof. Ritesh Singh, Prof. Purnima Singh, Prof. N.K. Chaddha, Prof. R.B Solanki (Vice Chancellor, Jind University), Prof. Shahnawaz, Prof. Sheema Alim, Dr. Samina, Dr. Arvind, Garima, Dr. Korsi, Dr. Parul, Dr. Shefali, Dr. Kanika, Dr. Vanita Sondhi, Dr. Sabeen, Dr. Baiju Gopal, Dr. Naved Iqbal and Dr. Roopali Sharma for the moral support and feedback whenever I needed them. My most special thanks to my valuable family and friends J.K Mishra, Ashok Kumar, Vivek Deep, Prof. Dharmendra and Somendra, for providing constant understanding and moral support during the course of this book.

I would also like to place on record my sincere thanks to Surendra Kumar, who is like an elder brother to me, and my friend Atulya Sharma for keeping me motivated while I was involved in my work.

I would like to express my deepest appreciation for my PhD students Nisha and Swati. Completion of this work would not have been possible without their support. I very much appreciate the unparalleled moral support from my college students, colleagues in the Department of Psychology and my PhD students from Delhi University and Amity University.

I gratefully acknowledge the assistance and insights from Lubna and Anvitaa for their valuable support throughout my work. I derived great pleasure while working with them, and words are insufficient to describe their ethical professionalism. Discussions with Sanjay K. Singh, Sanjeev Roy, Dr. Himanshu, N.K. Singh and Dr. Rajeev Verma have been illuminating and insightful.

I am indebted to my wife Swati for her love, prayers, caring and sacrifices for educating and preparing me to complete this work. Her encouragement when times get rough are much appreciated. I express my special thanks to my lifelines, son Kanishk and daughter Kriti, who always provide me emotive strength irrespective of circumstances. My other family members, especially my elder brother L.P. Singh and younger brother Manoj, provide me moral support in all my initiatives.

Finally, I dedicate this work to my parents, the source of my eternal strength in life.

1

INTRODUCTION TO MEDIA PSYCHOLOGY

Learning objectives

After reading this chapter, you will be able to understand:

- The nature and scope of media psychology
- The media in attitude and behavior of the people
- The relationship between psychology and communication
- The role of media on family and body image
- The role of media on social interaction
- Early and contemporary media theories
- The Indian perspective of media psychology

1.1 Defining the field of media psychology

Despite the pervasive presence of media in everyday life, the study of mass media has not received due recognition in mainstream psychology. How our behavior is being shaped by the various communication gadgets such as computers, mobile phones, television, print media and radio is critical to our patterns of behavior and interaction. Media is playing a key role in our lives influencing attitudes, work, entertainment, culture, health-care, education, personal relationships and other significant activities of our life. Indeed, nothing worth doing is untouched by the lens of mass media. Contemporary life is unseparated from the influence of media. All our activities are affected directly or indirectly by the various forms of mass media. Media are vehicles of information and communication and a close link exists between communication and behavior. Media psychology is a new interdisciplinary area of knowledge combining studies in the field of psy chology, sociology, mass communication, information technology and linguistic. It describes and explains human behavior conditioned by individual and group communication.

Russian researcher ZhiZhina (2010) views media psychology as a subject area related to phenomenology and law, and as a mechanism of regulation and development of a personality in the media world. In general, the field focuses on the media environment and its influence on individuals, groups, psychological health and change in the psychic conditions of people at large. It also studies the perceptual, emotional and motivational components of media texts which carry the importance of creating mass opinion and transformation of the worldview.

Media psychology attempts to understand the influence of media texts in forming the image of people and organizations. People as media consumers are influenced by conscious and unconscious motivations, needs and emotions. Media psychology tends to explore the relationship and psychological pattern of human behavior in a multicultural global media space. Media psychology is not limited to mass media content; it is extended to all forms of mediated communication and its impact on human behavior. Thus, it encompasses the process of perception, cognition and attention.

Media psychology may be defined as a field dealing with all forms of mediated communication and its effect on human behavior. Mass media is a congregation of technologies that helps in the process of communication from a source to receiver. In general, there are five main types of mass media sources, i.e. newspaper, radio, magazine, internet and television which have received attention. The field of media studies has grown in many dimensions that deal with the content, concepts and effects of various media including mass media.

1.2 Presence of media in everyday life

Whenever we are planning for important activities related to our needs, media visibility plays a crucial role in our decision-making. So many permutations and combinations of actions are possible with the life navigated through the lens of mass media and without.

What careers we choose is not always a product of our attitude to perform best in a particular field, but the amount of publicity, conformity and status expectations compel a person to choose a career contrary to the personality of that person. It is no wonder that some of the most talented people had to settle for a career which was the antithesis of their potential and thus could not experience the optimum growth of their personality. A great deal of unhappiness is due to the internalization of the values that are represented through the lens of mass media. The fear of maintaining synchronicity with the public opinion created by mass media acquires a significant place in the minds of people and isolation from public images and ideas becomes a source of pain caused by the burden of maintaining mental independence from the dominant surroundings. To a large majority of the people, the surroundings in which they find themselves are sympathetic and they adapt to the existing belief and customs. Not only is it true in the choice of career, but media-related representations also pervade our opinions about deciding who or what is a good teacher, good student, good university, good business, good political ideology, good moral characteristics and so on.

There is a great deal of homogenization, and conformity of doing things in our lives, due to images created by media domination. The definition of a good life may have thousands of versions expressed by individual discretion, and all may be relevant. The media may prescribe certain things like a good house in the city, a big car, studying in English medium school, having lots of IT gadgets at home and so on. This danger of uniformity imposed upon us, presented as an only possible solution or prescribed mode of social existence, is a faulty notion, as a man without a car can also lead a happy life and a person with a small house in a small town with a big library or a big farm can also be happier. In modern times of swiftness of locomotion and communication, people are less connected and less dependent upon their geographical neighbors and family members. People of science are more valued in the intellectual community as compared to those pursuing professions of the arts, film, literary activities and agriculture. This happens because the images of scientists are considered more progressive and powerful, which has created this brand in the minds of the people through various forms of communication and the modernist ethos of society. The agricultural laborers and peasants who cultivate land are less valued though they plow, they sow and they reap, which is very useful for them as well as for the rest of the society. But today it is very rare in a country like India to find parents who want their children to become agriculturists. Whereas mechanical work in an IT company, even when the large amount of work is uninteresting, repeating the same mechanical operation with minimum variation and human imitative, is considered a more sophisticated and valued profession to pursue. Rural youth now desire to find work in towns in the atmosphere of factories and urban pollution, leaving the solitude and serenity of rural habitats relatively free from pollution.

Promoting a brand through a media vehicle in the society at large gives it a necessity character by the repeated promotion in the public spaces, and repeated exposure of brand finds its place in the minds of the people.

1.2.1 Influence of media in attitude and behavior

Consumer's attitudes and perceptions are influenced directly and indirectly placing products in the advertisements in a deceptive manner. It is also true that consumers' views regarding the acceptability of advertising differ across different product categories.

The persuasiveness of media messages are scientifically planned and programmed for different age groups and ethnic identities. The product's placements are organized in such a manner that children when watching these messages get influenced by the persuasive intent of the messages.

Several studies by media researchers have found a strong linkage between the product placement through TV advertisements and children's brand preferences. For example, children playing video games or watching television may develop a liking for a certain food item.

Braun-LaTour and Zaltman (2006) put forward a "memory integration paradigm" that affirms that existing attitudes and values, prior knowledge, relevance, semantics and the advertising context all play a role when advertising messages are processed by the adults. The persuasiveness of media messages are one of the few studies to compare children's implicit versus explicit memory for product placement using a film clip showed a significant increase in children's likelihood of selecting Pepsi over Coca-Cola when given a choice (Auty & Lewis, 2004). With the advent of interactive media, children spend more time playing with internet-related games on mobile phones as compared to watching television. Nowadays the focus of market strategies has shifted from television to in-game product placement allowing interactivity as a key factor.

The stories that television offers are often interesting and amusing. They stir a variety of emotions in the viewers. Whatever programs and serials, even fictional ones, that we do watch on television on a regular basis have enduring effects on our memory and behavior. Most of the fictional representations on television present distorted reality than the real-life situation. It is no surprise that through internalization TV related facts are imitated by the people who watch television for a significant period. Though the degree of effect also varies from person to person depending upon activities outside the home, socio-cultural context and family environment. But it is a largely accepted fact that long hours of TV viewing will have an impact on the judgments related to the topics that television-related exemplars provide. It is advisable to differentiate between light viewing and heavy viewing patterns while estimating the effects of TV. Story characteristics play an important role in transportation through narratives. One of the postulates of the transportation imagery model (Green & Brock, 2002) holds that the medium and context in which a narrative is delivered can affect that narrative's capacity to transport, particularly since a given medium can limit imaginative participation. Narratives have been especially good in the area of health research publicity by stimulating self-relevant emotions. Morgan, Movius and Cody (2009) found that network television media dramas such as *House* and *Grey's Anatomy* were effective at influencing viewers' knowledge of and intentions towards personal organ donation, a highly emotional topic. It is important to note that narrative as a medium influences attitude through the emotional involvement of viewers. Whenever people are glued to TV sets watching some advertisements, the viewers are invited to imagine a fictional world that undermines critical thought about the product and enhances positive feelings about it.

Phillips and McQuarrie (2010) label this imaginative involvement of viewers as images grotesque (directly opposed to simple, pleasant, mundane or cheerful) and propose that part of their effectiveness lies in their transporting nature. The entertainment education model of fictional narratives can be as effective as factual ones in changing beliefs on several occasions. Messages from purely fictional worlds can effect real attitudes and actions. Of course, personality factors and level of awareness also play a crucial role in the degree of differences to which an individual is persuaded by the themes in a specific narrative.

FIGURE 1.1 Keeping strong with family bonds.
Source: Retrieved 21 June 2020 from https://www.dvidshub.net/image/3045833/keeping-strong-with-family-bonds

1.2.2 Media and family

The relationship between mass media and family functioning has acquired complex dimensions in recent times. Family health, family well-being and family life satisfaction depend upon leisure-time interaction of the members in a family, a large portion of which is being consumed by media. To achieve ideal family well-being, different needs of a family such as affective involvement, roles and responsibilities, problem-solving and communication need to be addressed. The interpersonal and intrapersonal needs of children and other generations are different, and they require the sharing of emotional aspects to resolve them. Family communication climate may affect the formation of attitudes and values requisite for social behavior and individual self-confidence.

Media images pervade our perception of young children who are more impressionable in getting social scripts from mass media. They may get distorted images of reality. Nowadays if one wants to understand family dynamics, the media interaction pattern should be taken into mindful consideration.

1.2.3 Media and body image

Instagram is currently a very popular social network site, especially among teenagers. It allows its users to share photos and videos with others. Starting up in 2010, Instagram attracted more than one billion users by June 2018, and people up to the age of 34 years comprise nearly 70 percent of the total users (Instagram, 2018). Even though Instagram is the most significant sharing application on the internet, it has received very little academic attention.

It is easily possible for the user to manipulate images to a perfect picture mode which creates negative influences among users. Research has indicated that both boys and girls (adolescents and adults) compare the images with their peers. This tendency for social comparison has cognitive and behavioral consequences. When people perceive others to be more similar to themselves, identification and related cognitive and behavioral consequences are more likely to occur owing to the interaction of social media platforms. There is a growing tendency that the users of the social media platform often manipulate their appearances in the pictures they post online. Adolescent girls are often found to be particularly vulnerable to being influenced by their media images due to psycho-social characteristics of the developmental stage.

Earlier research mainly focuses on thin-ideal body images among young girls and women with the influences of advertisements. The media models might cause a "thinness fantasy" (Myers & Biocca, 1992) by inspiring women for whom thinness is self-relevant. This trend among adolescents and young girls is growing at a fast pace in India and all over the world due to the ease of transportation of images at the global level. It is also noticeable across families that children are spending much of their time viewing and manipulating Instagram images for long durations every day. As Steele has stated, "whereas 50 years ago a teen's family, friends, school, and the church probably were the primary influences on his or her attitude, values and belief about sexuality, today teens have access to a fifth powerful influence the ubiquitous mass media" (Steele, 1999, p. 135). These statistics indicate an increase in "the depiction of sexual content in family hour programming – constantly over the last 20 years – up 118 percent since 1986 and 270 percent since 1976" (Kunkel et al., 1996).

Regarding sex on TV, researchers Kunkel, Eyal, Finnerty, Biely and Donnerstein (2005) reported that there are "correlations between watching television programming high in sexual content and the early initiation of sexual intercourse by adolescents". Heavier viewers of sexual television content had increased perception of the frequency with which sexual behavior occurs in the real world. Adolescents who viewed television dramas laden with sexual content tended to rate description of casual sexual encounters less negatively than teens who had not viewed any sexual content.

A longitudinal panel study with a nationally representative sample demonstrated a causal relationship between adolescent exposure to sexual talks and behavior on television and the acceleration of sexual activity including intercourse (Kunkel et al., 2005).

These studies and facts indicate a paradigm shift in the behavior of individuals, families and society and the resulting impact on the psycho-social and moral fabric of the society. The institution of marriage is at a crossroads, with an increasing rate of divorce and the essential bond of trust and commitment gradually decreasing. Millions of children are becoming innocent victims of divorce, which is also indirectly related to media influence.

Manning (2005) has referred to the findings of Schneider's study, commenting that "A majority of internet users in the United States are married males, more than half of Americans (172 Million) use the internet and 20–23 percent of users go online for sexual purposes".

1.2.4 Media's role in social interaction

A growing number of young children use a variety of media devices and applications at home (Jones & Park, 2015) and at an increasingly younger age. The traditional situation of one television per family accessible at a fixed location at home with limited interactivity and predefined content has changed and we are now increasingly witnessing a situation in which family has access to several media devices. The dynamics of parental mediation has become more challenging in the times of contemporary media evolution. The parental mediation of digital media is a dynamic and complex process that is co-constructed by the parents and the children in which both the users influence each other's media usage patterns.

A conflict of values takes place among the children and parents while using digital media poses a paradoxical situation to the intrafamily interaction. The changing media landscape affects children's and parent's leisure time as well as their social interaction patterns.

There is a growing erosion of actual social responsibilities with the rapid growth of the internet and mobile communication technology. In twenty-first-century global cities, unprecedented opportunities for access to information and communication through mobile communication technologies poses new neurological, psychological, behavioral and health burdens on people (Carr, 2011; Gergen, 2000; Klingberg, 2008; Misra & Stokols, 2012; Turkle, 2012). As a consequence, information and communication technologies have created a new category of sensory overload (Misra & Stokols, 2012).

In contrast to place-based sources of sensory stimulation, cyber-based overload originates from information and communication transactions from a variety of sources such as mobile phones, YouTube, laptops, tablets and other forms of networked technologies. Cognitive overload resulting from the division of attention demanded by information and communication technologies effects individuals' working memory, increasing distraction and making it difficult for them to distinguish between relevant and irrelevant information. Experiments and field studies on the impact of multitasking on cognitive abilities have found that the divided attention limits information acquisition (Rockwell & Singleton, 2007) and leads to poorer retention and learning (Hembrooke & Gay, 2003; Poldrack & Foerde, 2008).

Field studies in organizational environments have revealed the fragmentation of knowledge workers' work routine caused by the emergence of information and communication technologies. People routinely check for the new email

FIGURE 1.2 Social media interaction.
Source: Shankbone, D. (2014). Flickr. https://www.flickr.com/photos/shankbone/12263334196

and messages every 5–10 minutes and frequently enough which affects their concentration.

1.2.5 Media's dangers to human life

People use mobile phones while driving, resulting into accidents, and teenagers risk lives by clicking "selfies" from dangerous spots. Such incidents are regularly reported by the media.

The pervasive use of social media has sparked concerns about the effects of these websites have on users' mental health (e.g. O'Keeffe & Clarke-Pearson, 2011; Pantic, 2014). The American Academy of Pediatrics voiced particular worries (O'Keeffe & Clarke-Pearson, 2011), warning that the use of social media can lead to depressive symptoms. A growing body of research studying social media from a social comparison perspective suggests that browsing other positive posts has negative effects on mood and happiness with the feeling that others have a better life. However, some researchers indicate positive emotional responses among viewers. It is also important to understand that there are individual differences in how messages are processed and the varying effects on the viewers. Other mediating factors such as family environment and socio-cultural context do affect the pattern of media messages on viewers.

With the rapid pace of urbanization and technological development over the past few decades, people are not sufficiently engaged in pro-environmental actions owing to detachment from the natural world. The degree to which people feel connected to nature tends to be a robust predictor of happiness (e.g. Zelenski & Nisbet, 2014) and engagement in pro-environmental behavior (e.g. Dutcher et al., 2007; Nisbet et al., 2009). Digital altruism is a concept where prosocial behavior can be enhanced with the effective use of technology.

1.3 Psychology of entertainment media

There is a strong practice of incorporating a product or service in the process of media consumption by viewers and doing promotional activity by various organizations. The product or service is integrated in such a way that it gets incorporated into the story, and the mere presence of the product in a story generates promotional values for the product. The sponsors of the product adopt a disguised method to advertise the products through media stories. Marketers and advertisers focus on perceived goals of branding to persuade consumers' attitude and their products. When consumers realize communication as a persuasion attempt, their attitude acquires a critical component while making opinions but in the situations when products are integrated into the media stories, it has a larger impact on consumer's attitudes.

The role of advertising is to inform and persuade, but how product integration is woven into movies, television shows or other social media platforms increases its impact on consumers. Russell (1998) characterized product integration in a three-dimensional framework consisting of purely visual, auditory or verbal and the third one is the degree to which integration is connected with the plot of the story.

As Baker (1999) explained, effective classical conditioning is a matter of pairing unconscious stimulus (e.g. beautiful scene) with the conditioned stimulus (e.g. brand of product) such that the good feelings associated with the scene are transferred to the brand. And as McCarty (2004) has observed "a good product placement may be one that fits with the story in such a way as to make us forget that it is there to persuade us and this idea of fit product placement is critical and relates to the notion of seamlessness" (pp. 50–1).

It is no wonder that the fictional stories media tells its consumers can be arousing, can be heartrending, and may elicit strong emotions. Every piece of information that is attended and processed by consumers has the potential to be reflected in our behavior moderated by the factors of motivation and ability.

The images are more than an idea; it is a vortex or cluster of fused ideas. It is a very common practice these days to use images as a propaganda technique. More recently, research has revealed that watching one's own avatar (a digital twin) exercise increases the odds that a person will exercise in real life (Fox & Bailenson, 2009). This imitation of one's digital doppelganger is known as the Proteus effect.

The stereotyped characterization of women in the media often degrades them and portrays them as secondary to men. Research has shown that exposure to visual imagery and the associated stereotype in that imagery automatically activates consistent behavior (Chartrand & Bargh, 1999).

Underrepresentation and negative representation of women leads to women's marginalization. Socio-cultural norms for ideal and appropriate representation highlight greater importance to physical appearances. The majority of female images portrayed as standard and idealized are tall, thin and young. This appearance contingent self-worth leads to body dissatisfaction and increases undue concern for others' perceptions. A huge market of cosmetics and physical fitness programs focus on fashion, weight loss and cosmetic surgery to acquire those idealized images.

1.4 Media and values

For both Durkheim and Weber, values were crucial for explaining changes at social and personal levels. There are multiple values with varying degrees of importance in a given society. The values carry a varying level of importance in a given society. There are some values that hold universal importance, such as achievement, power, benevolence, altruism and honesty. Actions in pursuit of values have practical, psychological and social consequences. With the constant increase in media exposure among teens and the older generation, conflicts between values have also widened.

An intergenerational preference pattern has also emerged among varied users of different age groups. The continuous increase in media exposure of the teens has resulted into intergenerational conflicts of values. However, benevolence values promoting co-cooperativeness and supportive relations do not get adequate reinforcement due to the lack of face-to-face relations and the deceptive mode of interaction through social media. Intrinsically motivated values receive limited attention, and extrinsically motivated values get more attention on the social media platform owing to advertisements on mass media platforms.

The availability of internet-related platforms present people with a bigger world. Teenagers now update their stories on a regular basis, and it has become an utterly essential part of daily social life. Social network sites like Facebook, Twitter and Instagram are the cool places for teenagers. Teens are looking for a place of their own to make sense of the world beyond their family and society of elder persons. The networked lives of teen and contemporary youth are becoming normative. Networked publics formed through social media sites serve a similar function as playgrounds, clubs or parks served for the previous generation of teenagers.

The design and architecture of the environment evaluate certain types of interaction to occur, and these properties or characteristics of the environment are known as affordances. The networked public spaces are different from traditional physical public places. There are certain striking characteristics of networked public spaces which include longevity, visibility and spreadability. In networked public spaces, visibility of any shared content is too large, and interactions are often public by default, private through effort. Media messages can be easily spread, forwarded to a large section of people following certain techniques. Someone who misbehaved with an official on an airplane may go viral and acquire a lifelong image of that person from what may be a temporary emotional outburst of that person. Sometimes something is said in a particular context and the message highlighted removes the context, which can lead to faulty interpretations. The person might get branded by a particular description highlighted on social media. This description may be the completely untrue version of the values that the person holds for his life. Too much dependence on technology-driven communication has its own limitations, and a balanced view will lead us to analyze the dynamics of social media interaction properly.

1.5 Social media, self-presentation and privacy debate

Social media is a moving landscape that has affected the lives and practices of many people and will continue to play a significant role in shaping diverse aspects of society. Contemporary youth are growing up in a cultural milieu in which the majority of life decisions are directed by interaction on social media. It also varies from the interaction pattern of the individual.

Self-presentation on social media is also fabricated in terms of name, location, age and income, etc. As Erving Goffman has noted, the social rituals in self-presentation involve "Impression Management". He argued that the impressions we make on others are a product of what is given and what is given off. People decide what to share and what not to share on the basis of understanding of social situations and the context. Impression management online and offline operates as a social process.

The rise of the internet and social media has led to a new debate over privacy and public sharing among different generations of people about morality. Parents, teachers and religious preachers frequently keep on highlighting the moral dangers to society and a generalized tag of immodesty is attached to the people of the younger generation. This does not mean that the teens of today don't care for privacy, but it is a matter apart that they don't care much about political correctness and avoid paternalistic attitudes. Taking a structuralist view, Westin (1967) has defined privacy as the claim of individuals, groups or institutions to determine for themselves when, how and to what extent information is communicated to others. This privacy is the voluntary and temporal withdrawal of a person from the general society.

Many parents believe that being a good parent means being all-knowing about their children is their right, which amounts to surveillance, and this habit of parents is also equated with responsibility. This may lead to a situation termed as parental noise. Many teens also have an issue with their Facebook account password as they don't want to share it with their parents. The issue of trust comes into play, affecting the relationship between parents and the children. Entertainment, information and society functions of teens are fulfilled through media platforms, which the elders often consider to be an addiction – though in some cases overdependence on social media platforms hardly affects the performance of the children. Ivan Goldberg (1995) coined the term "internet addiction disorder". There is a wide gap in the perception and perspectives that exist between teens and parents of what society should look like. The real contextual issue of the safety of a girl child is rarely discussed. The dangers of walking alone in a town or going alone in the parks have also contributed to children's engagement to the networked public created through social media.

1.6 Media psychology theories

1.6.1 Marshal McLuhan's theory

McLuhan's (1911–1980) famous book *In Understanding Media: The Extension of Man* described the terms "hot" and "cool" medium to describe print and electronic media respectively. Hot media stimulates people to perform or at the very least desire cathartic acts in the future, such as political unrest. Cool media of electronic medium stimulate people to the simultaneity of here and now in a constant succession of immediate occurrences. McLuhan coined the famous phrase "The medium is the message", arguing that the nature of a medium shaped and controlled human action. He also used the massage analogy, suggesting modern audiences enjoy media as soothing, enjoyable and relaxing, but in reality such pleasurable experiences by its deceptive nature perpetuates an age of anxiety.

1.6.2 Excitation transfer theory (Dolf Zillmann)

Zillmann (2006) stated "Residual excitation from essentially any excited emotional reaction is capable of intensifying any other exciting emotional reaction". The degree of intensification depends on the magnitude of residues prevailing at the time.

Zillmann (1971) stated that "communication produced excitation may serve to intensify or "energize" post-exposure emotional states". Excitation transfer theory is based on the assumption of ambiguity of excitation responses which are differentiated only by what emotions the brain assigns to them.

1.6.3 Uses and gratification theory

The concept of gratification through media usage was proposed by Lazarsfeld and Stanton (1949).

Herzog (1944) has drawn attention to quick programs and gratification derived from listening to soap operas. Suchman (1942) focused on the motives for getting interested in serious music on the radio. Wolf and Fisk (1949) focused on the development of children's interest in comics.

Extending a bifunctional view of the audience, the media or media content is usually viewed dichotomously as predominantly fantasist–escapist or informational educational in significance.

Lasswell (1948) had proposed a four-functional interpretation of media serving the functions of surveillance, correlation, entertainment and cultural transmission for individuals and society as a whole.

Katz, Gurevitch and Haas (1973) proposed that mass communication is used by individuals to connect themselves via instrumental, attentive or integrating relations with different kinds of others (self, family, friends, nation, etc.).

McQuail, Blumler and Brown (1972) put forward a typology consisting of the following: diversion (including escape from the constraints of routine and the burdens of problems and emotional release), personal relationships (including substitute companionship as well as social utility), personal identity including personal reference, reality exploration, value reinforcement and surveillance.

All of these theoretical perspectives related to media use and gratification indicates gratification from the media content, exposure and social contexts. Each mode of media transmission renders some kind of satisfaction for the audience, whether it is the creative impulse, family togetherness, civic participation or something else. But it does yield an impact on the audience.

Katz, Blumler and Gurevitch (1973) have identified the following five components of uses and gratification theory

1. Media competes with sources of satisfaction.
2. The goals of mass media can be discovered through data and research.
3. Media exists within the audiences.
4. The audience is conceived as active.
5. Judgments of mass media should not be expressed until the audience has time to process the media and their content on their own.

As Luskin (2002) has pointed out, the specialty of media psychology flows from applying understood theories in psychology in the use of pictures, graphics and sound in any form of communication technology. Media psychology encompasses the study of believability and the suspension of disbelief, situational cognition, assessment learning, mapping, feedback, reinforcement, mastery and persistence.

Luskin (2002) addresses the following distinctive and specialized areas of application:

1. Synesthetic: the study of stimulating and combining one sense with another.
2. Semiotics: communication through identification, manipulation and the use of symbols.
3. Semantic: understanding the use, effects and implication of the word.

THINK BOX

- Can you think of various domains in our life which is untouched by the lens of mass-media?

1.7 Early communication theories: four traditions in the history of ideas

1.7.1 Rhetoric

Rhetoric is the art of persuasion or convincing the people for a particular line of thought. The process of rhetoric is based on the engagement with the audience and the demand of situations. Communication includes writers/speakers, the audience and the text. This is a unique approach to data in terms of genre, differences, definition and comparison to places attends to the possibilities and diverse ways of thinking about the data. It is considered as the oldest tradition of ideas guiding humanities research and from antiquity, till the nineteenth century it remains very influential even in the contemporary times to it is getting attention.

Aristotle (384–322 BC) defined rhetoric as "faculty of observing in any given case the available means of persuasion". Its impact on communication and cultural research can be understood with the help of three concepts of ethos, logos and pathos.

The rhetorical tradition refers to five stages in preparing a speech (Quintillian 34–100 AD)

1. *Inventio* (the collection and conception of subject matter)
2. *Dispositio* (its linguistic articulation or arrangement)
3. *Elocutio* (style and presentation)
4. *Memoria* (memorizing the resulting configuration of forms and content)
5. *Actio* (performing the speech)

Of the five stages, the invention recognizes a strong relationship between knowing something and knowing how to communicate about the same. For instance, certain ways of speaking are appropriate in the playground, others in a courtroom and still others in a party-like situation. Each context has its own purpose and subject matter, both of which are given material shapes in speech. Disposition and elocution provide the concrete procedures in shaping the speech.

While addressing the audience through action, a speaker draws attention to three means of persuasion:

- Ethos
- Logos
- Pathos

These concepts emphasize the (ethical) character of the speaker, the (logical) quality of his/her arguments and the (more or less) pathetic emotions which the speech is designed to evoke in the listeners respectively. It is important to appreciate that these three means are present in any given act of communication but in different measures and combinations, depending on the purpose and hence the genre of communication.

The concept of *topos*, which classical rhetoric considered as one part of the invention, is of special interest as it is a thought which pervades modern humanities as well. Topos means places and implies that commonplace is actually commonplace in a familiar terrain that speaks sharing with their audience. It is a common understanding of reality as text and of text as a spatial and temporal universe that can be searched for traces and cues.

According to Aristotle, rhetoric is the source of knowledge. So many rhetorical concepts were redeveloped from their oral sources and applied to literary forms of communication.

The rhetorical tradition has remained an important source of ideas regarding the nature of both face-to-face and technology-mediated communication. Kenneth Burke developed the view of language as action (Burke, 1950, p. 99) and of literature as both social and aesthetic phenomenon (Burke, 1957). Duncan (1968) and Edelman (1971) applied the mass media theories of rhetorical communication for the purpose of political communication.

James Carey (1989) has suggested that technologically mediated communication serves to create and maintain a community. Rhetorical conception of communication as an action has provided one of the conceptual and methodological bridges between humanistic research on media texts and social-scientific research on communication practices.

1.7.2 Hermeneutics

Hermeneutics originally focused on the interpretation of sacred and legal texts and has developed into an influential school of thought in continental philosophy and applied social research. Initially, Immanuel Kant (1724–1804) had argued that there is no access to uninterpreted or a theoretical world of knowledge, but rather that the mind actively makes sense of the world based on prior conceptual frameworks. It paved the way for the development of the concept of hermeneutics. Friedrich Schleiermacher (1768–1834) was one of the first philosophers to theorize that hermeneutical thinking is a universal and natural part of being human in a social world rather than simply an application of the strategies for interpreting texts. He further distinguished between two types of interpretation: acts of interpretation that happens all the time as people encounter texts or the world around them and on which they act without much thought, and the complex texts or situations where understanding is not very clear and for which a doctrine of interpretation-hermeneutics is required.

There are both the possibilities of understanding and interpreting as natural ability. Hermeneutic theory of understanding is needed to explain the socio-cultural and political contexts related to an event. Hence the process of understanding became a core issue in social science research. The significant contributions by Wilhelm Dilthey, Emilio Belti and Eric Donald Hirsch Jr. have led to the development of hermeneutics as a methodological approach.

Paul Ricoeur (1913–2005) and Jurgen Habermas are also associated with critical hermeneutics. The theory of critical hermeneutics implies that any text can reveal the meaning of an author and power system, as well as ideology, is evident in the author's expression as well as in the reader's interpretation. Uncovering the ideological traces from a critical and reflective process allows readers and the authors to create more empowering interpretations.

Philosophical hermeneutics is a way of thinking and an intellectual tradition that lends itself to an inquiry. The basic nature of a phenomenon of interest is revealed through the conduct and analysis of the interview that allows participants to share their stories. An important goal of this method is to understand the meaning and to make sense of the experience Heidegger's (1971) idea of language, as something different from question answers exchanges.

Hans-Georg Gadamer (1900–2002) has distinguished between preunderstanding and understanding. The form of the proposition in itself is not suited to express speculative truths. Even the model proposition "snow is white" seems strange to me from this viewpoint. Who uttered this, even if it is true? I am only interested in asking about the precondition of human communication, namely that we really rise to understand what the other thinks about something (Gadamer, 1922, pp. 129–30). For Gadamer the past has a truly pervasive power in approaching understanding. His specific emphasis is not on the application of a method by a subject but on the fundamental continuity of history as a medium encompassing every such subjective act and the object it apprehends. Prejudices function as a limit to the power of self-consciousness. It is not so much our judgments as it is our prejudgments that constitute our being. During discourse, a fusion of horizons takes place between the speaker and listeners.

The truth, the horizon of the present, is conceived in constant formation in so far as we must constantly test our prejudices. The encounter with the past and the understanding of the tradition out of which we have come is not the last factor in the testing. Hence the horizon of the present does not take place at all without the past. There is just a little horizon of the present in itself as there are historical horizons which we would have to attain. Understanding is always a process of fusing such alleged existing horizons in themselves. In the working of traditions, such fusions occur constantly. The difference between methodological sterility and genuine understanding is imagination, that is, the capacity to see what is the questionnaire in the subject matter and to formulate questions that extend the subject matter further. The precondition of this capacity is that one is open to be questioned by the text to be provoked by it to risk involvement in a dialogue that carries him beyond his present position. The meaning of a text surpasses its author not occasionally but always as described by Gadamer. Understanding is considered a reproductive procedure but rather, it is always a productive procedure.

1.7.3 Phenomenology

Phenomenology is the study of consciousness as experienced from the first-person point of view. The phenomenological approach studies the structure of various types of experience from perception, thought, memory, imagination, emotion, desire, embodied action and linguistic activity. The structure of these forms what Husserl (1859–1938) called "Intentionality" that is the directedness of experience towards things in the world. Husserl (1913) mentioned the concept of "life world", and in order to gain a better understanding of life world, one should perform "reduction" of various types in order to capture its qualitative essence. Experience can't be broken into units; rather, phenomenological reduction involves bracketing (epoch) of experience as a whole from its incidental circumstances. Husserl's main ambition was to reinvent philosophy as a science in the formal sense of the form. Another proposition of Husserl was his attempt to close the subject–object divide. He stated that human consciousness or intentionality is always intentionality of something, not a mental state or entity that forever separated from external entities.

Husserl also highlighted the concept of the horizon which is the configuration of a life world at a given moment, pointing both past and future in time. A horizon includes a set of interpretive categories that an individual possesses owing to his/her socialization and acculturation. These are historical and culturally specific frameworks of expectation that guide interpretation of particular texts.

Some film studies have taken their lead from phenomenological bracketing of experience and have gone on to bracket film texts in order to get their essential experiential qualities that resemble the multifold life world (Deleuze, 1986, 1989). Phenomenology and radical hermeneutics may help to capture the distinctive feature of an increasingly mediatized modern existence.

1.7.4 Semiotics

Semiotics is a science that studies "the life of signs within the society" (Saussure, 1916, 1959, p. 16). A sign is the combination of a concept and a sound image; signs, then consist of two parts. For example, the sign "Tree" consists of

1. The concept of a leaf – the sort of object that is referred to as a leaf.
2. The sound image of leaves.

This is not the physical sound made when somebody says the word leaves, but the psychological imprint of the sound. One can recite the word "leaves" to him- or herself in his/her imagination without actually saying it, and the ability to do this means that the sound and image are a psychological phenomenon rather than the physical sound when the word is spoken. Saussure also describes the word signified to denote a concept and word signifier to denote the sound – the image signified and the signifier together forms a sign.

Saussure argued that there is an arbitrary relationship between signifier and signified. There is no particular reason why signifiers are used to denote particular concepts. It is apparent that different words are used to signify grass. Although signifiers are arbitrarily associated with the signified, people can't choose what words to use to signify a particular concept. Thus, an individual can't decide to start calling a mountain a playground and continue to be understood by others. Signs are handed from one generation to the next. Saussure comments: "No society, in fact, knows or has ever known language other than as a product inherited from preceding generations". Saussure considers language as a social phenomenon shared by the members of a social group and passed down to children.

According to Saussure the interrelation between the paradigmatic and syntagmatic axes gives rise to two specific forms of expression and representation-metaphor and metonymy very useful in the analysis of media as textual messages. Metaphor generally means saying one thing while intending other things. Metaphors are active in understanding. We use metaphors to group areas of experience, like "life is a journey".

According to Lakoff and Johnsen (2003), metaphors have entailments that organize and uniquely express that experience and that create necessary realities. Metonymy entails using a name to stand for the larger whole; in other words, it is the process by which a single sign evokes the full syntagm to which it belongs. To conclude, Saussure referred to the science of sign, not as semiotics but semiology.

1.8 Contemporary media theories

1.8.1 Linguistic and communicative theories

Language has always been a major source of conversation among people and has acted as a means of persuasive logic and the way we should live in this world.

The way people play with language is an effective way to communicate with a particular community. It is also important to note that in most cases, slang, banter and jokes are not ill-structured "secondary" forms of communication, but are coded means of crafting the specific type of exchange within a given community.

According to Wittgenstein, every word we speak is part of a language game. You will understand the language being used only if you are familiar with the language game. That is why Wittgenstein believes that religious language is meaningful, but only to the religious believers.

Wittgenstein stated that meaningful language and words have different uses and meanings in different contexts. He warned against prescriptivism and being stuck in a singular way of thinking. Wittgenstein thought that one could not stand outside a game and legislate about it or attempt to impose the rules of another game. You can't play basketball as if it is football.

1.8.2 Humanistic research tradition: arts research

Arts-based research involves an emotional and cognitive response to experiences, sense, temporality and space, based upon imaginative and creative perspectives. Researchers try to decode the meaning through critical inquiry of the meaning and value of societal artifacts and actions with different actors in the society to play. The act could be understood as the site and source of extraordinary and privileged insight. It was also realized that appreciation of arts and aesthetics was limited to certain classes and categories of people. Habermas (1969, 1989) argued that the arts enter into a cultural public sphere that is different from but nevertheless feeds into the political public sphere that debates and adjudicates issues of power and privileges.

The positioning of arts as a world into itself challenged and questioned the autonomous and consensual status of artworks. Social science research involving critical inquiry also took into account the social, political and critical aspects of pedagogy to enact theoretical stances of dialogic experiential, transactional, emancipatory, class and gender theories. Museums emerged, alongside libraries and the press, as institutions of record, but also of diversion for the general public.

The cultural heritage of the nineteenth and twentieth centuries was conveyed through the central carrier of stage entertainment. However, modern media acted as a new form of cultural infrastructure which also blurred the distinction between high and low cultural forms. Analytical models and methods as derived in part, from the psychology of perception and applied to different historical art forms (Arnheim, 1974; Gombrich, 1960) provided essential tools for examining from the perspective of color and iconographic conventions in film and television.

As Marshall McLuhan said, the medium is the message. Visual media texts carry formal "messages" that help to form a particular perspective of the world. Media studies also try to explore the junctures between artwork, artists and their sociocultural context with the help of empirical evidence. Arnold Hauser (1951) in his book *Social History of Art*, presented an account of the development and meaning of art from its origin in the Stone Age to the Film Age. He highlighted the role of ideologies and economic influences on cinema. John Berger (1972) described that photograph always need language and require a narrative to make sense. In his book *Ways of Seeing*, he wrote "The relation between what we see and what we know is never settled". He described the continuities between post-Renaissance European paintings of women and imagery from latter-day poster and "girlie" magazines, by juxtaposing the different images and showing how they similarly rendered women as objects.

Media-oriented images of digital art and internet art have strong interconnections with everyday life objects elevated in art forms. Sculpture and architecture have classic lessons to teach the designers and students of virtual worlds (Rush, 2005).

1.8.3 Literary criticism

As a formalist movement in literary theory, this approach focuses on the importance of closely reading a piece of literature, mainly poetry, to understand how it functions as a "self-contained" object. New criticism coined by John Crowe Ransom was developed by a group of American critics who tried to systematize the study of literature to develop a system centered on the rigorous study of the text itself. The method used by the new criticism approach involved a close reading, putting attention to formal aspects such as rhythm and theme. The new critics intentionally ignored the author, the reader and the social context.

The concept of intertextuality is an important contribution of structuralism to media and communication research. Mikhail Bakhtin provided a major theory of discourse in the twentieth century. His concept of polyphony (borrowed from music), which literally means multiple voices, is important. In an author's writing, there is a plurality of consciousness. Bakhtin highlighted Dostoevsky's dialogical principles as counterposed to the monologist (single thought discourse) also known as homophony or single-voice.

The dialogical world is always in an intense relationship with another's word being addressed to a listener in anticipation of a response. As many standpoints exist, the truth requires many incommensurate voices; from Bakhtin's point of view, the social world is made up of multiple voices. On a social scale, Bakhtin criticized Saussure who views language as a closed system. He highlighted the concept of heteroglossia of multiple everyday speech types.

Bakhtin's view is against the position that language is simply a means of communicating information. Any language is mediated by the social field of interacting ways of seeing between each speaker and the world. Thus particular choices within a national language constitute particular speech genres. Speech genres include such zones of language as journalistic studies, religious dialects and ideological systems. Each genre embeds in its language particular social value, worldview and intentionality as well as space-time references (chronotopes).

1.8.4 Linguistics

Linguistics is the scientific study of human natural language. It is concerned with the nature of language and communication. There are five important subfields of linguistics.

1.8.4.1 Phonetics

This subfield of linguistics studies the structure and systematic patterning of sounds for clear pronunciation in human language.

1.8.4.2 Lexical structure or morphology

It is the study of the internal structure of words and the relationship among words.

1.8.4.3 Syntactic information

It is the study of words grouped into phrases and internal structure of sentences and the relationship among internal parts.

1.8.4.4 Semantic information

For every word, we have learned a meaning that automatically comes to our mind. For example, to know the word "sister" is to know that it has a certain meaning. Semantics is the study of the nature of the meaning of individual words and the meaning of words grouped into phrases and sentences.

1.8.4.5 Pragmatics

It is the study of the use of words in the actual context of discourse and conversation.

1.8.4.6 Message model of linguistic communication

The speaker acts as a transmitter, and the hearer acts as a receiver of information. Communication is successful when the hearer decodes the same message that the speaker encodes, and communication is unsuccessful when a decoded message is different from the encoded message.

1.8.4.7 The inferential model of linguistic communication

According to the inferential model of linguistics, communication is successful when the hearer, upon hearing an expression, recognizes the speaker's communicative intentions.

Media linguistics is a research instrument in collecting and examining evidence about media and communication. Thus, language is both an object and a tool of analysis.

Scholars have been trying to conceptualize and examine this reconfiguration of media environment to the same degree rediscovering the importance of interpersonal communication both in and around mass media (Gumpret & Cathcart, 1986; Scannel, 1991).

Media linguistics studies the speech behavior of mass-communication participants and specific areas, textures and genres of media texts. Internet linguistics studies new language styles that emerged due to the internet, such as Short Message Service (SMS). Computer-mediated communication (CMC) accords importance to linguistics in understanding such a new style of communication.

1.8.5 Sociolinguistic perspective

Crystal (2005) emphasized the positive power of creativity using a language in internet ecology. We can notice a high degree of informal and personal communication with the emergence of internet communication. According to Crystal, sociolinguistics of the internet can be evaluated through five interconnected themes.

- Multilingualism: the internet provides a platform for various languages of the world interacting on a common platform.
- Language change: the change in language is influenced by the limitation of technology and socio-economic priorities.
- Conversation discourse: the social interaction pattern is also influenced by the discourse taking place on the internet platform.
- Stylistic diffusion: stylistic diffusion of language takes place with various linguistic forms converging on the same platform of the internet.
- Metalanguage and talk linguistics: these also give rise to the formation of a new type of language combining features of various socio-cultural and linguistics contexts.

1.8.6 Educational perspective

Crystal (2005) also talks about the educational impact of internet linguistics. New abbreviations reduce time in communication. It led to the rise of acronyms such as "lol" (laughing out loud) and "gtg" (got to go). It has been found that people who regularly texted displayed a wide range of vocabulary and this may lead to a positive impact on their reading development.

1.8.7 Stylistic perspective

The stylistic perspective looks at the internet as a medium through which new language phenomena have arisen. The traditional writing words can appear in static format, whereas in the internet model, words may appear in different colors and font sizes.

Chinese and Korean languages have already experienced English-language infiltration leading to the formation of their multilinguistic internet lingo. There is also a possibility of extinction of certain language forms due to their continued absence from the digital platform and domination such as English with its continued growth of usage of digital platforms.

1.9 Film studies

Before the 1960s, film theory was normally distinguished into two traditions, i.e. realism and formalism.

Munsterberg's (1916) work on film or photoplay explored the aesthetics of film and its relationship among art film and nature of thought. He explained that the photoplay tells us the human story by overcoming the forms of the author world, namely space, time and causality, and by adjusting the vents to the forms of the inner world, namely attention, memory, imagination and emotion (p. 129). For Munsterberg "film operates like the human mind" (Langdale, 2002, p. 9) and like art, both film and human mind transform and do not copy reality.

In writing about the nature of art, mind and film, Munsterberg borrowed from philosophical discourses of his time. Taking a cue from Wertheimer's phi phenomena, Munsterberg begins with the experience of movement and depths–illusions in a film which he sees as super additions that the mind supplies to a series of flat surfaces of still photos.

In films, the flashback embodies the act of memory. Imagination is similarly intimated in the flash-forward as a cinematic technique As Carroll (1988) has observed in the matter of film depth and motion, psychologists tell us we add something to the visual array, whereas with the close-up, the selecting is something that is done for us.

Langdale (2002) also observed a crucial difference between suggested thought in film and imagination, as the two were equated by Munsterberg. Langdale further writes, the suggestion is a "stealth-thought" that originates from an "external" source meant to "instigate specific association, taking their pace like intruders alongside association that really do spring from our own mind" (2002, p. 19).

Munsterberg's contribution to the psychology of film and media is considered largely behaviorist. Though Munsterberg's theory was criticized, his psychology of film based upon aesthetics of thought and perception has its unique place in understanding film studies.

1.10 Post-modernist theories as an aesthetic style

The interpretational model suggests that audiences filter the messages, whatever media messages they receive. Buckingham (1997) argued that someone with a higher level of television literacy might be able to read "behind" the screen images and sounds. According to Buckingham, a person with a higher level of media literacy can also categorize programs knowing their conventions, and being aware of its narratives enables one to understand the motivations and intentions of program producers.

Croteau and Hoynes's (2001) concept of discursive resources suggests that different groups of people in society have access to different sets of discursive resources for decoding media messages. Stuart Hall argued that each culture in a society has a different way of classifying the world and media. The meaning of the powerful images is encoded as they operate within the framework of consensus.

Hall has shown that media messages can be coded differently. He described the following codes:

- The hegemonic code is the preferred reading encoded by media professionals.
- The professional code interprets messages according to the culture of the professional group to which the viewer belongs.
- The negotiated code modifies but does not totally reject the preferred reading.
- The oppositional code is one in which the viewer comprehends the message but rejects it.

1.11 Postmodernism and media

The French theorist Lyotard (1984) has argued that the aim of enlightenment thinkers has been abandoned in contemporary societies. People no longer believe in grand theories of science and progress. The grand plans for the future of humanity in all areas of life and diversity are questioned. Lyotard brings in the notion of language games that serve to justify or legitimate people's behavior in society. According to him, meta-narratives of human emancipation, self-fulfillment and social progress created by the French Revolution and Marxism are no longer valid. From Lyotard's perspective, postmodernist society is based on the production and exchange of knowledge that is saleable. For Jean Baudrillard (1988), the communication/media revolution meant that people are engulfed by the information to such an extent that the distinction between reality and the world image which portrays it breaks down into a condition he called "hyperreality". Baudrillard noted that signs in human culture have passed through four mains stages (Baudrillard, 1981, 1994)

- In the first stage, signs (words, images, etc.) are a reflection of basic reality.
- In the next stage, the sign masks and perverts some basic reality. The image becomes a distortion of the truth but they have not lost all connection with things that really exist.
- In the third stage, the sign marks the absence of some basic reality.
- Finally, the sign has no relation to any reality whatsoever: it is its pure simulacrum. A simulacrum is an image of something that does not exist and has never existed.

1.12 Scope of this book

My intention in this book is to identify and illustrate what are arguably major tradi-tions of scholarly inquiry in the field of media psychology. The principal purpose is to provide fundamental understanding of the subject and relevant issues that may have had a seminal influence in the field of media psychology and communica-tion research. The chapters included in the book represent dominant paradigms in the field of media psychology and attempt to highlight interconnections between media and different aspects of socio-cultural existence. An important purpose of this book is to introduce and provide key sources and illustrate material regarding the major dimensions of media psychology research.

Major dimensions of media psychology research include such topics as media research methods, media consumer behavior, media and society, media and cul-ture, media's advertising, media messages, media effects and critical issues in media and consumer behavior. It is important to highlight that major ideological trajectories has been provided in various chapters of this book, as media operates in a multi-interest society which has a wider influence on different sections of society.

This book devotes a full chapter on early and contemporary media theories in its introduction chapter. The second chapter of this book explores the relations between media and consumer behavior. The multiplicity of different researchers and theories provide a substantial understanding of the topic comparing a range of diverse perspectives. Interactive technologies of social media derive from the con-cept of human-machine exchanges. It refers the relationship between social struc-tures and its constituent factors in which alternative social structures and entirely other positive worlds may be articulated. Networked forms of communication have transformed the intimate and social spheres functioning, creating a relatively auton-omous sphere of existence.

The third chapter highlights different media research that has emerged and taken shape in the field of media psychology. The whole of meaning transmitted through media sources is more than the sum of information. All communication occurring in a social context has implications for social actions.

The fourth chapter, covering media and society, involves new degrees of freedom in the management of everyday communication, which requires a nuanced understanding of how people balance different social contexts against each other. The conduct of everyday life is being affected by the dominance of media, influencing children, youth and families. How people integrate the affor-dances of personal media into their conduct of everyday life is shaped by the interplay of media and personal factors. Media content, exposure to the media and the social context plays an important role in shaping the attitudes and behav-ior of people. The social and environmental circumstances that lead people to mass media has short-term and long-term behavioral implications for different sections of the society. Media plays a crucial role in establishing and reinforcing value systems through the persuasiveness of its messages. Mass media's influence on children, youth and family has effects on their attitudes and behavior. The overall influence of mass media has increased drastically in recent times. These effects have both positive and negative implications which have been described in this chapter.

The fifth chapter on media and culture conveys the idea that media practices lead to emergence of cultures. The media culture has created concepts of popular culture which is a result of mass culture. Mass media consists of diversified media forms intended to reach the large masses. Media produces new cultural elements through propaganda, advertising and entertainment. The nature and authenticity of the cultural influence of media have been discussed in a critical way, as has media generally. Changes in the external environment with the advent of media perpetuate and develop new patterns of culture. Cultural relationships in this age of media dominance are detached from geographical and local boundaries. Popular culture more often than not takes into account moral and social values as represented in traditional culture.

The sixth chapter covers the media and advertising. Advertising media is the process of influencing the consumers' purchase decisions through effective communications programs. The advertising process has the capacity to improve the sales of products. Advertising effectiveness depends upon the factors of cognition, affect, awareness, interest and desires. The hierarchies of effect models include Cognition (C), Affect (A) and Behavior (B), which is the path to persuasion. Other models also describe advertisement on the basis of Awareness-Interest-Desire-Action. This chapter highlights the psychological factors of creating brand awareness and purchase behavior by consumers. Emotions, gender, culture, age, group and the personality profile of the individual play an important role in the customer's purchase decision. Some items are bought on the basis of high emotional involvement, while others are purchased on the basis of a rational decision. The profile of the audience, what the placement of ads should be and the type of media to be used are planned for different demographics. No single model can work in every type of situation; hence, good planning is required for effectiveness of the advertisement programs.

The seventh chapter on media messages analyzes the texts which can have an impact on the audience's moods and actions. Rhetoric has the ability to enhance the persuasiveness among the audience. The impact of messages are also improved in storied form of narratives, cultural analysis of messages describes to decode the culture, ideology power meaning associated with the messages. The psychoanalytic perspective looks from the perspective of analyzing unconscious desires. The queer perspective tries to uncover the meanings surrounding human sexuality. Media usage patterns have short-term and long-term effects on identity, women, violence and other aspects. People related their self-identity and social identity through media platforms, which are well articulated in the eighth chapter on media effects. The reader will comprehend the differential effects of media through variations in usage patterns. A large variety of aggressive and violent behavior patterns can be imitated through media, but mediational factors also contribute to its varying impacts.

The last chapter discusses the crucial issues of citizenship, pedagogy, digital storytelling and digital altruism, which are relatively less researched topics and nascent in its origin. Media citizenship has changed the social and institutional dynamics which is widely influenced with citizens' journalism and citizens' empowerment.

THINK BOX

- Which media theory has wider applications in our day to day life?
- Critically examine the similarities and differences between traditional and contemporary theories of mass media?

1.13 Critical evaluation and the Indian perspective

In the Indian context, people are using the internet. They are spending more and more time in online communication for handling their daily life routines and social and professional activities. People of all ages are using the internet, and lives between home and work have made people act as virtual communities conducting businesses, exchanging knowledge and sharing emotional bonding, gossip, etc. All kinds of propaganda are also done, and suddenly some people or an organization becomes important through validation in social media. Celebrities are appreciated and trolled for good and bad reasons, and it both empowers socio-economic positioning and endangers it. In some situations, people combine, cooperate, collaborate, create work opportunities and spread messages on the world platform. It is no surprise that the internet accomplishes us as we wake up, as we breakfast, as we are eating in restaurants. It comforts us when we are alone, and depending upon our choices of material we engage, it can relax us or stress us. At times it helps us to remove the boredom of being alone. Even at times, it may challenge us. Our whole life pattern seems to be simultaneously preoccupied and surrounded by online sociability along with offline. Young and old, men and women, rich and poor are significantly engaged in this medium and its consequences. There is a significant decline in social capital – mutual obligations and trust, and offline physical activities by the people. Online products and related businesses have grown phenomenally in size. A broad range of gratifications, from excitement to political activism and entertainment, is derived by the users. With the availability of smartphones, it is now becoming an integral part of one's life to own it and use it almost 24/7, except sleeping hours. A large number of children and adolescents are also becoming dependent on their use, and parents are having a tough time controlling the online activities of their children along with balancing their own.

The use of social media has become a dominant feature to highlight government programs and political activities. The information received from the satellites is also being used for weather predictions. The use of mass media for political campaigns during elections has also acquired significant share as other modes of campaigning. At times social media messages without their authenticity check are being used. It also creates problems of social conflict in certain situations. Mass media, social media and other forms of internet-mediated communication have become a part and parcel of people in the Indian context, and this new avatar of modern-day communication has become a reality. It will be better to know micro and macro ramifications of this medium instead of ignoring and offering generalizations which will take us far from understanding its advantage.

People from all walks of life – ranging from the tea vendor using the Paytm facility for his customers, to students using e-learning applications for education, to business houses advertising their products, to music companies highlighting their products through social media – have had social media become a part and parcel of their daily lives. Activists highlighting the ideological debates and politicians and taking the help of social media to propagate their views on a daily basis have become the order of the day. We can expect more changes in social interaction, participation and engagements on media platforms increasing in quality and complexity. A detailed understanding of these dynamics will help us understand it better. The use of the official Twitter handle of government offices shows the increasing importance of mass media in governance. So many apps have been launched by the government to highlight and implement social welfare schemes. Most organizations have social media platforms to highlight their activities and achievements. It is becoming more important with the passage of time and has acquired various dimensions. The field of media psychology is widening in its scope, and a balanced approach is required to understand the media dynamics and its implications for people.

THINK BOX

- Can you highlight the role of mass-media in body-image identity?

Key points

- Media psychology is a field dealing with all forms of mediated communication and its effects on human behavior.
- People's attitudes, perceptions and behavior are directly and indirectly influenced by media messages.
- Media plays a crucial role in determining family relations, body-image, social interactions and values.

- Self-representations and social media have acquired increased importance in the contemporary period.
- Important media theories include excitation transfer theory, users and gratification theory and cultivation theory.
- Early communication theories include four important traditions of rhetoric, hermeneutics, phenomenology and semiotics.
- Contemporary media theories include linguistic theories, sociolinguistic theories and film theories.
- Postmodernist theories highlighted the role of media in shaping people's behavior.
- The educational perspective of media has far-reaching potential.
- The realm of mass media is all pervasive and it has implications in the Indian and global context.

Key terms

media psychology, thinness fantasy, product integration, stereotypical characterizations, impression management, phenomenology, semiotics, rhetoric, hermeneutics, hyper-reality

References

Arnheim, R. (1974). *Art and Visual Perception: A Psychology of the Creative Eye*. Berkeley, CA: University of California Press.

Auty, S., & Lewis, C. (2004). The "delicious paradox": Preconscious processing of product placement by children. In L.J. Shrum (Ed.), *The Psychology of Entertainment Media: Blurring the Lines between Entertainment and Persuasion* (pp. 117–33). New Jersey: Lawrence Erlbaum.

Baker, M.J. (1999). Argumentation and constructive interaction. In G. Rijlaarsdam & E. Espéret (Series Eds.) and P. Coirier & J. Andriessen (Vol. Eds.), *Studies in Writing: Vol. 5: Foundations of Argumentative Text Processing* (pp. 179–202). Amsterdam: University of Amsterdam Press.

Baudrillard, J. (1981). The precession of simulacra. In V.V. Leitch, W.E. Cain, L. Fink & B. Johnson (Eds.), *The Norton Anthology of Theory and Criticism* (pp. 1732–41). New York, NY: W.W. Norton Company.

Baudrillard, J. (1988). *The Ecstasy of Communication*. New York: Semiotext(e).

Baudrillard, J. (1994). The implosion of meaning in the media. In J. Baudrillard (Ed.), *Simulacra and Simulation* (S.F. Glaser, Trans., pp. 79–86). Ann Arbor, MI: University of Michigan Press.

Berger, J. (1972). *Ways of Seeing*. London: BBC and Penguin.

Braun-LaTour, K.A., & Zaltman, G. (2006). Memory change: An intimate measure of persuasion [Electronic version]. *Journal of Advertising Research*, 46(1), 57–72.

Buckingham, D. (1997). News media, political socialization and popular citizenship towards a new agenda. *Critical Studies in Mass Communication*, 14, 344–66.

Burke, K. (1950). *A Rhetoric of Motives*. Berkeley, CA: University of California Press.

Burke, K. (1957). *The Philosophy of Literary Form: Studies in Symbolic Action*. New York: Vintage Books.

Carey, J.W. (1989). A cultural approach to communication. In *Communication as Culture* (pp. 13–36). Winchester, MA: Unwin Hyman.

Carr, N. (2011). *The Shallows: What the Internet Is Doing to Our Brains*. New York: W.W. Norton.

Carroll, N. (1988). *Mystifying Movies: Fads and Fallacies in Contemporary Film Theory* (p. 262). New York: Columbia University Press.

Chartrand, T.L., & Bargh, J.A. (1999). The chameleon effect: The perception–behavior link and social interaction. *Journal of Personality and Social Psychology*, 76(6), 893–910.

Croteau, D., & Hoynes, W. (2001). *The Business of the Media: Corporate Media and the Public Interest*. Thousand Oaks, CA: Pine Forest Press.

Crystal, D. (2005). *How Language Works*. London: Penguin Books.

Deleuze, G. (1986). *Cinema 1: The Movement-Image* (H. Tomlinson & B. Haberjam, Trans.). Minneapolis: University of Minnesota Press.

Deleuze, G. (1989). *Cinema 2: The Time-Image* (H. Tomlinson & R. Galeta, Trans.). Minneapolis: University of Minnesota Press.

Duncan, H.D. (1968). *Symbols in Society*. New York: Oxford University Press.

Dutcher, D., Finley, J., Luloff, A.E., & Buttolph Johnson, J. (2007). Connectivity with nature as a measure of environmental values. *Environment and Behavior*, 39, 474– 93.

Edelman, M. (1971). *Politics as Symbolic Action: Mass Arousal and Quiescence*. Chicago: Markham Publishing.

Gadamer, H.-G. (1922). *Education, Poetry and History: Applied Hermeneutics* (D. Misgeld & G. Nicholson, Ed.; L. Schmidt & M. Ruess, Trans.). Albany, NY: SUNY Press.

Gergen, K.J. (2000). The self in the age of information. *Washington Quarterly*, 23, 201–14.

Goldberg, I. (1995). IAD. In M.E. Cinti (a cura di), *Internet Addiction Disorder un Fenomeno Sociale in Espansione* (pp. 6–7).

Gombrich, E. (1960). *Art and Illusion*. Princeton, NJ: Princeton University Press.

Green, M.C., & Brock, T.C. (2002). In the mind's eye: Transportation-imagery model of narrative persuasion. In M.C. Green, J.J. Strange, & T.C. Brock (Eds.), *Narrative Impact: Social and Cognitive Foundations* (pp. 315–41). Mahwah, NJ: Lawrence Erlbaum Associates Publishers.

Gumpret, G., & Cathcart, R.S. (1986). *Inter/Media: Interpersonal Communication in a Media World*. Oxford: Oxford University Press.

Habermas, J. (1969). *Protestbewegung und Hochschulreform*. Frankfurt am Main: Suhrkamp.

Habermas, J. (1989). *The Structural Transformation of the Public Sphere: An Inquiry into a Category of Bourgeois Society* (T. Burger, Trans. with the Assistance of F. Lawrence). Cambridge, MA: Polity Press.

Hall, S. (1973). Encoding and decoding in the television discourse. In P. Marris & S. Thornham (Eds.), *Media Studies: A Reader* (pp. 51–61). Washington Square, NY: New York University Press.

Hauser, A. (1951). *The Social History of Art*. London: Routledge & Kegan Paul.

Heidegger, M. (1971). Building, dwelling, thinking. In M. Heidegger (Ed.), *Poetry, Language and Thought* (A. Hofstadter, Trans.; pp. 143–62). New York: Harper & Row.

Hembrooke, H., & Gay, G. (2003). The laptop and the lecture: The effects of multitasking in learning environments. *Journal of Computing in Higher Education*, 15(1).

Herzog, H. (1944). What do we really know about daytime serial listeners? In P.F. Lazarsfeld & F.N. Stanton (Eds.), *Radio Research* (pp. 3–33). New York: Duell, Sloan & Pearce.

Husserl, E. (1913). *Ideas Pertaining to a Pure Phenomenology and to a Phenomenological Philosophy – First Book: General Introduction to a Pure Phenomenology* (F. Kersten, Trans.). The Hague: Nijhoff.

Katz, E., Blumler, J., & Gurevitch, M. (1973). Uses and gratifications research. *The Public Opinion Quarterly*, 37(4), 509–23.

Katz, E., Gurevitch, M., & Haas, H. (1973). On the use of the mass media for important things. *American Sociological Review*, 38, 164–81.

Klingberg, T. (2008). *The Overflowing Brain: Information Overload and the Limits of Working Memory*. New York: Oxford University Press.

Kunkel, D., Cope, K.M., & Colvin, C. (1996). *Sexual Messages in "Family Hour" TV: Content and Context*. Menlo Park, CA: Henry J. Kaiser Family Foundation.

Kunkel, D., Eyal, K., Finnerty, K., Biely, E., & Donnerstein, E. (2005). *Sex on TV 4*. Menlo Park, CA: Kaiser Family Foundation.

Lakoff, G., & Johnsen, M. (2003). *Metaphors We Live By*. London: University of Chicago Press.

Langdale, L. (2002). *Hugo Münsterberg on Film: The Photoplay – A Psychological Study, and Other Writing*. New York: Routledge.

Lasswell, H. (1948). In L. Bryson (Ed.). *The Structure and Function of Communication in Society. The Communication of Ideas* (p. 117). New York: Institute for Religious and Social Studies.

Lazarsfeld, P.F., & Stanton, F. (1949). *Communication Research 1948–9*. New York: Harper & Row.

Luskin, B. (2002). *Casting the Net over Global Learning: New Development in Workforce and Online Psychologies*. Santa Ana, CA: Griffin Publishing Group.

Lyotard, J.F. (1984). The postmodern condition: A report on knowledge translation from the French by Geoff Bennington and Brian Massumi. *Theory and History of Literature*, 10.

McQuail, D., Blumler, J., & Brown, J. (1972). The television audience: A revised perspective. In D. McQuail (Ed.), *Sociology of Mass Communications* (pp. 135–65). Middlesex, England: Penguin.

Misra, S., & Stokols, D. (2012). Psychological and health outcomes of perceived Information overload. *Environment and Behavior*, 44, 737–59.

Morgan, S., Movius, L., & Cody, M.J. (2009). The power of narratives: The effect of entertainment television organ donation storylines on the attitudes, knowledge, and behaviors of donors and nondonors. *Journal of Communication*, 59(1), 135–51.

Munsterberg, H. (1916). *The Photocopy: A Psychological Study*. New York: D. Appleton and Company.

Myers, P.N., & Biocca, F.A. (1992). The elastic body image: The effect of television advertising and programming on body image distortions in young women. *Journal of Communication*, 42(3), 108–33.

Nisbet, E.K., Zelenski, J.M., & Murphy, S.A. (2009). The nature relatedness scale: Linking individuals' connection with nature to environmental concern and behavior. *Environment and Behavior*, 41(5), 715–40.

O'Keeffe, G.S., & Clarke-Pearson, K. (2011). The impact of social media on children, adolescents, and families. *Council on Communications and Media*, 127(4).

Pantic, I. (2014). Online social networking and mental health. *Cyberpsychology, Behavior, and Social Networking*, 17(10), 652–7.

Phillips, J.B., & McQuarrie, F.E. (2010). Narrative and persuasion in fashion advertising. *Journal of Consumer Research*, 37(3), 368–92.

Poldrack, R.A., & Foerde, K. (2008). Category learning and the memory syst debate. *Neuroscience & Biobehavioural Reviews*, 32, 197–205.

Rockwell, S., & Singleton, L. (2007). The effect of the modality of presentation of streaming multimedia on information acquisition. *Media Psychology*, 9, 179–91.

Rush, M. (2005). *New Media in Art* (2nd ed.). London: Thames of London.

Russell, A.C. (1998). Toward a framework of product placement: Theoretical propositions. In J.W. Alba & J.W. Hutchinson (Eds.), *NA – Advances in Consumer Research* (Vol. 25, pp. 357–62). Provo, UT: Association for Consumer Research.

Saussure, F. (1959). *Course in General Linguistics*. New York: Philosophical Library.

Scannel, P. (1991). The relevance of talk. In P. Scannel (Ed.), *Broadcast Talk*. London: Sage.

Steele, J. (1999). Teenage sexuality and media practice: Factoring in the influences of family, friends and school. *Journal of Sex Research*, 36(4), 331–41. Retrieved from Communication & Mass Media Complete Database.

Suchman, E. (1942). An invitation to music. In P.F. Lazarsfeld & F.N. Stanton (Eds.), *Radio Research, 1941*. New York, Duell, Sloan and Pearce.

Turkle, S. (2012). *Alone Together: Why We Expect More from Technology and Less from Each Other*. New York: Basic Books.

Westin, A. (1967). *Privacy and Freedom*. New York: Atheneum.

Wittgenstein, L. (1961). *Tractatus Logico-Philosophicus* (D.F. Pears & B.F. McGuinness, Trans.). London: Routledge and Kegan Paul.

Wolf, K., & Fisk, M.(1949). The children talk about comics. In P.F. Lazarsfeld & F.N. Stanton (Eds.), *Communications Research* (pp. 3–50). New York: Harper and Brothers.

Zelenski, J., & Nisbet, E. (2014). Happiness and feeling connected: The distinct role of Nature Relatedness. *Environment and Behavior*, 46, 3–23.

Zhizhina, M. (2010). *Subject Area and Main Tasks of Media Psychology: Video Conference on Media Psychology in Russia: Problems and Prospects*. Saratov: Saratov State University.

Zillmann, D. (1971). Excitation transfer in communication-mediated aggressive behavior. *Journal of Personality and Social Psychology*, 7(4), 419–34.

Zillmann, D. (2006). Dramaturgy for emotions from fictional narration. In J. Bryant & P. Vorderer (Eds.), *Psychology of Entertainment* (pp. 215–38). Mahwah, NJ: Erlbaum.

2

CONSUMER BEHAVIOR
AND PSYCHOLOGY

Learning objectives

After reading this chapter, you will be able to understand:

- Consumer behavior and its theories
- Consumer behavior and its relationship with psychology
- Consumer culture
- Consumer culture and identity
- Interactive emerging technologies
- Interactive media
- Virtual social media
- Self-representation in social media
- Critical evaluation in the Indian context

2.1 Introduction

Consumption refers to the goods, services, energy and resources that are used by people, institutions and societies. Consumer behavior is linked with the rising level of consumption around the world of all kinds of resources, including food, clothing, cars, air conditioners, refrigerators, washing machines, motorbikes, airplanes, plastic, electricity, internet service, etc. The rising level of consumption can have negative consequences, leading to depletion of natural and environmental resources. There have been glaring differences in inequalities in consumption between the world's rich and poor countries. The world's total consumption is shared by a minority of the population from the developed nations. The share of consumption by undeveloped and underdeveloped nations has remained significantly low. It has been argued that industrial capitalism sets societies on a "treadmill of production" leading to environmental damage, using natural resources at a rapid rate and generating a high level of pollution and waste (Schnaiberg, 1980). However, in the twentieth century, it was modern consumerism which kept that treadmill running faster in this direction.

2.2 Consumption: need or greed

To some extent, consumption is necessary for survival, but contemporary forms of consumption are assuming different shades. Consumption and consumerism are strongly related to the process of mass production, which became prominent with the advent of capitalism. In 1776 Adam Smith (1723–90), in his famous book *The Wealth of Nations*, highlighted the importance of specialization of labor in the manufacturing of pins. Other important contributions highlighting the importance of specialization of labor included Eli Whitney (1797), inventor of the cotton gin; and Brunei, whose machine tools were designed and built by Henry Maudslay, who is also known as the father of the machine tools industry. By the middle of the nineteenth century, machine-assisted manufacturing, division manufacturing and division of labor became established factors of growth and production. Frank B. Gilbreth and his wife Lillian Gilbreth began their studies on time and motion to achieve more economy of effort, combined with the studies of Taylor; and Henri Fayol's (1916) concept of organization and supervision gained wider acceptance.

There was a significant turn in the history of civilization with the mass production concept. Henry Ford (1913), the US industrialist, integrated the mass production concept as an integrated and coherent process. Mass production was based upon the principle of division of production operation, standardization of component parts, systematic planning and well-planned distribution and market,

FIGURE 2.1 Shopping mall centre.
Source: Stojanovic, D. (n.d.). Needpix. https://www.needpix.com/photo/281222/shopping-mall-center-shop-sale-buy-market-business-consumer

and it led to the search for a large number of consumers. Nowadays with the application of robotics and artificial intelligence, a large number of products with the least amount of human intervention are being produced. Automatic production in the agricultural sector – cultivating and harvesting, followed by the techniques of preserving and packaging food products – drew heavily on mass production. Before the advent of mass production techniques, goods were produced only for limited needs, and the concept of long-term storage of products was not a common practice.

With the growing need for more and more products, capitalist giants grew in numbers and also started exploiting natural resources. The pollution generated by factories of mass production become a threat to the environment. Plastic pollution and electronic waste led to the generation of greenhouse gases which ultimately effected global warming and posed a threat to one's climate, air and water. This complex dynamics of mass production is determined by factors such as urbanization, globalization and competition among capitalist giants. Debates on genetically modified foods, global warming and other manufactured risks have presented a scenario in which humankind finds itself in a trap of human-made creations. Ulrich Beck (1992, 1999, 2002) argues that conflict related to the distribution of wealth is losing its significance as environmental risks rise to prominence. He further argues that more people are beginning to realize that their fight for a share of the "wealth cake" is futile if the cake itself is poisoned as a result of pollution and environmental damage.

2.3 Definition of consumer behavior

According to Walters (1974), "A consumer is an individual who purchases, has the capacity to purchase goods and services offered for sale by marketing institutions in order to satisfy, personal or household need, wants or desires". Consumption got channelized from need to greed with the practice of mass-production being adopted by the modern business organization. Walters (1974) has defined consumer behavior as "the process whereby individuals decide whether, what, when, where, how and from whom to purchase goods and services". Schiffman and Kanuk (1997) view consumer behavior as "The behavior that consumers display in searching for, purchasing, using evaluating and disposing of products, services and ideas".

The importance of understanding consumer behavior is also echoed in a statement by Assael (1995): "Consumers determine the sales and profit of a firm by their purchasing decisions. As such their motives and actions determine the economic viability of the firm". Consumer behavior is a complex phenomenon of psychosocial and economic factors. The purchasing tendency of a consumer is decided and determined by a combination of factors that include the economic status of the person, psychological needs and social factors.

2.4 Models of consumer behavior

It is an extremely difficult task to uncover the reasons why people are subject to many influences, and the most important factor is the psyche, which eventually leads to overt purchase responses. People are guided by economic and social perspectives and a consumer's rationalization of a purchase decision is also guided by group norms, references and values.

2.4.1 Veblenian socio-psychological model

According to economist Thorstein Veblen (1857–1929), human beings conform to the group and cultural norms. Veblen also described members of society's "leisure class" whom he hypothesized, were influenced by the desire for prestige rather than utilitarian need fulfillment. Veblen provided a behavioral explanation for conspicuous consumption motivated by an attempt to advertise wealth.

For Veblen, human behavior and consequently consumer behavior is in a state of continuous evolution depending upon socio-cultural and economic environments. Kotler (1965) has classified the Veblenian analysis in the leisure class "as a social psychological model" in which man is seen primarily as "a social animal conforming to the general forms and norms of his larger culture and to the more specific standards of the subcultures and face to face groupings to which life is bound. His wants and behavior are largely modeled by his present group membership and his aspired group membership".

Veblen's theory highlighted that more important factors motivating purchasing behavior were prestige-seeking and status as compared to any intrinsic factors, and it rejected any kind of hedonistic explanation of consumer behavior as proposed by classical and neoclassical economic theories proposed by Adam Smith, David Ricardo (1772–1823), Vilfred Pareto (1848–1923), John Clark (1847–1938), Irving Fisher (1883–1946) and J.M. Keynes (1883–1946). This approach of satisfying two master motives of pleasure and pain was rejected in the Veblen model and highlighted the importance of non-hedonistic motives such as family affection and loyalty or social status.

Veblen had described a man "as not simply a bundle of desires that are to be saturated but the rather coherent structure of propensities and habits which seek realization and expression in an unfolding activity" (Veblen, 1898). Thus Veblen argued that the possession of property becomes the basis of popular esteem, therefore, it also becomes a requisite to the complacency which we call self-respect (Veblen, 1899). Campbell (1995) has noted that Veblen's clearest arguments were that wealth confers honor, and the individual is esteemed in proportion to wealth they possess, while individual self-esteem depends on the esteem accorded by others. According to Veblen, respect accorded by neighbors also motivates a person to strengthen his self-respect and by becoming rich.

2.4.2 Pavlovian learning model: classical conditioning

Any relative permanent change in behavior that can be attributed to experience is called learning. A form of learning in which reflex responses are associated with new stimuli is called classical conditioning. In brief, Ivan Pavlov observed that meat powder caused reflex salivation in dogs. At first, the bell was a neutral stimulus which when ringed produced nothing but when paired with meat powder caused salivation. Pavlov repeated the sequences many times. Eventually (as conditioning took place), Pavlov's bell alone began to cause salivation. By association, the bell, which by nature did not affect salivation began to produce the same response that food did. Once a person or an animal learns to respond to a conditioned stimulus (CS), other stimuli similar to the CS may also trigger a response. The value of stimulus generalization is easy to understand; for example, a child who gets burned while playing with a matchbox. Learning principles predict that the sight of a lighted matchbox will become a conditioned stimulus for fear.

The result of Pavlovian research led to a stimulus-response model of human behavior. There have been numerous applications of the Pavlovian concept to consumer behavior. The laws that characterize classical conditioning are the following:

2.4.2.1 Acquisition

The period in conditioning during which a response is reinforced is called acquisition.

2.4.2.2 Extinction

If the unconditioned stimulus never again follows the conditioned stimulus, conditioning will extinguish. Repetition of the conditioned stimulus without reinforcement is called extinction.

2.4.2.3 Generalization

Once a person or an animal learns to respond to a conditioned stimulus, another stimulus similar to the conditioned stimulus may also trigger a response. Stimulus generalization greatly affects our behavior. For instance, if you happen to meet a person who looks like your enemy, your initial attitude and feeling towards the person may be influenced by generalization.

2.4.2.4 Stimulus discrimination

It is an important part of learning. It is the learned ability to respond differently to similar stimuli.

2.4.2.5 Vicarious conditioning

Vicarious classical conditioning occurs when we observe another person's emotional reactions to a stimulus and, by doing so, learn to respond emotionally to the same stimulus. For example horror movies probably add to fear of snakes, caves, spiders, height and other terror-provoking situational stimuli. Being simply told that snakes are dangerous may not explain the child's emotional response. More likely, such fears are learned by observing others as they react fearfully when the word snake is mentioned or a snake image appears on television (Ollendick & King, 1991).

2.4.2.6 Marketing application of the Pavlovian model

In the case of the introduction of a new brand in the market, Pavlovian principles can be used. The organization introducing a new brand may attempt to form new habits for its new brand by extinguishing existing brand habit. This can be achieved by the use of strong cues for the product being introduced. Another approach in which the Pavlovian model offers insight is in the form of guidance for advertising strategies. Repetition in advertising is an effective technique to sufficiently arouse the individual consciousness towards the product.

Repetition in advertising also has two desirable effects. Repetition (or frequency of association), firstly, combats forgetting and, secondly, provides reinforcement while the consumer becomes selectively exposed to advertisements of the product after purchase.

2.4.3 Freudian psychoanalytic model

According to the Freudian model, the behavior is driven by unconscious, biologically based urges that demand gratification. People continue to carry the unconscious residue of unresolved infantile conflicts and make the appropriate choice for the original desired object when the situation is favorable. Freudian assumption of "depth psychology" led to fascinating analysis of everyday phenomena of dreams, jokes and the slip of the tongue. His concepts of Id, Ego and Superego are frequently used to explain personality and behavior. The personality of a person develops in response to four major sources of tension: physiological growth process, frustration, conflict and threat. Identification and displacement are two main methods by which the individual learns to resolve frustrations, conflicts and anxieties. Identification is a method by which a person takes over the feature of another person. The child identifies with parents as they appear to be most important during the early years of childhood. During different developmental stages, people tend to identify with those whose accomplishments are more in line with their current wishes. The process of identification takes place unconsciously.

The process of displacement takes place when an original object choice is not achieved and a new object choice is formed as a substitute.

Freud pointed out the development of civilization was made possible by the inhibitions of primitive object choices and the diversion of instinctual energy into the socially acceptable and culturally creative channel. A displacement that produces a higher level of cultural achievement is called sublimation.

In the marketing of brands, psychological factors of identification and displacement are applied to create a brand value for their products which can be easily integrated by consumers. It is not an irony that poor and middle-class persons are shown the dream of becoming like a rich person by identifying themselves with certain products that work in reality.

2.4.4 Maslow's hierarchy of needs

Maslow (1967, 1970) proposed a theory of human motivation hierarchy of needs. Lower-level needs are more dominant, known as deficiency motivation and triggered by some deficit or lack within the person. Higher-level needs are called growth motivation, which is a person's striving to achieve goals and personal growth.

The lowest level of needs in Maslow's hierarchy theory consists of hunger, sex, thirst and other drives with somatic basis. As Maslow stated, "a want that is

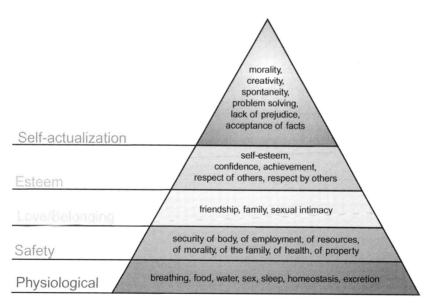

FIGURE 2.2   Maslow's hierarchy of needs.
Source: https://commons.wikimedia.org/wiki/File:Maslow%27s_hierarchy_of_needs.svg

satisfied is no longer a want. The organism is dominated and its behavior organized by unsatisfied needs. If hunger is satisfied, it becomes unimportant in the current dynamics of the individual" (1970, p. 38).

The next set of needs to emerge is that of safety needs, which include security, protection from fear and need for structure. The third set of needs to emerge consists of the belongingness and love needs. These represent the need for friends, family and "affectionate relations with people in general". Maslow referred these needs to our deeply animal tendency to herd, to flock, to join, to belong (1970, p. 44). Maslow suggested that "the thwarting of these needs is the most commonly found in case of maladjustment and more severe pathology" (1970, p. 44).

The fourth level according to Maslow's hierarchy theory includes two sets of esteem needs, representing our needs for self-esteem and esteem for others. The first set includes desires for achievement, mastery, confidence, competence and independence. The second set includes the needs for respect and esteem from others, which consist of the desire for fame, status, dominance, attention and dignity.

In Maslow's hierarchy, need for self-actualization is considered the highest level of need. Maslow described that when all four basic, deficiency needs have been satisfied, a new discontent and restlessness will soon develop unless the individual is doing what he individually, is fitted for – what a man can be, he must be (1970, p. 40). In Maslow's use of the term, self-actualization refers to "The desire to become more and more what are idiosyncratically is to become everything that one is capable of becoming" (1970, p. 46). It is important to recognize that self-actualization does not entail a deficiency or lack of something external: rather, it represents "Intrinsic growth of what is already in the organism . . . Development then proceeds from within rather than from without, and paradoxically the highest motive is to be unmotivated and unstriving" (1970, pp. 134–35).

Maslow's theory is useful in marketing strategy, since it provides an understanding of consumer motivations, primarily because consumer goods often serve to satisfy each of the needs levels. The relevance of need theory indicates need priorities of the consumers. However, this theory can't be generalized at a universal level, and a lot depends upon the cultural and individual differences of consumers.

2.5 Models for consumer behavior

The models of consumer behavior are useful in many ways. The explanatory variables are specified, that is, in the minds of the people. The relationship between variables and the sequences of cause and effect of the variable are specified. By showing explicit relationships between variables, a tentative view of behavioral phenomena is offered. In addition, consumer model research findings are integrated to archive specific goals. Evaluations of a particular model can be carried out about its impact and failure on the consumers. Some of the main models of consumer behavior are described in the following.

2.5.1 Bettman information processing model (1979)

A theory of human rationality must attach due importance to the content of the decisions as well as procedural rationality, or the ways in which decisions are made. According to Simon (1990), rational human behavior is shaped by the structure of the task environment and the computational capabilities of the actor. As regards the decision process, the view that preferences and beliefs are frequently constructed as needed on the spot, rather than simply retrieved from memory, is becoming increasingly accepted and has important implications for the understanding, assessment and improvement of decisions (Payne, Bettman & Schkade, 1999). This model focuses on the information processing perspective. It analyzes the type of information used by consumers and how the decision is arrived at by consumers based on information. How consumers do the perceptual coding, processing and memorizing of information is also given paramount importance in this model. Runyon and Stewart (1987) pointed out a strong correlation between processing capacity and education, intelligence and previous experience. Also, it has been noted that consumers are often interrupted and do not behave single-mindedly when pursuing a goal.

2.5.2 Nicosia model

This model was developed by Nicosia (1966). It describes that messages from advertisement agencies first influence the predispositions of consumers towards the product or service and that depending upon contextual circumstances, the consumer will develop a certain attitude towards the product. The consumer may search for the product after becoming influenced by the evaluation of the product. If the consumer is satisfied after an evaluation, he may develop a positive attitude resulting in the purchase of the product, and in case of not being satisfied, the customer may not be inclined to purchase.

2.5.3 The Howard-Sheth model

Howard and Sheth (1969) used the term buying behavior, and not consumer behavior. The model has four major components: stimulus Input (Input variables) Hypothetical construct, Response outputs (output variable) and Exogenous variable. It also described significant stimuli (brand) and the social stimuli on the information about the product in the social realm. The hypothetical construct in this model deals with perceptual constructs and learning constructs.

The perceptual constructs describe how a consumer obtains and processes information received from input variables. The learning constructs includes the consumer's goals, preferences, standards for evaluating alternatives, information and buying intentions. Output variables represent a possible response to stimuli by the consumer, which includes five variables – namely attention, brand comprehension, attitude, intention and purchase. Exogenous variables are not directly part of the decision-making process by consumers, but it includes other factors of time, personality traits, financial status and importance of the purchase. The model shows the complexity of the process of consumer behavior.

2.5.4 The Engel, Blackwell, Miniard model (EBM)

Engel, Blackwell and Miniard (1995) identified three broad decision processes-based reasoning underlying consumer behavior which includes extended, limited and wide-range problem-solving. The model highlights the importance of individual differences, environmental influences and psychological processes in the decision-making process of a consumer. Decision-making is influenced by need recognition, search for alternative evaluation, purchase, consumption and post-purchase alternative evaluation as well as divestment. The decision-making process is a result of a combination of factors that influences consumer behavior. Consumer behavior is a complex process dependent on a variety of factors varying with context and culture. The role of psychological factors occupies paramount importance in this process. It is important to highlight the factors of price perception and perceived quality as a contributor to consumer behavior.

2.5.5 Belief-expectancy and valence model

Developed by Rosenberg (1956) and Fishbein (1963), this model is used to predict attitude preferences. Intentions are verbally reported and are also considered important factors for the attitude/behavior link. Personality factors and their dimensions such as the need for achievement, self-concept, self-actualization and interpersonal relationships are also contributory factors to understand the dynamics of consumer behavior. Brand loyalty has been a powerful factor in influencing consumer behavior. Innovations and considerable importance of new products have also been an important influencing factor for consumer behavior. On a daily basis new researches, techniques and strategies are being adopted to influence consumer behavior.

2.6 Consumption and happiness

Consumption and happiness are strongly associated. The term "subjective well-being" is often used interchangeably with the more colloquial term "happiness". This construct refers to people's cognitive and affective evaluation of their lives

(Diener, 2000). In principle, it is the most democratic evaluation, as it allows each individual to decide for himself or herself whether they have a good and worthwhile life. Research suggests that although happiness has a strong genetic component, about 50% of the differences between people in their life happiness can be attributed to external factors (Weiss et al., 2008). It is perhaps not surprising that a major emphasis in economic studies is on the links between income and subjective well-being. The extent to which consumption contributes to happiness is a matter of intense debate.

Though cross-sectional micro-data analysis suggests a positive and statistically significant correlation between life satisfaction and income, the magnitude of these associations is generally small. The relationship between money and happiness is weak at best (Layard, 2005).

Indeed, differences in the personal income of individuals explain less of the difference in reported well-being than a range of other factors, such as employment, family relationship, health, education and income inequality (Di Tella & Macculloch, 2005). Increased consumption of goods that are not available with a person, such as purchasing a house, car and television, may increase well-being by reducing material hardship or making life easier. Consumption of certain "conspicuous" goods may increase happiness by increasing status (Charles et al., 2009; Veblen, 1899). Expensive clothing, jewelry, automobiles, (even) licensed weapons, membership of elite clubs and resorts, expensive vacations and aesthetic pursuit of golf and billiards are characterized as status goods and may be related to happiness. Consumption of such products and hobbies are linked to happiness through its effect on social relationships. A social relationship does bring happiness to an individual (Diener & Biswas-Diener, 2002; Putnam, 2000). It is also suggested that consumption and happiness do not happen in a vacuum and strong social identification and recognition are necessary to add a happiness dimension. Increase in life satisfaction is not possible through the mere accumulation of material goods.

People who are more oriented towards the consumption of market goods for the sake of materialism (and conversely less oriented towards relational goods) report a lower level of subjective well-being (Kasser, 2002). Economists have long argued that consumption data are a superior measure of permanent income and overall material well-being than are income data (Meyer & Sullivan, 2003).

THINK BOX

- Are consumption and happiness directly linked in your opinion?
- What is the role of social factors for enhancement in life satisfaction in your opinion?

2.7 Work and happiness

Doing work is also among the causes of happiness or causes of unhappiness. According to the nature of the work and the abilities of a person, the degree of both happiness and unhappiness varies. Work is desirable in most of the situations to earn income and sustain our livelihood. At the same time, it reduces the burden of boredom. It has been found that idle rich people suffer boredom at the cost of doing nothing or the least. To fulfill one's ambitions and deriving continuity of purpose is one of the most essential ingredients of happiness in the long run. One of the causes of unhappiness among intellectuals these days is that so many of them whose skill is the antithesis of their instinctual choice find no interest in the role. If you ask many of the people who work in media, in the information technology sector or for marketing companies, the majority would endorse the view that they are doing it for the sake of livelihood. Such types of work can't bring any satisfaction, and in this process of doing something antithetical of his/her interest, in the long run, may make them cynical.

The idea of a good life in Indian tradition emphasizes the continuous achievement of knowledge and work towards good actions. The concept of happiness is also guided by cultural factors. In individualistic cultures, the main focus of satisfaction is related to a single person, whereas in a collectivistic culture, the group is valued above the individual.

Possessing compassion helps the person to succeed in life, and according to Eastern culture, this is a good virtue. In moving toward the aim of a good life, compassion plays a key role in Eastern cultures. The attainment of compassion means "to transcend preoccupation with the centrality of self". In Buddhist teachings, when people reach a state of nirvana, they have reached a state of peacefulness entailing "[c]omplete harmony, balance and equilibrium" (Sangharakshita, 1991).

Similarly, in Confucian teaching, harmony is viewed as crucial for happiness. Confucius had high praise for individuals who were able to harmonize. It has been noted that leisure spending across the culture is associated with a higher level of happiness through its aesthetic and social effects. Although people may not realize it always, it is a fact that leisure and recreation is the largest industry in the world. A variety of activities like sports, gardening, crafts and other hobbies related activities exist at a national and a global level.

Perceived freedom of mind during leisure activities enhances the intrinsic motivation of individuals. Perceived competencies are also derived through consistent participation in recreational activities. People also experience skill development through regular participation in such activities. Human health, too, is benefitted by taking part in recreational activities; especially outdoor activities can greatly improve physical health.

THINK BOX

- Does doing work always bring happiness in your opinion?
- Are there differences in satisfaction levels among individualistic and collectivistic cultures?

2.8 Comparison and happiness

Consumer theory of happiness has also strong characteristics of comparison and competition and a constant need for social validation. This tendency for showing luxury to others, whether a big house, car, job or any other achievement, is highlighted by people through personal efforts and social media. It is, in fact, a cry for attention and validation from others. Chasing social validation can never bring happiness, as it has a long unending list of valuables to be acquired. In another sense constantly seeking social approval may bring more disappointment, greater loneliness and lowered self-esteem. Nowadays children and adolescents want to purchase high-end technological gadgets, and they feel very bad about themselves owing to peer pressure. There are instances when children forgo eating and fight with parents to get a mobile phone of their choice, and this also applies to adults in some cases. People also tend to form an "us" and "them" category. In case of something not having with them, they tend to acquire those things. According to the equity theory posited by Adams (1963), people do not feel bad about themselves unless they perceive inequity in the related environment to which they belong.

Therefore, it appears that consumerism and the happiness relationship are paradoxical. The trend of having more and more is also determined by socio-cultural, economic and political factors. Money cannot buy happiness, and consuming more stuff does not necessarily improve our happiness. An important distinction is to be made between fundamental needs and non-essential needs. Researches and reality indicate people with higher income levels are not always happy as compared to the people of middle socio-economic status. The pressure of advertising also creates and manipulates our needs and pursuit of happiness, which is largely influenced by socio-cultural traditions and values of human fulfillment. We have too many materialist items in the market which are also playing disastrous effects on the climate. In the book *Climate Shock*, Gernot Wagner and Martin L. Weitzman (2015) highlighted the likely repercussions of a hotter planet. The city of Copenhagen is widely recognized as a leader in the global green economy. Copenhagen has experienced phenomenal growth while improving environmental performance and transitioning to a low-carbon economy. Human-induced climate change is possible through small changes. It is important to realize that happiness is not the sole venture of individuals, and true happiness can be only achieved through integrating an individual's aspirations and goals with nature.

2.9 Consumer culture and identity

People's engagement with social media, like Facebook, Instagram and Twitter, have impacted how individuals are related to one another.

2.9.1 Bedroom culture

Significant interaction of the virtual world with the real world is a hallmark of emergent contemporary culture. Mobile phones and internet-mediated communication are the basis of friendship, business and peer relations and has led to major cultural and identity consequences. The media have thrown up new rituals, replacing many old traditions and having an important impact on people's identity sculpture. Bedroom culture centered on the use of internet-related communication has also led to the construction of a new media home environment. The flourishing of bedroom culture encourages the privatization of media usage as everybody attempts to forge a world that is distinct from that of their parents. As Angela McRobbie (1978) argues, girls are socialized not to engage in crime and deviance through bedroom culture. This is because they are virtually trapped in their rooms. Bedroom culture involved engaging in consumer products that might improve their appearance or provide entertainment that could be enjoyed alone through music and other commercial products. Children's television viewing and interaction culture are quite different from the shared values of adult television culture. Children's television is often more a "reflection of adult interest as fantasies or desires" and their view of childhood, rather than what children would choose themselves.

Important behavioral changes have taken place in the lives of all three generations of people with the advent and dominance of media-mediated interaction. A new trend has been fueled by the continual multiplication of media goods at home, fostering a shift in media use from that of "family television" to that of individualized media lifestyles.

2.9.2 Privatization of leisure

Nowadays outside places are considered unsafe and have led to a decline in outdoor activities for children and youth. No public places, like gardens, parks, schools, police stations, even temples and churches, are considered safe places to visit alone. You can't trust anybody these days and fear of the outdoors is expressed by parents in urban and rural areas.

The fears about children's crime in public places exemplify society's requirement for an "indoor child" which will not only keep children but also the public safe.

Thus, children face not only practical and material but also discursive constraints on their lived activities. Their media preferences are decreasingly shared with their parents, for "the modern family ideology (promotes) families in which the goal of individual self-realization overshadows community solidarity and stability" (Gadlin, 1978). As media gadgets have multiplied in a home, the interaction of family and practices that enhance intra-family attraction have altered.

2.9.3 Identity

In the changing preference of lifestyle, bedroom culture and privatization tendencies, our identity formation has also undergone a sea change.

In adolescence, the concern with self-identity is of primary importance. Children and adolescents have developed a special preference towards identity, protecting and embellishing their own spaces distinct from adult scrutiny and intervention. Personal ownership of media-friendly gadgets in the bedroom dramatically increases in the early teenage years.

These images of self-sufficiency and control figure prominently in young people's conversation of their bedroom and private space, and any type of interference by the elders in this personal territory is experienced as a violation of privacy. During earlier times, collectivity principle as regards family choices used to be the dominant principle. Nowadays distinct space, time and preferences possibly maintaining distinct identities need to be respected to help the family sustain its unity.

2.9.4 Technology and identity

Critical theorists such as McLuhan and Benjamin Enzensberger envisioned the democratic potential of the increased communication capacity of radio, film and television. Mitchell Kapor, former developer of Lotus 1.2.3, claims that the information superhighway opens qualitatively new political opportunities because it creates new loci of speech: The crucial question is, who controls the switches? There are two extreme choices. Users may have indirect or limited control over when, what, why and from whom they get information and to whom they send it. That's the broadcast model today, and it seems to breed consumerism, passivity and mediocrity. Or users may have decentralized, distributed, direct control over when, what, why and with what they exchange information. That's the internet model today, and it seems to breed critical thinking, activism, democracy and quality. We have an opportunity to choose now (Kapor, 1993, p. 5) in the information superhighway model a shift towards a decentralized network of communication-making senders, receivers, producers, consumers, rulers and ruled, upsetting the logic of the understanding of the previous media age. In the present media ecology subject, constitution occurs through the mechanism of interactivity. According to Rheingold (1993, p. 61), cybernauts know what they are looking for, and finding in the same surprising ways not just information, but instant access to ongoing relationships with a large number of other people. Rheingold terms the network of relations that came into existence on internet bulletin boards "virtual communities". Virtual communities are on the ascent, and real communities with their traditional rituals are on the decline. In the case of the nation-state, generally regarded as the strongest group identification in the modern period and thus perhaps the most "real" community of this era, the role of imaginary has been fundamental (Anderson, 1983). People connect with the stranger and try to establish a bond without much of traditional social boundary languages. Huge cultural exchange is happening on the screen, with less inhibition decoding the identities of others and unpacking our own identities.

The rigid boundaries of caste, creed and gender are not static, and a level of fluidity of exchange occurs in electronic communication. Technology is breaking down the notion of a few-to-many communication. It is also a fact that some communicators are more powerful than others, but the big idea behind cyber-tales is that many people are talking to many people.

The stories are becoming more and more idiosyncratic interactive and individualistic, told in different forums to diverse audiences in different ways (Katz, 1994). The constraints of broadcast oligopolies are being broken by the World Wide Web, which allows the simultaneous transmission of text, images and sounds. Social relations networks on internet media are much larger, hence fundamental principles of group psychology can't be applied on social media platforms. Dunbar's (2012) social brain hypothesis states that cognitive capacity and neocortex size determine complex social interaction and therefore the size of social networks. He concludes that the "natural" social group size for humans is approximately 150 (Dunbar, 2012), but nowadays people maintain multiple networks and numbers in the thousands in their contact lists, hence authentic social interaction is not possible through these media. Social media platforms allow the users to broadcast information via different modes like Facebook, Twitter and Instagram and avails the response from others in the form of comments and likes. Social media conversation entails the flow of content across social media platforms and the mixing of local and remote social spheres. This effectively expands the conversation into many-to-many interactions. This ability to broadcast the information about self has increased, but the quality of a relationship is also affected. Sometimes the message being broadcast through these media can't convey the identity and seriousness of attention it deserves. Thus, the level of satisfaction from a particular broadcast may not provide satisfaction to the sender, and a gap in expectations and its fulfillment occurs. Though self-disclosure has long been associated with increasing relational intimacy (Altman & Taylor, 1973) self-disclosure via social media can negatively impact the relational quality.

> **THINK BOX**
>
> • Do you think advancement in technology has improved the satisfaction levels of people in society?

2.9.5 Lack of commitment and attachment

There are possibilities of commitment loss owing to multiple relational contexts of families, friends, acquaintances and strangers. The broadcast quality of social media platform intersects with spatial boundary management processes because it alters the level of control an individual has over the intended audience for disclosure (Tufekci, 2008). It becomes difficult at times to manage coherence in one's identity due to the unpredictability of responses from the audience.

Self-categorization, that is, identifying oneself as a member of a particular social grouping, is a basic component of group identity. In a social media platform, it is difficult to find a match as a category owing to the diversity of identity of its members. It further lacks a positive in-group attitude about the members of a social media platform. Theoretically, a strong sense of belonging to a group is assumed to include feeling comfortable with one's ethnicity and having positive feelings about one's group membership (Tajfel & Turner, 1986).

Positive feelings for one's group contribute to happiness; however, lack of commitment about one's media group does not offer scope for happiness in a genuine sense. Values also determine one's closeness to the group and Identity. It is difficult to arrive at a consensus regarding values of users of social media owing to different value preferences. Whatever group identity consensus is achieved on social media platforms through developmental and situational changes turns out to be a stage of identity diffusion. Research on intergroup attitudes has been guided by contact with other groups that will, under certain conditions, lead to a more positive attitude towards members of the group (Hewstone & Brown, 1986). Also, contact among groups can contribute to positive intergroup outcomes, including expressed liking (Wagner & Machleit, 1986) and lowered anxiety (Stephan & Stephan, 1989).

But such studies can't be generalized to social media networks owing to the diversity of group members and wide differences in interaction patterns adopted by them. Media messages certainly have great potential to influence the attitude-behavior and identity of the people.

2.10 Interactive and emerging technologies

Emerging technologies include a variety of technologies such as educational technology, information technology, nanotechnology, biotechnology, psychotechnology, robotics and artificial intelligence. Emerging technologies are characterized by novelty, innovation and relatively fast growth with a degree of persistence, and its impact on a socio-economic and cultural spectrum.

Theorists like Ray Kurzweil (2005) are techno-Utopians who believe that emerging and converging technologies could and will eliminate poverty and abolish suffering. Some theorists such as Martin Ford (2009) argue that as information technology advances, robots and other forms of automation will ultimately result in significant unemployment as machines and software begin to match and exceed the capability of workers to perform most routine jobs.

A fundamental assumption in educational literature is that interaction and communication between and among participants in the learning process are critical to achieve productive outcomes. It is also emphasized that technology has an inherent benefit as compared to other educational resources, and suitable development in technology can help interactive instruction to be more effective.

In the current environment, the tendency is to focus on learner-centered development and prototype to determine the operational parameters of the final product. The objectives of an interactive learning project involves prototyping by using the technique of approximations. Another task for supporting the interactive application is to merge the prototype and production tasks into a single activity.

2.10.1 Psychotechnology

Psychotechnology refers to any application of technology for psychological purposes or to any way of using the psychological process for the desired outcome. Medical uses of "psy-tech" for pain control, immune system enhancement, and accelerated healing are already into existence. Our survival in the age of cutthroat competition can be vastly improved with the help of technology in improving creativity and decision-making. Psy-tech can also contribute to humans through products and services that can reduce stress. For instance, activities of music, dance and singing are heavily influenced by technology, and it ultimately helps people inducing altered states.

2.10.2 Video games and their implications

In general, there is a negative view ascribed to video games and computer games in society. Even in 1969, we had computational technology linked with networking used for games in a version of Spacewar! This game ran on PLATO, originally a computer-based educational system developed in the 1970s.

Later on in the mid-1980s, the Bulletin Board System (BBS) called the Door allowed users to access a variety of games. In 1979 the first MUD (Multi-User Dungeon) was developed by Richard Bartle and Roy Trubshaw while they were at Essex University. At the beginning of online gaming, structures were influenced by fantasy literature like *The Lord of the Rings* (1954) but later adaptations were more focused. In the later years, MMOG's with titles like Meridian 59 (1996) and Ultima Online (1997) provided a large number of players around the world to game together. PUGO host numerous games that are produced by Plains Exploration & Production Company. Other titles, like Puzzle Pirates or KartRider are also popular among the players. These days there are more than thousands of games that are popular among users of different age groups, and, to name a few: Bubble Shooter, Fireboy and Watergirl, 1001 Arabian Nights and Ludo Legend. Snail Bob is another great series of online games that provides the player to a series of epic adventures. There are also a different categories of games, such as makeover games, mobile games, puzzle games, simulation games, skill games, family games, girl games, boy games and so on. All kinds of games available online can be found under a prominent category of sports, action, arcade, racing, adventure, girl games, boy games and kids games.

Online gaming has become very popular across all sections of people, especially the youth and children. Today gamers seek more and more interactive ways to participate in online gaming. Player Unknown Battle-Grounds (PUBG) is an online multiplayer battle royal game developed and published by PUBG Cooperation, a subsidiary of South Korean video game company Bluehole. PUBG has over 30 million active users daily and is a chart-topper on Android and iOS handsets alike in India. In August 2018, India saw its first case of Bengaluru clinic treating a 15-year-old boy for PUBG addiction. PUBG was first launched in December 2017 on gaming consoles and then in March 2018 on smartphones. In each round at the game, PUBG Parachutes 100 players onto a virtual island where teams of two fight each other to the death until only one survives. PUBG games were banned in Tamil Nadu's Vellore Institute of Technology in its men's hostel. In January 2019 a statewide ban on PUBG was issued across primary schools in Gujarat owing to children's studies being adversely affected. In February 2019, 11-year-old Ahad Nizam filed a Public Interest Litigation (PIL) at the Bombay high court through his mother, alleging that the game perpetuates violence, aggression and cyberbullying. Goa's information technology minister, Rohan Khaunte, also labeled the multi-player game "a demon in every house" and called to curb its spread in the coastal state. Currently, at $290 million (Rs 2070 crore) business, India's gaming industry will be worth over $1 billion by 2021, a KPMG study estimates.

India's obsession with PUBG, particularly among adolescents and early youth, is rising fast, as are games created by the Chinese publisher Ten Cent Games. People are using PUBG in India mainly because they perceived it better than other games and everyone is talking about it. Students gain knowledge through game-based learning in math, social sciences, sciences and food-safety-related techniques. Nowadays clinicians and pediatricians use active gameplay as part of a strategy to get kids moving. Even teachers and physical education instructors make use of games to encourage activity and motivation in classrooms.

A large body of evidence indicates that computer and video games are engaging, interactive and educational, and critics, particularly those in obesity-prevention fields, continue to suggest limits on screen time (Krebs & Jacobson, 2003), without differentiating between sedentary screen time and active behavior encouragement by many video games.

2.10.2.1 The functions of play

Erikson (1977) proposed that play context allows children to experiment with social experiences and stimulate alternatives emotional consequences which can then bring about feelings of resolution outside the play context. Both Piaget (1962) and Vygotsky (1978) espoused strong theoretical links between play and development of social cognition. Gottman (1986) described development lists emphasizing that play constitutes an emotionally significant context through which themes of power and aggression, nurturance, anxiety, pain, loss, growth and joy can be enacted productively. The video games vary in the level of complexity and the extent of social interaction.

2.10.2.2 Cognitive benefits of gaming

A recently published meta-analysis (Uttal et al., 2013) concluded that the spatial skills improvement derived from playing commercially available shooter video games are comparative to the effect of formal (high school and university-level) courses aimed at enhancing these same skills. A 25-year longitudinal study with a US representative sample (Wai, Lubinski, Benbow & Steiger, 2010) established the power of spatial skills facilitating achievement in subjects like science, technology, engineering and mathematics. The "videogames are controlled training regimens delivered in highly motivating behavioral contexts … because behavioral changes arise from brain changes, it is also no surprise that performance improvement is paralleled by enduring physical and functional neurological remodeling" (Bavelier et al., 2011). The most robust effect on cognitive performance comes from playing shooter video-games and not from for example – puzzle or role-playing games (Green & Bavelier, 2012). Video games also seem to facilitate developing problem-solving skills.

2.10.2.3 Motivational benefits of gaming

Motivational styles characterized by persistence and continuous effortful engagement are found to be key contributors to success and achievement (Dweck & Molden, 2005). According to Dweck and Molden (2005), children develop a belief about their intelligence and abilities, which underlie specific motivational styles and directly affect achievement. Immediate and concrete feedback in video games (e.g. through points, coins, a dead-end in puzzles) serve to reward continual effort and keep players within what Vygotsky (1978, p. 86) called the "zone of proximal development".

The extent to which individuals endorse an incremental theory versus an entity theory of intelligence reliably predicts whether individuals in challenging circumstances will persist or give up respectively (Dweck & Molden, 2005). The entity theory of intelligence maintains that intelligence is an innate trait that can't be improved, and the incremental theory of intelligence prescribes that intelligence can be cultivated through effort and time. Video games use failure as a motivational tool, and a positive attitude towards failure makes a person more motivated for better performance.

2.10.2.4 Emotional benefits of gaming

Children having extremely positive feelings for gaming show that playing puzzle video games with minimal interfaces can improve players' mood, promote relaxation and ward off anxiety. Flow or transportation in another positive emotional experience described by gamers, during which they are immersed in an intrinsically rewarding activity.

2.10.2.5 Social benefits of gaming

In the virtual social community, video gamers utilize social skills. Given these immersive social contacts, we propose that gamers are rapidly learning social skills and prosocial behavior that might generalize to their peer and family relations outside the gaming environment (Gentile & Gentile, 2008; Gentile et al., 2009). Players seem to acquire many social skills when they play games that are specifically designed to reward effective cooperation, support and helping behaviors. It also needs to be understood that by playing and engaging in prosocial games, children will tend to replicate it in practical life situations.

2.10.2.6 Health benefits

One of the most important success stories of a game that had a significant impact on health-related behavior is the case of Re-mission (Kato, Cole, Bradlyn & Pollock, 2008) a video game designed for child cancer patients. The self-efficacy and adherence to treatment protocol were much higher in the group of child patients who played video games, designed for this purpose. Therapists currently use games and virtual reality for stroke rehabilitation (Saposmik et al., 2010).

2.11 Adverse effects of video games

There is a growing concern that children are becoming involved in screen time to the exclusion of creative play or time in natural environments. There are also obesity-related problems with high involvement in video game activity. Children are also spending a large amount of time playing video games, which adds to their excessive screen time and ignoring of basic physical activities. Excess engagements in video games can also lead to isolation, particularly for children who are introverts. It is pertinent to understand that simply highlighting video games as "good" or "bad" will not be the right approach to analyze the enormity of the issue. Again, generalizing them as "violent" or "prosocial" will also amount to overlooking the complexity of the new playground and the varied landscape of virtual interactions taking place in those games. How gaming influences player's cognitive, emotional and social domains needs to be addressed through future research and understanding of this subject. Internet addiction is not yet an officially recognized mental disorder.

Some warning signs of technology addiction include:

- A sense of euphoria while plugged in
- Difficulty in negotiating with friends and family
- Skimping on sleep
- Dishonesty about usage
- Feeling anxious, ashamed, guilty or depressed as a result of technology use
- Withdrawing from other activities that were once pleasurable

Physical symptoms of technology addiction may include:

- Weight gain or weight loss
- Carpal tunnel syndrome
- Headaches
- Neck or backaches
- Dry, red eyes

2.11.1 Risk factors

More knowledge about a particular addiction may be useful for handling the problem in a better way. Some factors indicate a tendency for high risk. Gender tends to influence the usage pattern of the internet. Men are more susceptible to compulsive behavior with online/video gaming, cyberporn and online gambling, while women are more likely to become addicted to sexting, texting, social media, eBay and online shopping, according to Dr. Kimberley Young.

2.12 Ways to overcome internet dependence

In her book *Internet Addiction: Symptom, Evaluation and Treatment*, Young (1999) has suggested methods for internet addiction treatment. Unfortunately, clinical evidence in support of her prescribed strategies are lacking.

Peukert et al. (2010) suggest that interventions with a family member or other relatives, like "community reinforcement and family training", could be useful in enhancing the motivation of an addict to cut back on internet use, although the reviewers remark that control studies with relatives do not exist to date. A multi-modal approach by using several types of treatment can be more effective. Orzack and Orzack (1999) mentioned that treatment for internet addiction needs to be multidisciplinary, including CBT psychotropic medication, family therapy and case managers, because of the complexity of these patients' problems. There can be other methods of diversifying one's activities to other preferred hobbies. The techniques of Yoga, meditation, sports and cultural activities are the basic methods through which one can divert his/her attention from a fixed activity, in this case internet usage.

Young's (1996) questionnaire of screening internet addiction has focused upon an excessive preoccupation with internet terms of engagement and time, losing one's control to regulate behavior and compromising personal and social relationships due to excess internet usage. Those people who do not find sufficient motivation in active life activities also rely on excess use of the internet. Young (1996) suggested that catastrophic thinking may contribute to addictive internet use in providing a psychological escape mechanism to avoid real or perceived problems. In the Indian context also, lots of students, while traveling in the metro and even in school and colleges, are hooked to internet activity, ignoring important academic assignments. Even in the office, internet misuse is a serious concern among HR managers. Now monitoring devices are being installed to check for internet misuse by employees for non-official purposes.

2.13 Virtual social media

New forms of communication with interactive collaborative communications and multi-user communities for social networking are known as social media. These virtual social networks are essentially communities aiming to formulate socio-cultural-economic existence.

The virtual community is a social network of individuals in which people interact online to pursue mutual interests and goals. Such communities are social aggregations that emerge from internet-mediated communication in which people engage, deliberate and established personal and social relationships. The realm of the public sphere has enlarged with the advent of computer-mediated communication. Ben Bagdikian (1920–2016) argued that media monopoly will result in the control of the world's media, namely newspapers, magazines, books, broadcast stations, movies, recordings and videocassettes in the hands of a few corporate giants.

2.13.1 Panopticon

We now have the freedom to pursue virtual media platforms to express our view, which is not limited to geographical boundary limitations. Panopticon was the name for an ultimately effective prison, seriously proposed in eighteenth-century Britain by Jeremy Bentham. Bentham's panopticon is the architecture figure, who was regarded as the founder of utilitarianism and an advocate of the separation of church and state, freedom of expression and individual legal rights. According to Bentham, panopticon is a way to trace the surveillance tendencies of disciplinarian societies. The basic setup of Bentham's panopticon consisted of a central tower surrounded by cells, and having a watchman in the central tower. In the cells are prisoners or workers or children, depending on the use of the building. The tower shines a bright light so the watchman can see it, but prisoners are unable to see the watchman and consequently assume that they are always under observation. Though Bentham could not see a panopticon prison built in actuality, in the 1920s the closest thing to a panopticon prison was built – the Presidio Modelo complex in Cuba, which was infamous for corruption and cruelty and is now abandoned.

In the panopticon, the inspector exposes himself to the eyes of prisoners as little as possible. All of his power over the prisoners derives from his invisibility, or more precisely, his invisible omnipresence. One goal of panopticism was to spread throughout the social body, and social media performs this accordingly. The panopticon was only capable of holding a single prison on an imaginary basis, but social media watches millions at the same time, avoiding any physical confrontation which is also an important feature of panopticism. Social media has altered the social order of users' lives. The social order of society has become an integral part of user lives. Social media, however, is more realistic, and there are differences in terms of actual needs of the people associated being served more effectively. Social boundaries of the interpersonal relationships are changing with the new modalities of ambient and always-on sociability and enhanced by the architectural features of the social environments sustained by virtual media social networks.

Social media conversation can take place between individuals and groups, and the flow of content may involve local and global topographical spheres. Self-disclosure is an important feature of intimate social interaction, which people do not do on a social media platform very easily hence affecting the quality of social relationships. Social media platforms' messages are also unidirectional, hence allowing less scope for creation of consensus and negotiation to a common objective.

THINK BOX

- Does social media interfere with our freedom or does it helps improve autonomy and freedom?

2.13.2 Boundaries and social media

Social boundaries include the spatial, temporal and relational limits that define us as separate from others. Karr-Wisniewski, Wilson and Richter-Lipford (2011) identified five areas that challenge an individual's boundary regulation processes in social media environments, which are networks, territories, disclosure, relationships and interactions. Some theorists argue that friendship is a sacred thing, and that its sanctity is compromised on social media platforms. Some social scientists agree and have described SNS relationships as "Belief" and "Tangential" characterized by "ambient Intimacy" (Hesse-Biber, 2010) where we are surrounded indirectly by friends but lack true connections. Although online sharing has increased a lot, the importance of intimacy can't be equated with sharing. In some cases, sharing too much can be detrimental to relationships, and social psychology theorists argue that interpersonal boundaries are vital to both personal well-being and relational development.

SNS build social capital, the intrinsic value of participating in social exchange, through emotional support and access to new information and people. But one of the most obvious issues emerging from the impact of social network site use is the challenge of boundary lines that denotes where the relationship begins and ends.

Many types of negative activities happening on social networking sites, such as privacy breaches, ridicule, sexual advances and abusive words result in a feeling of disappointment and negative experiences. It is a very common practice by SNS users to withdraw from SNS for some time or forever. According to Altman (1975), interpersonal boundary regulations are the key to maintaining an appropriate level of interaction within one's social environment. Privacy is conceptualized as an interpersonal boundary process by which a person or group regulates interaction with others, by altering the degree of openness of self to others. According to Altman, in most of the relationships, primary mechanism of interpersonal control used to negotiate boundaries are personal space, territory, verbal behavior and non-verbal behavior. Who can access my information on SNS is a big issue, and there are several categories like only me, specific individuals and friends, everyone to settle this subject of privacy on social networking sites. The disclosure boundaries should be handled with privacy settings on SNS. Facebook also allows users to specify whether or not one's friend, can "comment on posts", "friends can check me into places", and other boundary negotiation issues. It is important to understand that despite so-called free flow of ideas, on SNS users have to struggle a lot deciding and determining relational boundaries. How to regulate it to the advantage of users who keep searching for innovative ways, and this whole dynamics of social media interpersonal interaction, is far more complex than it appears to be.

2.14 Self and social representation

Self-representation is an image of how one sees oneself resulting from how others see the individual, and to a great extent these traits are consistent with the self-image of the person. Psychologists Carl Rogers and Abraham Maslow talked about self-concept in detail. The self-categorization theory was developed by John Turner, who stated that the self-concept consists of two levels, a personal identity and a social identity. Self-concept can alternate rapidly between personal and social identity. The normal understanding of self-representation includes one's beliefs, thoughts, feelings, ideas, desires, actions and values. Social and clinical psychologists use the concept of self very frequently to describe human behaviors. Thagard (2014) has proposed a view of the self as a multilevel system consisting of social, individual, neural and molecular mechanisms. According to social identity theory, one psychological basis of group discrimination is that people identify with some groups and contrast themselves with other groups that are viewed less favorably (Tajfel, 1974).

The concept of "looking glass self" or "reflected appraisals" the idea that people come to see themselves as others see them (Markus & Kitayama, 1991; Mead, 1934) talked about westerners' "independent self-construals" and Asians' "interdependent self-construals". Andersen and Chen (2002) described a "relational self"in which knowledge about self is linked with knowledge about significant others. In most of the definitions of self, self-presentation occupies a central place which is a result of individual and social in self-presentation. People have a basic need for relatedness, for belonging to groups of people that they care about. Social approval is also strongly associated with the concept of self-representation. Baumeister (1998) stated people use self-representation to construct an identity for themselves. McGuire and McGuire (1996) stated that every type of identity needs social validation when people focus on positive aspects of themselves, their state self-esteem increases. Leary's sociometer theory proposed that the very existence of self-esteem is due to the need to monitor the degree to which one is accepted and included by other people (Leary & Baumeister, 2000). Social acceptance and rejection also affect our well-being, although self-representation seems to be a private matter but is closely interlinked with societal influences. According to Aron's self-expansion theory, self-expansion is a motivation to enhance potential efficacy (Aron et al., 1991, p. 105).

2.15 Internet

In understanding what Gidden's (1991) called the "project of the self" children and young people are experiencing the internet as a valued new place for social exploration and self-expression (Holloway & Valentine, 2003). The relation between politics and environment's everyday experiences can no longer be recognized without the internet's intrusive ubiquity. Self-authoring becomes a dominant practice adopted by teenagers with less regard to mainstream public opinion.

2.16 Social, economic and cultural impact of social media

The concept of geography is turning into digital geography having dramatic socio-economic and cultural impact on the lives of the people. Wires are disappearing with the wireless revolution and virtual modes have entered in paper in clothes in highways, in education, in politics and business and the very fabric of our existence today. Telecommuting and mobile communication are making the office environment more ephemeral. In many different ways, businesses are operating in a digital, interconnected space of flows (Castells, 1996) that has permitted a fine-grained division of labor, taking advantage of optional combinations of (high) skills (Laws) wages in various places around the world (Grossman & Rossi Hansberg, 2006; Scott, 2006).

A whole set of people from the information technology sector are being employed from third world countries providing much cheap labor. This "great unbundling" of tasks has sparked fears that nearly all jobs will disappear from high wages countries (Baldwin, 2006).

As IT has become cheaper, faster, better and easier to use, a large number of works in Indian and global contexts are being performed with the help of digital applications. Death of distance created by digital applications has allowed many educational organizations to use e-learning material from as far away as the USA and Europe thanks to broadband networks and computer-aided design. For a worker, telework centers and tele-cottages provide a third place, neither home nor business locations, where they can connect with their employer, whether government or business. An exceptional development pattern of business process outsourcing has taken place in India in the IT sector. Broadband technologies are enablers of the digital economy leading to the huge marketing potential of the products.

Some activities like farming, mining and forestry have not been greatly affected by digital technologies. Media, entertainment, electronic commerce, call center services, financial services, automobiles and aircraft have huge marketing potential of their products through social media and digital technology.

2.17 Impact of digital technology

E-learning is becoming an effective substitute of classroom learning. It is an interactive method of providing education through electronic media. The use of images, sounds, texts and video are making the learning more interesting for the students.

There are several e-learning platforms, and by 2022 this industry will turn into a huge market. Some of the popular e-learning platforms in India include BYJU's, Dexter Education Edumcamp solutions, IGNOU, NIIT, NIOS, Edukart and Zeus learning, and they pose a tough challenge to the traditional education system. The emergence of cloud computing and the rising popularity of big data and learning analytics are major trends which are challenging the dynamics of the online education market in India.

People are using social media for entertainment. There is a sea change in the behavior of the people, and the choice of entertainment is heavily influenced by social media platforms and their messages. The kinds of posts on social networking sites also influence the choice of music by the users of social networking sites.

2.17.1 Digital altruism

The digital landscape is always surrounded by its negative influences, but digital altruism is about using digital technologies for the support and growth of virtues and ethics. Digital altruism involves forming and promoting social good of charity for the poor. Education for uneducated provides harmony in times of conflict. It has been found that during times of natural disasters like floods, earthquake and typhoons, people do a lot of philanthropy work with the use of social media platforms. Many of us also send health tips for good health by experienced doctors and important research journals.

THINK BOX

- Can the concept of digital altruism be used to overcome poverty in India?

2.17.2 Social media and social unrest

In the Indian context, from Kashmir to Kanyakumari, we always keep noticing the paradox of fake news and real news on various social media platforms. Malicious propaganda and misleading polarizing views which do not exist in reality are reported on an everyday basis, and various law-enforcing agencies keep requesting and instructing CEOs of social media platforms to control this menace. Many fake referendums concerning issues of national integration are propagated in a prejudiced manner, doing enormous damage to the stability of the parties concerned. Which video is uploaded by whom and promoted in such subtle manners that it does the harm and concerned parties struggle for damage control. The user bases of Facebook, Twitter and YouTube are global and generate revenue globally. The societal impacts of malicious minded propaganda may have far-reaching implications. Fake accounts and Facebook-fueled misinformation and rumor mongering take place at regular intervals, creating hatred and conflicts in the society. So many interested parties work against each other to plant stories in social media which can raise tension, fears and tempers regarding the economy, fiscal health, poverty, and unemployment and if such stories sustain for a long period of time, it can impact the voting behavior of people in elections.

Digital disinformation is becoming an existential threat to democracy and to the civil society at large. One fake video can lead to a state of communal, caste or race frenzy; hence this medium of promoting free speech takes its toll on freedom by being an antithesis to it. Malicious actors exploit such a forum in the garb of free speech, promoting ideology of hate and disintegration of social harmony. Social media's filtering and sorting algorithms have so far failed to curtail this menace of making the correct distinction between information and disinformation to a large extent. Fake news also becomes worst in the form of paid news, which is banned by law but still happens, and certain conspirators do it despite legal restrictions. Left unchecked, this problem of genuine and fake is going to multiply in the times to come, posing a serious threat to authenticity and credibility of such platforms. It is affecting the lives of the people at large, and digital media platforms have acquired more complex dimensions than its intended objectives of promoting free and fair communications to all. Political propaganda, social life stories, product advertising people's opinion, capability for critical thinking, consumerism, biases and prejudices and altruism have a powerful impact on the democratic ethos of our society. This is such a dynamic platform that any kind of censorship is not easily possible or desirable, but it certainly poses some questions about these platforms and its effectiveness in the long-term goals of social harmony.

THINK BOX

- Is social media playing a negative role in maintaining broader social harmony across communities?

2.17.3 Ola-Uber and mass impact

The driving profession witnessed a huge employment opportunity in the recent years with the emergence of the Ola-Uber taxi service. Similarly, learning apps greatly reduced the demands for tutors at homes. Another huge decline in the recruitment of security guards due to emergence of CCTV cameras is also a case in point in Indian context. Lots of small-type eateries became irrelevant with the growth of online eateries. India witnessed a significant growth in start-up companies. E-commerce growth has a huge impact on traditional businesses of clothes and street hawkers business. The print industries of newspapers are also facing tough times with mobile app–generated news portals. In the Indian context, a large number of laborers migrate to cities and want to send money to their parents. Through pay phone and several other digital transaction apps, people can send money to their native places without any worries. Similarly, education apps are now reaching the remote rural areas of the country where students can get advantage of good-quality learning. Another good application is the use of apps for farmers to get free consultation with experts. Through government schemes like Jan-Dhan Yojana, money is being directly transferred into the accounts of direct beneficiaries.

It will be apt to suggest that digital technologies have both advantages and disadvantages, and striking a good balance is the need of the time.

2.18 Indian context and critical evaluation

Consumer behavior is an important area of research in the field of media psychology. Consumer society has deep-rooted implications for our psychosocial, cultural and economic aspects of life. Consumerism has affected overall happiness, and a growth of materialism in Indian society can be easily noticed. Consumerism has also contributed to ecological degradation. Gaming activity becoming a global phenomenon has also affected Indian society. A large number of children and adults are using gaming activity, and it has some emotional issues. Internet dependence has also emerged as a major problem in children, youth and adults in our society.

Social media has permeated to all sections of people, affecting their lives in different ways. Nowadays, the identity of a person and almost all other activities, social, cultural and professional, are being conducted through the lens of social media. It will be unwise to generalize its effects and implications on the Indian masses. People are adopting this platform for advantages to conduct their activities and more researches are needed to ascertain its implications in present and future. People in India are moving to online shopping for big and small necessities. Even people living in the rural areas have started buying online products. In India, social media bans in many parts of the country on various time periods have also posed security challenges to law-and-order agencies. Social media has also contributed positively in the empowerment of the Indian masses.

2.18.1 Case studies in Indian context

"Swiggy India; Voice of Hunger" is a food delivery app that has become a leading player with immense popularity and fan following. This brand used innovative techniques to engage with customers in exciting ways and it has a large number of followers to date. Lok Sabha Election's 2019 "Main Bhi chowkidar" was branded as a major campaign logo in their social media profile which received the attention of millions on Twitter, Facebook and other social media platforms.

A "Pay Attention" campaign was launched by Avon India, a beauty company, to raise awareness among Indian women about breast cancer. They intentionally launched the program one month prior to the International Month of Breast Cancer in October to register their presence among social media users. Avon posted a video of breast self-examination (BSE) of a woman which generated wide discussions on social media platforms. Support from celebrities on social media helped the brand get more attraction among viewers and the result was that 10,000 women got breast examinations in different cities of India.

Shaadi.com has a huge number of followers on Instagram, Facebook and Twitter. This is a digital platform for everyone to connect and share. Couples post their one common thing which eventually brings them together.

2.19 Summary

Consumer behavior is the cornerstone of a capitalist society because it allows the growth of consumption in different shades. Consumption as a need or greed is highly influenced by social status and fulfillment of prestige needs. Several methods of consumer behavior highlight varying aspects resulting in the purchasing behavior of individuals. Several techniques, strategy and technology along with psychological factors are used to grasp the attention of consumers and increasing their propensity to purchase. Consumption of goods and services is not directly related to happiness, and happiness can be derived from social factors as well. Work and happiness are closely related if a person can relate with himself, the job which he is doing otherwise can also become a source of stress. Social comparison is a strong contributing factor for the rise of consumerism, as constantly seeking social approval may bring disappointment. Consumer culture has also resulted in the emergence and growth of bedroom culture. Leisure activity is one of the largest industries in the world. Technology is also providing so many facilities of online shopping, online entertainment, online management of travel, online education, etc. It is also interfering with the time and privacy of individuals. The new emergence of virtual social media has entirely changed the dynamics of human behavior. Virtual environments are interactive, playing the role of social activities on digital platforms being used by people of all ages. Similarly, the video games industry has proliferated at wider levels in society. Some of these videogames are interactive and educational while others are addictive and harmful. There are motivational and problem-solving skills improvement benefits associated with video games. Some children and adolescents are becoming dependent of internet and video games which is adversely affecting their wellness.

Social media can also become a tool for promoting prosocial behavior with the use of digital altruism applications. It can also play a dangerous role with rumors and propaganda affecting the peace and harmony in society. It is suggested that technology in itself is not bad, but how we use it to our advantage depends a lot on our awareness and understanding.

Key points

- The consumer is an individual who purchases goods and services to satisfy personal and social needs.
- Consumer behavior tendency is also influenced by self-esteem, self-respect and social status factors
- Psychological theories explaining consumer behavior can be understood with the help of Pavlovian theory, Freudian theory and Maslow's hierarchy of needs.
- Important models explaining consumer behavior include information processing model (Bettman), the Nicosia model, the Seth model and the EBM model.
- Consumption and happiness are not positively correlated to each other.
- Consumer culture plays a crucial role in the identity formation of people.
- Interactive technologies provide scope for novelty and innovation for the users.
- Psycho-technology refers to the application of technology for bringing behavioral changes.
- Contrary to popular perception, video games have both advantages and disadvantages.

Key terms

consumer behavior, consumer culture, hierarchy of needs, belief-expectancy, bedroom culture, psycho-technology, social networking sites, panopticon, looking glass self, digital altruism

References

Adams, J.S. (1963). Toward an understanding of inequity. *Journal of Abnormal and Social Psychology*, 67, 422–36.

Altman, I. (1975). *The Environment and Social Behavior: Privacy, Personal Space, Territory, Crowding*. Monterey, CA: Brooks/Cole Pub. Co.

Altman, I., & Taylor, D.A. (1973). *Social Penetration: The Development of Interpersonal Relationships*. Oxford, UK: Holt, Rinehart & Winston.

Andersen, S.M., & Chen, S. (2002). The relational self: An interpersonal social-cognitive theory. *Psychological Review*, 109(4), 619–45.

Anderson, B. (1983). *Imagined Communities: Reflections on the Origin and Spread of. Nationalism*. London: Verso.

Aron, A., Aron, E.N., Tudor, M., & Nelson, G. (1991). Close relationships as including other in the self. *Journal of Personality and Social Psychology*, 60, 241–53.

Assael, H. (1995). *Consumer Behaviour and Marketing Action*. Ohio: South-Western College Publishing.

Bagdikian, B. (2004). *The New Media Monopoly*. Boston, MA: Beacon Press.

Baumeister, R. E. (1998). The self. In D.T. Gilbert, S.T. Fiske, & G. Lindzey (Eds.), *Handbook of Social Psychology* (4th ed., pp. 680–740). New York: McGraw-Hill.

Bavelier, D., Green, C., Han, D., Renshaw, P., Merzenich, M., & Gentile, D. (2011). Brains on video games. *Nature Reviews: Neuroscience*, 12, 763–8.

Beck, U. (1992). *Risk Society: Towards a New Modernity*. New Delhi: Sage.

Beck, U. (1999). *What Is Globalization?* Cambridge: Polity Press.

Beck, U. (2002). The cosmopolitan society and its enemies. *Theory, Culture and Society*, 19(1–2), 17–44.

Campbell, C. (1995). Conspicuous confusion? A critique of Veblen's theory of conspicuous consumption. *Sociological Theory*, 13(1), 37–47.

Castells, M. (1996). *The Rise of the Network Society: The Information Age: Economy, Society, and Culture* (Vol. 1). Oxford: Blackwell.

Charles, K.K., Hurst, E., & Roussanov, N. (2009). Conspicuous consumption and race. *The Quarterly Journal of Economics*, 124(2), 425–67.

Di Tella, R., & MacCulloch, R. (2005). Partisan social happiness. *Review of Economic Studies*, 72(2), 293–367.

Diener, E. (2000). Subjective well-being: The science of happiness and a proposal for a national index, *American Psychologist*, 55(1), 34–43.

Diener, E., & Biswas-Diener, R. (2002). Will money increase subjective well-being? A literature review and guide to needed research. *Social Indicators Research*, 57(2), 119–69.

Dunbar, R.I.M. (2012) "Social cognition on the Internet: Testing constraints on social network size". *Philosophical Transactions of the Royal Society*, 367(1599), 2192–201.

Dweck, C.S., & Molden, D.C. (2005). Self-theories: Their impact on competence motivation and acquisition. In A.J. Elliot & C.S. Dweck (Eds.), *Handbook of Competence and Motivation* (pp. 122–40). New York: Guilford Press.

Engel, J.F., Blackwell, R.D., & Miniard, P.W. (1995). *Consumer Behavior* (8th ed.). Fort Worth, TX: The Dryden Press.

Erikson, E.H. (1977) *Toys and Reasons: Stages in the Ritualization of Experience*. New York: W.W. Norton & Co.

Fayol, H. (1916). *General and Industrial Management*. Paris: Institute of Electrical and Electronics Engineering.

Fishbein, M. (1963). An investigation of the relationships between beliefs about an object and the attitude toward that object. *Human Relations*, 16, 233–9.

Ford, M.R. (2009). *The Lights in the Tunnel: Automation, Accelerating Technology and the Economy of the Future*. Lexington, KY: Acculant Publishing.

Gadlin, H. (1978). Child discipline and the pursuit of self: An historical interpretation. In H.W. Reese and L.P. Lipsitt (Eds.), *Advances in Child Development and Behavior* (pp. 231–61). New York: Academic Press.

Gentile, D., Anderson, C., Yukawa, S., Ihori, N., Saleem, M., Lim, K., Shibuya, A., Liau, A., Khoo, A., Bushman, B., Huesmann, L., & Sakamoto, A. (2009). The effects of pro-social video games on prosocial behaviors: International evidence from correlational, longitudinal, and experimental studies. *Personality and Social Psychology Bulletin*, 35, 752–63.

Gentile, D., & Gentile, J. (2008). Violent video games as exemplary teachers: A conceptual analysis. *Journal of Youth and Adolescence*, 9, 127–41.

Gottman, J. (1986). The world of coordinated play: Same- and cross-sex friendship in young children. In J. Gottman & J. Parker (Eds.), *Conversations of Friends* (pp. 129–91). New York: Cambridge University Press.

Green, C.S., & Bavelier, D. (2012). Learning, attentional control, and action video games. *Current Biology*, 22(6), R197–R206.

Hesse-Biber, S.N. (2010). *Mixed Method Research: Merging Theory with Practice*. New York: Guilford Press.

Hewstone, M., & Brown, R. (1986). Contact is not enough: An intergroup perspective on the "contact hypothesis". In M. Hewstone & R. Brown (Eds.), *Social Psychology and Society: Contact and Conflict in Intergroup Encounters* (pp. 1–44). Cambridge, MA: Basil Blackwell.

Howard, J., & Sheth, J.H. (1969). *The Theory of Buyer Behavior*. New York: Wiley.

Kapor, M. (1993). Democracy and the new information highway. *Boston Review*, October/November.

Karr-Wisniewski, P., Wilson, D., & Richter-Lipford, H. (2011). *A New Social Order: Mechanisms for Social Network Site Boundary Regulation. AMCIS 2011 Proceedings – All Submissions, 101.*

Kasser, T. (2002). *The High Price of Materialism*. Cambridge, MA: MIT Press. doi:10.1542/peds.2007-3134.

Kato, P.M., Cole, S.W., Bradlyn, A.S., & Pollock, B.H. (2008). A video game improves behavioral outcomes in adolescents and young adults with cancer: A randomized trial. *Pediatrics*, 122(2), 5–17.

Kotler, P. (1965). Behavioral models for analyzing buyers. *Journal of Marketing*, 29(4), 37–45.

Krebs, N.S., & Jacobson, M.F. (2003). Prevention of pediatric overweight and obesity. *Pediatrics*, 112, 424–30.

Kurzweil, R. (2005). *The Singularity Is Near: When Humans Transcend Biology*. New York: Viking.

Layard, R. (2005). *Happiness: Lessons from a New Science*. London: Penguin Books.

Leary, M., & Baumeister, R. (2000). The nature and function of self-esteem. *Advances in Experimental Social Psychology*, 32, 1–62. https://doi.org/10.1016/S0065-2601(00)80003-9

Markus, H., & Kitayama, S. (1991). Cultural variation in the self-concept. In G.R. Goethals & J. Strauss (Eds.), *Multidisciplinary Perspectives on the Self*. New York: Springer-Verlag.

Maslow, A.H. (1967). A theory of metamotivation. *Journal of Humanistic Psychology*, 7, 93–127.

Maslow, A.H. (1970). *Motivation and Personality* (2nd ed., pp. 40–70). New York: Harper & Row.

McRobbie, A. (1978). Working class girls and the culture of femininity. In Centre for Contemporary Cultural Studies (Ed.), *Women Take Issue*. London: Hutchinson.

Mead, G.H. (1934). *Mind, Self and Society*. Chicago: University of Chicago Press.

Meyer, B.D., & Sullivan, J.X. (2003). *Measuring the Well-Being of the Poor Using Income and Consumption*. NBER Working Paper No. 9760.

Nicosia, F.M. (1966). *Consumer Decision Processes: Marketing and Advertising Implications*. Englewood Cliffs, NJ: Prentice Hall.

Ollendick, T.H., & King, N.J. (1991). Origins of childhood fears: An evaluation of Rachman's theory of fear acquisition. *Behaviour Research and Therapy*, 29(2), 117–23.

Orzack, M.H., & Orzack, D.S. (1999). Treatment of computer addicts with complex co-morbid psychiatric disorders. *Cyberpsychology and Behavior*, 2(5), 465–73.

Payne, J.W., Bettman, J.R., & Schkade, D.A. (1999). Measuring constructed preferences: Towards a building code. *Journal of Risk and Uncertainty*, 19, 243–70.

Peukert, P., Sieslack, S., Barth, G., & Batra, A. (2010). Internet and computer game addiction: Phenomenology, comorbidity, etiology, diagnostic and therapeutic implications. For addictives and their relatives. *Psychiatrische Praxis*, 37(5), 219–24.

Piaget, J. (1962). *Play, Dreams, and Imitation in Childhood*. New York: W.W. Norton & Co..

Putnam, R.D. (2000). *Bowling Alone: The Collapse and Revival of American Community*. New York: Simon and Schuster.

Rheingold, H. (1993). *The Virtual Community: Homesteading on the Electronic Frontier*. Reading, MA: Addison-Wesley.

Rosenberg, M.J. (1956). Cognitive structure and attitudinal affect. *Journal of Abnormal and Social Psychology*, 53, 367–72.

Runyon, K.E., & Stewart, D.W. (1987). *Consumer Behavior and the Practice of Marketing* (3rd ed.). Columbus, OH: Merrill, USA.

Sangharakshita. (1991). *The Three Jewels: An Introduction to Buddhism*. Cambridge: Windhorse Publications. (Orig. pub. Rider, 1967)

Saposmik, G., Teasell, R., Mamdani, M., Hall, J., McIilroy, W., Cheung, D., Thorpe, K., Cohen, L., & Bayley, M. (2010). Effectiveness of virtual reality using Wii gaming technology in stroke rehabilitation: A pilot randomized clinical trial and proof of principle. *Stroke: A Journal of Cerebral Circulation*, 41, 1477–84.

Schiffman, L.G., & Kanuk, L.L. (1997). *Consumer Behavior*. New Jersey: Prentice Hall.

Schnaiberg, A. (1980). *The Environment: From Surplus to Scarcity*. New York: Oxford University Press.

Simon, H.A. (1990). Organizations and markets, Department of Economics, Carnegie-Mellon University, Pittsburgh, PA 15213, U.S.A. *Mathematical Social Sciences*, 20(3), 306.

Stephan, W.G., & Stephan, C.W. (1989). Antecedents of intergroup anxiety in Asian-Americans and Hispanic-Americans. *International Journal of Intercultural Communication*, 13, 203–19.

Tajfel, H. (1974). Social identity and intergroup behaviour. *Social Science Information*, 13, 65–93.

Tajfel, H., & Turner, J.C. (1986). The social identity theory of intergroup behavior. In S. Worchel & W.G. Austin (Eds.), *Psychology of Intergroup Relation* (pp. 7–24). Chicago: Hall Publishers.

Thagard, P. (2014). The self as a system of multilevel interacting mechanisms. *Philosophical Psychology*, 27, 145–63.

Tufekci, Z. (2008). Can you see me now? Audience and disclosure regulation in online social network sites. *Bulletin of Science, Technology & Society*, 28.

Uttal, D., Meadow, N., Tipton, E., Hand, L.L., Alden, A., Warren, C., & Newcombe, N. (2013). The malleability of spatial skills: A meta-analysis of training studies. *Psychological Bulletin*, 139(2), 352–402.

Veblen, T. (1898). Why Economics is not an Evolutionary Science. *History of Economic Thought Article* (Vol. 12).

Veblen, T. (1899). *The Theory of the Leisure Class*. New York: Macmillan.

Vygotsky, L.S. (1978). *Mind in Society: The Development of Higher Psychological Processes*. Cambridge, MA: Harvard University Press.

Wagner, G., & Weitzman, M. (2015). *Climate Shock: The Economic Consequences of a Hotter Planet*. Princeton, NJ: Princeton University Press.

Wagner, U., & Machleit, U. (1986). "Gestarbeiter" in the Federal Republic of Germany: Contact between Germans and migrant populations. In M. Hewstone & R. Brown (Eds.), *Contact and Conflict in Intergroup Encounters* (pp. 59–78). Oxford: Blackwell.

Wai, J., Lubinski, D., Benbow, C.P., & Steiger, J.H. (2010). Accomplishment in science, technology, engineering, and mathematics (STEM) and its relation to STEM educational dose: A 25-year longitudinal study. *Journal of Educational Psychology*, 102, 860–71.

Walters, C.G. (1974). *Consumer Behavior Theory and Practice*. Illinois: R.D. Irwin.

Weiss, A., Bates, T., & Luciano, M. (2008). Happiness is a personal(ity) thing: The genetics of personality and well-being in a representative sample. *Psychological Science*, 19, 205–10.

Young, K.S. (1996). *Internet addiction: The emergence of a new clinical disorder. Paper presented at the 104th annual meeting of the American Psychological Association,* August 18, 1996, Toronto, Canada.

Young, K.S. (1999). Internet addiction: Symptom, evaluation and treatment. In L.VandeCreek & T.L. Jackson (Eds.), *Innovations in Clinical Practice* (Vol. 17). Sarasota, FL: Professional Resource Press.

3

RESEARCH METHODS

Learning objectives

After reading this chapter, you will be able to understand:

- The importance of research
- The concepts used in research methods
- Quantitative research methods
- Perspectives of qualitative research
- Different methods of qualitative research
- Application of research methods in the field of media psychology
- Critical evaluation

3.1 Importance of research in media psychology

Mass media is an integral aspect of contemporary life, having physical, psychological, social, cultural and economic effects on its users. Several questions arise, like how much time do people spend with a particular medium? Does it have the effect of bringing change in attitude and perceptions of the people? Does the excessive use of medium have harmful psycho-social effects? What are the advantages of mass media? Media research includes a whole range of study about the development of media, information about the users and its effects on users. In recent years media researches seeks and analyzes consumers' changing tastes, values and lifestyles. The influence of media on modern societies is very powerful, and it is not one way. Media research is an objective and systematic way of collecting information and analyzing it. Mass media performs the functions of information, education and entertainment. In this process, mass media has the ability to socialize its viewers and activate people to action. If we imagine hundred great persons in our country, most of them would be the people who have been given a great deal of media exposure. Mass media has the ability to focus public attention, influence voting behavior, change attitudes, expose claims and sell products and ideas.

Mass media research for health and wellness reasons is also important as researchers are still learning how technology is affecting people in both positive and negative ways. There are studies being conducted to evaluate the side effects of social media usage on adolescents and children. We also find researches describing the dependence on the internet and its implications of psychological aspects of anxiety and sleep disturbances.

Mass media researches are also being carried out to explore the positive aspects of technology for our educational and health objectives. Media research has drawn substantially on semiotics to account for the distinctive sign, types, codes, narratives and modes of address such as the newspaper, television, or the internet. Good research should be systematic, verifiable, reliable, valid and able to contribute to knowledge. Research is considered as a cyclical process and states the relationship among chosen variables.

Generally, the goal of media research is to understand audience behavior and how media-mediated communications are dynamically related to each other. Nowadays, the involvement and engagement of people from daily to professional needs are carried out through various platforms of mass media. Media users as consumers are a big interest to the advertisers and all kinds of business organizations. How technology is affecting people in both positive and negative ways is an area of major concern for the researchers and promoters of research by big business organizations. Media content, concepts and broadcasts have tremendous potential to persuade the minds of media users. The rise of electronic media and its influence on human behavior has social, political and economic implications.

Research plays a vital role in discovering new realities and good research achieves this objective effectively. The use of scientific methods of research can provide us with the ability to analyze the field of media psychology objectively and develop a balanced view of the results of studies related to this field.

3.2 Key concepts related to media research

3.2.1 Theory

A good theory has unity, and it consists of problem-solving strategies that can be applied to a range of circumstances. The most important use of a theory is its practical applications which are coherent, systematic and predictive.

A good theory is also about unifying variables which explains a great number of observations within a given framework. Hong et al. (2010) define theory as "a comprehensive explanation of an important feature of nature supported by facts gathered over time" (p. 23).

Theories are also integrated into its completeness with the support of empirical adequacy. A theory is empirically adequate if appearances "are isomorphic to the empirical substructures of some model of the theory" (Mohler et al., 2008). A theory is not an empirical model but is based upon a host of assumptions and presumptions, what Kuhn (1962) called a paradigm and later called a disciplinary matrix. The knowledge gained through experiences and senses to the study of reality is also a part of the theory.

3.2.2 Deduction

Deduction is a method of reasoning which moves from particular to general. It is also concerned with developing a hypothesis based on existing theory, and a research strategy to test the hypothesis. By the use of a deductive approach, the researcher may explain the causal relationships between concepts and variables.

3.2.3 Induction

Inductive theory is a method in which researchers generalize to a broad statement using experiments and other methods with reasonable levels of certainty.

3.2.4 Empiricism

Empirical research is based on the ideals of observing the phenomenon in the social world and generates knowledge about them. The central focus of empirical theories is on logical positivism as an ontological framework which suggests that social phenomena can be studied objectively, verified and generalized in the line of principles of natural sciences.

3.2.5 Nominalism

Nominalism refers to the denial of the existence of abstract entities. It is a philosophical position that also suggests that abstract concepts do not exist in the same way as physical and tangible material.

3.2.6 Realism

Realism suggests that entities are of a certain type of objective reality completely independent of our conceptual schemes and beliefs. Realism can be contrasted with anti-realism, denying the objective reality of entities, with nominalism being the idea that abstract concepts and general terms have no independent existence except existing only as names, and with idealism being the concept that the external world is an illusion and it is the mind which exists.

3.2.6.1 Platonic realism

It was articulated by the Greek philosopher Plato, who suggested that universals do exist, and they do not exist in the ordinary mode of existence of space and time but outside of space and time.

3.2.6.2 Moderate realism

Moderate realism represents a midpoint between Platonic realism and nominalism suggesting that there are no separate realms of universals, but they are located in space and time.

3.2.6.3 Aesthetic realism

It was developed by American poet and critic Eli Siegel (1941), who suggested that the reality of the world has a beautiful structure that unifies opposites like a great work of art should and can, therefore, be liked honestly.

3.2.6.4 Moral realism

Plato, Immanuel Kant and Karl Marx were moral realists, and contemporary philosophers G.E. Moore and Ayn Rand (1905–82) say moral realism is an ethical view that there are objective moral values which are independent of our perception of them.

3.2.7 Epistemology

Epistemology is concerned about the basic questions of what is knowing and what is knowledge. It is the theory or science of the method of producing knowledge. Several distinctions of knowledge gradually emerged, including induced perfection and imperfection, explicit and tacit, private and public, a priori posteriori and analytic and synthetic propositions: "knowing that" and "knowing how". Wittgenstein (1958), Russell and G.E. Moore prescribed analytic propositions defining knowledge as justified true belief.

Another important approach to knowledge considers knowledge as historically and discursively contextualized. This pragmatism was proposed by C.S. Peirce and William James, while neo pragmatism was proposed by John Dewey. Another tradition of knowledge known as post-structuralism advocates that knowledge is a product of societal tradition. German Martin Heidegger's (1889–1976) view of hermeneutic phenomenology concerns the meaning of "being" as "in itself" being temporally situated and suggests a pre-figured existence of all knowledge.

3.2.8 Ontology

Ontology is the science or study of being and deals with the nature of reality. Principal characteristics of ontology include questions such as, what is a thing? What are the meanings of being? Ontological dichotomies also include concepts like universals and particulars, abstract and concrete objects, idealism and materialism and so on. Ontology is figured in the Samkhya School of Hindu philosophy from the first millennium BC (Larson, Bhattacharya, & Potter, 2014).

For Aristotle (384–322 BC), there are four ontological dimensions:

1. According to the various categories in ways of addressing a being as such
2. According to its truth or falsity
3. Whether it exists in and of itself or simply comes along by accident
4. According to its potency movement or finished presence (Studtmann, 2007, Aristotle's categories)

3.2.9 Positivism

French philosopher Auguste Comte (1798–1857) described positivism as an approach of observable evidence as the only form of scientific knowledge. According to the positivistic approach, the logic of inquiry remains the same across disciplines whose aim is to predict observables through human senses which are value-free and should not be treated as common sense. Positivism strongly relies on the principles of science which are deterministic (X causes Y) and mechanistic. It relies on empirical methods and it can be measured. Wilhelm Dilthey (1833–1911) opposed the assumption that only explanations derived from science are valid. Anti-positivism theorists Max Weber and George Simmel rejected the doctrine of positivism based on "scientism".

3.2.10 Praxis

This is an action-oriented research method in which theorizing should be aimed at changing the status quo through action. Karl Marx (1818–83) takes other philosophers to task, criticizing them for not translating their theorizing into concrete action writing. Marx, in a movement against idealism and metaphysics, proposed a "practical critical" activity that combines theory with practice, where no thinking can be isolated from social practice. Marx describes two types of praxis: one is unreflective, which enables capitalism to thrive and another is reflective, that allows the oppressed class of labor the potential to emancipate and change the status quo.

Antonio Gramsci (1891–1937), famous for his *Prison Notebook*, proposed that hegemonic culture propagates its values and norms so that they become the "common sense" values of all and thus maintaining the status quo. For Gramsci, the philosophy of practices explains the struggle that people participate in to gain a critical perspective. The praxis intervention method prioritizes this unsettling of the set-old mentality, especially where the old mindset prevalent in the social world is suspected of having sustained or contributed to their suffering or marginality (McLaren & Farahmandpur, 2000).

3.2.11 Interpretivism

Interpretivism is one form of qualitative methodology. It has different auditions in different disciplines. Schutz, Cicourel and Garfinkel (phenomenological/sociology, the Chicago School of sociology) and Malinowski (anthropology) are often attributed to the origin of the interpretive paradigm. This approach relies heavily on observation and analysis of existing texts. It holds that meanings emerge during the research processes and what we know is always negotiated with cultures, situations, social context and relationships with other people. A dialogue is created between lived experiences and practical aspects requiring an ethos of respect for the voice actions and text. The interpreter moves between examining the congruities and incongruities using paradigm cases, thematic analysis and exemplars.

In brief, interpretivism focuses on understanding the practical worlds, situated understanding and embodied lived experiences. The interpreter uses participant observation, video and audiotapes, interviews, films and biographies to gather the data for interpretation.

3.2.12 Constructivism

This view holds that knowledge is constructed with a learner's active participation. From a psychologist's point of view, the theories of Dewey, Piaget and Jerome Bruner support this viewpoint. From this point of view, everything that we know in the social world is determined by the interaction of politics, values, ideologies, religious beliefs and language, and it is not a result of a simplistic objective world. From the radical constructivist point of view proposed by Glasserfeld, there is no absolute external environment; it is only perceived environment in each individual's mind.

3.2.13 Deconstructionism

Deconstructionism is an approach to understand the relationship between text and meaning, originally proposed by philosopher Jacques Derrida (1976/1967) in his book *Of Grammatology*. There is an assumed bias in the binary mode of expression: good/bad, male/female. Deconstructionism is the active antithesis of everything, and authorized traditional values and concepts are critically evaluated. Deconstruction manifests itself in the process of writing rather than in the product. Deconstruction takes place; it is an event that does not await the deliberation consciousness or organization of a subject (Derrida, 1976, p. 274).

Derrida also described that the opposition between speech and writing is a manifestation of the logocentrism of Western culture. The assumption is that there is a realm of "truth" existing before and independent of its representation by linguistic signs. The logocentric assumption of truth and reality as situated outside the language system develops from deeper prejudices which Derrida calls the "metaphysics of presence". What we perceive as total realities are often combined with interactive conflicts between meanings of different types. Deconstruction allows us to analyze not only rhetoric and performative aspects of language use, what the text says, but also exploring the relationship and potential conflict between what a text says and what it does. It favored an approach to inspire a suspicion of established intellectual categories and skepticism about the possibility of objectivity.

THINK BOX

- Describe the importance of research in media psychology.
- Also, discuss the qualities of a good research.

3.3 Quantitative research methods

3.3.1 Process of quality quantitative research

The following stages characterize the general framework of research:

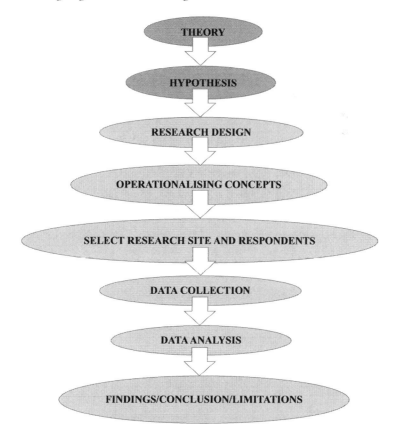

As noted earlier, theory is described as an explanation of observed regularities that can operate at a general and abstract level. It is also defined as a set of principles on which the practice of an activity is based. It is also described as a supposition or system of ideas intended to explain something, especially one based on general principles – for example, Newton's theory of gravitation and Einstein's theory of relativity.

3.3.1.1 Hypothesis

A hypothesis is a supposition or explanation for a phenomenon as a starting point for scientific investigation. A good hypothesis must be clear and be capable of being tested. The most important function of the hypothesis is to provide a framework for testing and experimentation. The hypothesis clarifies the links between variables (Bryman, 2008).

3.3.1.2 Concept

A concept represents the building block of the theory which indicates the points around which research is conducted. There are numerous examples of concepts, such as emotional satisfaction, leadership, expectation of the audience, academic motivation and quality of life. For example, we can differentiate people's usage patterns of media technology and varying patterns of usage may be linked to the behavior of the people. In different contexts, the concept of cultivation may be used to describe distinctive patterns of perceptions or beliefs that individuals who are heavy media users hold and that distinguish these from the perceptions and beliefs held by light media users (Gerbner et al., 1986; Wober and Gunter, 1988).

A concept used in quantitative research can be measured. In other words, concepts may provide explanations for certain aspects of the social world that we wish to explain in the form of independent or dependent variables.

3.3.1.3 Measurement

Measurement helps in delineating differences between people in terms of characteristics in question. The degree to which media-related advertisements affect the buying behavior of people is a good example. Measurement devices provide a consistent technique to find out the differences.

Measurement provides more precise estimates of the degree of relationship between concepts. A construct comprises a combination of concepts. It is often used to describe the personality type of individuals. For example, the personality construct of "sensation seeking" is used to distinguish between people who seek varying levels of optimal stimulation from their environment (Zuckerman, 1994).

3.3.1.4 Variable

A variable is an empirical representation of a concept or construct. The foundations of quantitative research are variables, and there are three main types of variables: dependent, independent and control. Every successful scientific experiment must include specific types of variables. An independent variable is a variable that the experimenter manipulates to experiment. The dependent variable is the measure of response or outcome. It is therefore also known as the "effect" or criterion variable. There must be an independent variable that changes throughout an experiment, a dependent variable which is observed and measured and a controlled variable which must remain consistent and unchanging throughout the experiment.

Let us assume that a researcher is experimenting to test the effect of noise on the clarity of hearing. In this case, noise itself will be an independent variable, which the researcher can alter. The dependent variable will be the clarity of hearing that a researcher observes in relation to the independent variable. A controlled or constant variable does not change throughout an experiment. The control variable in this experiment will be the architecture of the place and other conditions like temperature. If these factors were not constant, the researcher may not be able to judge the effects of noise on the clarity of hearing.

Essentially, a control variable is what is kept the same throughout the experiment and is not of primary concern for the experimental outcome. Any change in a control variable in an experiment would invalidate the correlation of the dependent variable (DV) with the independent variable (IV), thus skewing the results.

In experimental designs, the term control variable is described as a variable that has no importance and it constitutes an extraneous third factor that is either controlled or eliminated. A confounding variable is an outside influence that changes the effect of dependent and independent variables.

Strategies to reduce or control confounding variables are as follows:

- Randomization (aim remains a random distribution of confounders in the targeted study)
- Restriction of subjects with the bias of confounding factors
- Matching of individuals or groups with the aim of equal distribution of confounders

3.3.1.5 Statistical strategies to eliminate confounding effects

- *Stratification*: stratification aims to fix the level of confounders and produce groups within which the confounder does not vary.
- *Multivariate models*: multivariate models can handle a large number of covariates and also confounders simultaneously. For example, in a study that aimed

to measure the relation between obesity and diabetes, one could control other co-variates like age, sex, smoking and alcohol.

- *Logistic regression*: logistic regression is a mathematical model that can give an odds ratio which is controlled for multiple confounders. The special thing about it is that it can control numerous confounders if there is a large sample size.
- *Linear regression*: the linear regression analysis is also a statistical model that can be used to examine the association between multiple covariates and a numeric outcome.
- *Analysis of covariance*: analysis of covariance (ANCOVA) is a type of analysis of variance (ANOVA) that is used to control for potential confounding variables.

3.3.1.6 Reliability and validity

Reliability in psychology refers to the consistency of a measure of a research study or measuring test. For example if a person weighs themselves during the course of a day, they expect to see a similar reading. Three factors are prominently involved in considering whether a measure is reliable:

- *Stability*: this consideration indicates whether a measure is a stable over time. That means if we administer a measure to a group and then re-administer it, there will be a little variation in the results due to time factor.
- *Internal reliability*: the main point is whether the indicators that make up the scale or index are consistent, whether respondents' scores on any one indicator tend to be related to their scores on the other indicators.
- *Inter-observation consistency*: this may arise in situations and activities where there is more than one observer and there is a possibility that there is a lack of consistency in their decisions. Reliability can be established by carrying out repeated tests of phenomena and relationships between phenomena, by repeating such tests among different groups of people with the same results, and by having several research run the same test (Siegel & Hodge, 1968).

3.3.1.7 Split-half reliability

Spilt-half reliability is a test for a single knowledge area that is split into two parts, and then both parts are given to one group of students at the same time. The scores from both parts are correlated. A reliable test will have a high correlation. Alternatively, a researcher could construct two different questionnaires to measure the same concept and administer both to the same group of respondents.

This is called multiple forms (Goode & Hatt, 1952) or alternate forms (Sellitz et al., 1976) reliability.

3.3.1.8 Cronbach's alpha

Cronbach's alpha is a commonly used test of internal reliability. It essentially calculates the average of all possible split-half reliability coefficients. A computed alpha coefficient will vary between one (denoting perfect internal liability) and zero (denoting no internal liability).

3.3.1.9 Validity

Validity refers to the issue of whether an indicator that is devised to gauge a concept measures that concept. The validity of the measurement tool (for example, test of intelligence) is the degree to which the tool measures what it purports to measure. The concept of validity was formulated by Kelley (1927, p. 14), who stated that a test is valid if it measures what it claims to measure.

3.3.1.10 Types of validity

1. *Face validity*: a researcher who develops a new measure should establish that it has a face validity that the measure reflects the content of the concept in question. For example, a measure on emotional intelligence might be verified with the people working in this area to act as judges to determine whether on the face of it, the measure seems to reflect the concept concerned.
2. *Concurrent validity*: concurrent validity means that a measure is associated with another indicator that has already been shown to be valid. Thus, a new measure of job satisfaction may be related to high performance.
3. *Predictive validity*: in this, the researcher uses a future criterion measure rather than a contemporary one used in concurrent validity.
4. *Construct validity*: in this type of validity, the researcher is encouraged to deduce a hypothesis from a theory that is relevant to the problem under study.
5. *Convergent validity*: in this type of validity, a measure is gauged by comparing it to the measures of the same concept developed through other methods.
6. *Ecological validity*: ecological validity is related to the question of whether social scientific findings apply to people's everyday natural social contexts. As Cicourel (1982, p. 15) has put it: "do our instruments capture the daily life conditions, values, attitudes and knowledge base of those we study as expressed in their natural habitat".

3.3.2 Levels of measurement

These are measures to represent numerically the degree of attributes under study in a systematic and controlled manner. Stanley Smith Stevens (1946) developed the best-known typology with four levels or scales of measurement. Discrete variables can be measured at nominal and ordinal levels, while continuous variables can be measured at interval or ratio levels.

- *Nominal level*: nominal level differentiates between items or subjects only on their names. (Examples of this classification include gender, nationality, religion, etc.). The mode is the most common measure of central tendency for the nominal type of measurement.
- *Ordinal scale*: objects at this level of analysis are ranked along a dimension, such as smaller to greater and higher to lower, but does not indicate the distance that lies between these ranks. Dichotomous data such as healthy versus sick and dichotomous data consisting of a spectrum such as completely agree, mostly agree, or partially agree is used in this type of measurement. The median that is a middle-ranked item is allowed as the measure of central tendency in ordinal measurements.
- *Interval scale*: the interval scale allows for the degree of difference between items. One most commonly used example is temperature. For example, in terms of Celsius, it has two defined points, 0° and 100°, but 20°C can't be said to be twice as hot as 10°C. Similarly, an IQ of 50 and an IQ of 100 are not twice intelligent persons. The mode, median and arithmetic mean are allowed to measure the central tendency of interval variables.
- *Ratio scale*: in the ratio scale measurement, it is the estimation of the ratio between a magnitude of a continuous quantity and a unit magnitude of the same kind. The most powerful method of measurement involves a definite (unique and non-arbitrary) zero value. Time, speed and distance are examples of ratio-level scales. An object moving 20 miles an hour is moving twice as fast as one moving 10 miles an hour. The geometric mean and harmonic mean are used to measure the central tendency.

3.3.3 Survey research

Survey research refers to the process of researching data collection from respondents about their knowledge, beliefs, opinions, attitudes, values and behaviors. Survey research is a quantitative and qualitative method asking participants to report their thoughts and behaviors with considerable attention paid to sampling. Most of the survey research is conducted for opinion polls during elections, marketing research, or any other issue of social, political and economic importance.

In the media and communication context, surveys are used to ascertain media audiences' behavior. A classic study illustrating the early adoption of survey research regarding media influences was conducted by Lazarsfeld et al. (1944).

They surveyed American voters to try to understand more about the role of the media (radio and newspapers) during election campaigns.

Further research by Katz and Lazarsfeld (1955) utilized a survey to establish the significance of informal social networks in public opinion formation. A specific communication process consists of two-step flow of communication posited that the media have an indirect effect upon public opinion which operates through opinion leaders (Lazarsfeld et al., 1944). Some of the most common ways to administer surveys include mail, telephone and online interviews. Surveys can be divided into two categories i.e. descriptive and analytical.

The descriptive survey simply attempts to describe the current conditions or phenomena being studied. A census is conducted to define the general characteristics of the entire population. The descriptive surveys do not go into the roots of the problem; rather, they describe what exists at the moment.

The analytical survey also collects the descriptive data, but this is to examine relationships among variables in order to test the research hypothesis. Analytical surveys are carried out to investigate how a response variable is related to specific explanatory variables.

3.3.4 Sampling

A key aspect of quantitative research is a sampling. In research terms, a sample group of people, objects, or items are taken from a large population for measurement. In order to probe the research question, the researcher can't collect data from all the cases. Thus, there is a need to select a sample through sampling techniques and reduce the number of cases.

In brief, the sampling techniques can be described as follows:

- Probability sampling or random sampling.
- Non-probability or non-random sampling probability sampling: this means that every item in the population has an equal chance of being included in the sample.
- Simple random sampling: this is the most basic form of probability sampling, in which every case of the population has an equal probability of inclusion in the sample.
- Systematic random sampling: it is a method of sampling in which every *n*th case, person, or unit is drawn. For example, while surveying a sample of internet users, every 5th user may be selected from your sample.
- Stratified random sampling: in this sampling method, the population is divided into strata (or subgroups) and a random sample is taken from each subgroup. A subgroup is a natural set of items, for example, which can be based on gender, education, or occupation. Stratified sampling is used where there is a great deal of variation within the population. Its purpose is to ensure that every stratum is adequately represented.

3.3.4.1 Cluster sampling

Cluster sampling is a special case of stratification. It is advantageous for those researchers whose subjects are fragmented over large geographical areas, as it saves time and money (Davis, 2005). Subsequently, a random sample is taken from these clusters, all of which are used in the final sample.

3.3.4.2 Multistage sampling

It is a process of moving from a broad to a narrow sample using a step-by-step process. For example, if a real estate magazine wants to conduct a survey in India, it can simply take a random sample of homeowners in the entire population. This will be extremely time-consuming and expensive. A better alternative would be to use multistage sampling involving people from different geographical regions. Later on, these geographical regions can be chosen at random and subdivisions made at the district level also.

3.3.4.3 Non-probability sampling

The term non-probability sampling is used to describe all forms of sampling that are not conducted according to the canons of probability sampling. Non-probability sampling is often associated with case study research and qualitative research. In qualitative research small samples are used to examine a real-life phenomenon and statistical inference is not very relevant in this case.

3.3.4.4 Quota sampling

Quota sampling is a non-random sampling technique in which participants are chosen on the basis of pre-determined characteristics so that the total sample may have the same distribution of characteristics as the wider population. For example, the distribution of males and females is 46% and 54% in the total population, respondents are selected for the survey until the distribution is matched in the sample.

3.3.4.5 Snowball sampling

In the snowball approach to sampling, the researcher makes initial contact with a small group of people who are relevant to the research topic and then uses these to establish contacts and encourage others to participate. This approach is most applicable in small populations that are difficult to access due to their closed nature example secret societies and inaccessible professions.

3.3.4.6 Convenience sampling

Convenience sampling is selecting participants because they are often easily and readily available.

3.3.4.7 Purposive sampling

Purposive sampling is a method in which respondents are selected according to a specific criterion such as the purchase of a particular automobile. Purposive or judgmental sampling is a strategy in which particular settings, persons or events are selected deliberately to secure information which can be obtained from other sources.

3.4 Cross-sectional research

Cross-sectional studies or surveys measure both the exposure and outcome in a sample of the population at a point in time. It can be also defined as observational research that analyzes data of variables collected at a given point of time across a sample population. In the cross-sectional study, data are collected from people who are similar with respect to other variables except for the one variable which is under study.

Cross-sectional studies can be conducted to check the expenditure differences between the sexes regarding the purchase of cosmetic products or how people of different socio-economic status groups use internet-mediated communication. Cross-sectional studies may be entirely descriptive; for example, how a random sample of the cities across the state is assessed to check for pro-environment behavior amongst boys and girls.

A cross-sectional study is also analytical in which the researcher aims to investigate the association between two related or unrelated parameters. For example, to validate if school students in a school could develop stress owing to the school environment. But this may not account for stress factors related to home, and other factors.

In media violence studies, for example, respondents may be asked to identify or recall details about their television and cinema viewing and their aggressive disposition. Participants may be provided detailed lists of program titles and required to report the programs they like watching the best. In this approach, the assumption is taken that these people who prefer crime drama programs may have aggression tendencies but are not properly tested on scientific validity parameters.

Cross-sectional studies have been conducted among media professionals about journalists' working practices, job satisfaction among people employed in the media industries and their opinions concerning the impact of new communication technologies on the future of their businesses (Bergen & Weaver, 1988; Demers & Wackman, 1988; Ross, 1998).

3.5 Longitudinal research

Longitudinal research is a type of observational method in which data are gathered for the same group of subjects over a period of time which can take place for weeks, months or years. Most longitudinal studies related to disease examine the association between exposure to known or suspected causes of disease and subsequent morbidity. In the simplest design, a sample or cohort of subjects exposed to a risk factor is identified along with a sample of unexposed controls. Unlike cross-sectional studies, which look at different people, longitudinal studies look at the same person for a long period of time. In individual studies, individuals are tracked and studied. This type of study is used to survey people about their changing opinions and behaviors over time and can be evaluated at different stages of life.

3.6 Cohort studies

Cohort studies are done when people from certain age groups are studied to explore their different trajectories as they age. Rentz et al. (1983) conducted a cohort analysis of consumers born in four time periods, 1931–40, 1941–50, 1951–60 and 1961–70. These consumers were studied for the consumption of soft drinks, and a large cohort effect was noticed in the consumption pattern of soft drinks. Rosengren and Windahl (1989) also used cohort analysis as part of their in-depth longitudinal study of television usage by Swedish youngsters. They concluded that age was a prime factor involved in habitual television viewing.

3.7 Content analysis

Content analysis is an approach to the analysis of documents and texts that tries to quantify the data into categories. Content analysis is a research technique for the objective, systematic and quantitative description of the manifest content of communication (Berelson, 1952, p. 18). Content analysis is a technique for making inferences by objectively and systematically identifying specified characteristics of messages. The content analysis aims to produce quantitative accounts of the raw material in a systematic and objective manner.

Content analysis is profoundly affected by the nature of research questions under consideration. In the case of mass media, it tends to focus on the voice of significant actors in the production of information. What kind of person has produced the items, which are the main focus of the item, what kinds of emotive words are being used, what kinds of dramatic words are being used and other aspects need to be taken into account while doing content analysis.

Frequent use of certain words suggests indicative of a certain type of discourse such as safety, risk, fears, dangers, etc. Sometimes illness narratives are highlighted that leads people in large numbers seeking the support of curative practices.

3.7.1 Subjects, themes and coding

Each study should be classified on the basis of subjects and themes. There are two main elements in a content analysis coding scheme: designing a coding schedule and designing a coding manual. Imagine a student interested in the study of media mediated violence by youngsters. We can have tentatively following variables:

- Nature of offense
- Gender of perpetrator
- Age
- Social class of victim(s)
- Age of victim(s)

3.7.2 Coding manual

A coding manual is a statement of instructions to coders that also includes all possible categories for each dimension being coded. It provides the list of all the dimensions. The transparency of content analysis makes it an objective method of analysis. Clearly defined coding schemes and procedures help in replication and follow-up studies.

Five main purposes of content analysis have been identified (Wimmer & Dominick, 1994)

- Describing patterns or trends in media portrayals
- Testing hypothesis about the policies or aims of media producers
- Comparing media content with real-world indicators
- Assessing the representation of certain groups in society
- Drawing inferences about media effects.

One example of the use of a coding manual is an investigation of the extent to which films released in Britain between 1945 and 1991 were characterized by crime themes. In the case of news, it is particularly an analysis of the sources of quotes, comments or other material that can yield insights (Lasorsa & Reese, 1990). Neutrality and partiality factors can also be evaluated by analysis of the sources of news items.

3.8 Experimental designs

Most experimental designs require experimental units to be allocated to treatments either randomly or randomly with constraints as in blocked designs (Montgomery, 1989). A research design in which causal relation between manipulation of a variable and an assumed effect is investigated in a valid way by comparing an experimental group (with intervention) with a control group (without intervention) where both the groups are made statistically comparable with the help of randomizing. An experiment is a method of data collection designed to test a hypothesis under controlled conditions.

In the classic experiments, the effects of an independent variable upon the dependent variable are tested. As the researcher's main intention is in the independent variable, the participants must be measured on the dependent variable before and after the independent variable is administered (pre-testing and post-testing).

3.8.1 The Hawthorne effect

Participants perform better when they are in an experiment.

3.8.2 Demand characteristic

Participants try to give the answer to what they think is correct rather than the honest answer.

3.8.3 Placebo effect

Participants respond to the belief that they are receiving a drug, regardless of whether they actually are or not.

3.8.4 The double-blind experiment

The double-blind experiment is an experimental design in which the researchers do not know as to which group is the experimental group and which group its control group.

3.8.5 Pygmalion effect

People perform better when more is expected of them.

3.8.6 Selection of subjects

Randomization, matching and Quota matrix are used for the selection of participants in an experimental design.

3.8.7 Variations on experimental designs

3.8.7.1 One-shot case study

In this type of experimental design, a single group of participants is measured on a dependent variable following an experimental stimulus.

One group pre-test post-test design: in this type of experimental design, pretest is added for the experimental group but lacks a control group.

Static group comparison: this type of experimental design includes experimental and control groups but no pretest.

3.8.7.2 Quasi-experimental design

For example, if a researcher is examining the effects of meditation on studies, he/she might randomly assign participants to one of three independent variable conditions: those who do meditation, those who do exercise and those who do nothing. The prefix quasi-means "resembling". The quasi-experimental research is that research which resembles experimental research but is not true experimental research. Although the independent variable is manipulated, participants are not randomly assigned to conditions or orders of conditions. Quasi-experimental designs do not eliminate the problem of confounding variables and are more likely to be conducted in field settings where random assignment is difficult or impossible.

The most commonly used quasi-experimental design is the non-equivalent groups designs which require a pre-test and post-test for a treated and comparison group.

3.8.7.3 Factorial design

In many studies. researchers look at how multiple factors affect a given dependent variable both independently, and together it is called a factorial design. In factorial designs, two or more independent variables or factors are manipulated, and these factors may have two or more aspects to be considered in the analysis. A study with two factors that each have two levels is called 2×2 factorial design. When you have multiple independent variables in a single study, it is called factorial design.

THINK BOX

- Describe various types quantitative research methods used in media research.
- Do you think quantitative research method is an important tool to understand human behavior?

3.9 Critical evaluation of quantitative research methods

Quantitative research is more concerned with data analysis in terms of numbers. The key characteristics of this kind of research are operational definition, hypothesis and application. Quantitative research also allows objectivity and the ability to produce casual statements.

3.9.1 Limitations

Quantitative research is unable to tap the diversity and complexity of human experience. Its mechanistic approach reduces the notion of freedom, choice and moral responsibility. It also generalizes these facts claiming to be true to all which is in fact not possible. It is not objective because researcher's subjectivity and bias always play a role in the process of research.

3.10 Qualitative research

Shank (2002) defines qualitative research as "a form of systematic empirical enquiry into meaning" (p. 5). Denzin and Lincoln (2000) claim that qualitative research involves an interpretive and naturalistic approach: "This means that qualitative researchers study things in natural settings attempting to make sense of or to interpret phenomena in terms of the meaning people bring to them" (p. 3). Shank (2002) has used two metaphors as a different way of seeing research. The first is "window" to look through to get an accurate view of the subject, and the second is "lantern" which helps "shed light" in dark corners.

Qualitative research methods are necessary to tap the complexities of pluralities of life realities aiming to capture multiple voices and perspectives in a local context. Knowledge and practice are studied as local knowledge and practices (Geertz, 1993).

Beginning of qualitative research: Toulmin (1990) highlighted four tendencies for the emergence of qualitative research which included a return to the oral tradition, return to the particular, return to the local and return to the timely.

3.10.1 Research perspective in the field of qualitative research

The theoretical assumptions underlying qualitative research are based on three basic positions of symbolic interactionism, ethnomethodology and structuralist perspectives.

3.10.1.1 Symbolic interactionism

The term symbolic interactionism was coined by Herbert Blumer (1938). He summarizes the starting points of symbolic interactionism as three simple premises. The first premise is that human beings act towards things on the basis of the meaning that the things have for them. The second premise is that the meaning of such things is derived from – arises out of – the social interaction that one has with one's fellows. The third premise is that these meanings are handled in, or modified through, an interpretive process used by the person in dealing with the things encountered (Blumer, 1969, p. 2). The basic focus of this perspective is on reconstructing the viewpoint of participants from various points, providing importance to subjective views and also understanding autobiographical narrative in a local context.

3.10.1.2 Ethnomethodology

Harold Garfinkel, founder of this school, defines ethnomethodology studies as the analysis of everyday activities as members, methods for making the same activities visible, rational and reportable for all practical purposes that is "accountable" as organizations of commonplace everyday activities. The reflexivity of that phenomenon is a singular feature of practical actions, of prosocial circumstances of common-sense knowledge of the social structure and of practical sociological reasoning (Garfinkel 1967, p. 7). In order to uncover the methods through which interaction is organized researcher seeks to adopt an attitude of ethnomethodological indifference (Garfinkel & Sacks, 1970).

It is necessary to understand the dynamics of structure and context, and no element of conversation should be ignored as unimportant. In this method, attempts are made to capture the reality of conversation as it occurs without any intent to curtail it. The scope is enlarged from studying interactive practices to a concern with the embodied knowledge that emerges in such practices as well as in their results. Interpretative repertoires are also analyzed for their use of terms, images, speech and metaphors.

3.10.1.3 Cultural framing of social reality

Qualitative research can also be understood and appreciated with the cultural systems of meaning:

- *Poststructuralism*: structuralists' description of texts as realities has been questioned by the poststructuralists. Texts are not representative of objective reality; rather, a lot of interest of its producers is also included in the text. There are big gaps between the manifest representation of language and latent processes involved in the production which is a problem related to objective hermeneutics.
- *Construction of knowledge*: Schutz (1962, p. 5) begins with the following premise: "all our knowledge of the world in common sense as well as in scientific thinking involves constructs that is set of abstractions, generalizations, formalizations and idealizations, specific to the relevant level of thought organization". The radical constructionism of Glasserfeld is described as follows: that knowledge is related to the way in which we organize our experiential world and knowledge is a human construct.
- *Social Constructionism*: Schutz holds that "the exploration of general principles according to which man in daily life organizes his experiences and especially those of the social world is the first task of the methodology of

the social sciences" (1962, p. 59). He assumed multiple realities of which the world of science is only one and is organized partly according to the same principles of everyday life and partly according to other principles. Our worldview is achieved through coordination among persons, negotiations, agreements, disagreements, comparisons and so on. Treating the truth as absolute product of the individual mind is a mistaken notion, and this is largely a product of community traditions lodged in culture and history. The ability for critical reflexivity, questioning one's premises by suspending the obvious to multiple viewpoints, is the important aspect of constructionist consideration.

Objectivity is rarely possible due to the lack of value neutrality. Habermas in his influential volume *Knowledge and Human Interest* (1971) proposed that any research for knowledge favors certain political and economic goals over others. The inherent implicit values bias claims value neutrality by experts of different fields, be it a doctor, scientist or judge who always represents varied interests, myths, doctrines and values from their own vantage point.

3.10.2 Feminism and qualitative research

Qualitative research has been considered very useful for feminist researches in order to bring forth the complexities, subjectivities, structure and policies of our social organizations. Feminist researches aim to emancipate woman and their lives, and commitment to equality of rights.

Feminist research in general is characterized by both constructions of new knowledge and change in the situation of women. There can't be a precise agreement on defining feminist research, but the importance of consciousness-raising, reflection, subject/object to divide, acknowledging the role of social and historical processes, role of power relations and inequality of woman, role of mass media in the portrayal of stereotypes and intention to empower woman are all central concerns of feminist research. The use of predetermined categories in quantitative research results in an emphasis on what is already known and subsequently in the silencing of women's voices (Maynard, 1994).

The social and political goals of feminist research led to a preference for qualitative research "to focus on women's experiences and to listen and explore the shared meanings between women". No method can be considered as most appropriate for feminist research instead of more trust in context. Women's experiences grounded in reality should be the driving force for such researches.

3.10.2.1 Radical feminist perspective

In the late 1960s radical families redefined women's problems not as the symptoms of failure but as the symptoms of oppression by a system of male dominance. There was a constant effort in the direction of abandonment of "sex roles" as it was considered a major instrument of oppression and subordination of women.

Andrea Dworkin, a radical American feminist, questions the concept of "two discrete biological sexes" and suggests we are multi-sexed species and our gendered society structure stops as perceiving the continuum of sexes.

Some feminists contend that most languages are inherently patriarchal. Before the terms "sexism" and "sexual harassment" were coined, a woman had difficulty in talking about important features of their lived experiences that Betty Friedan (1963) called a problem with no name.

3.11 Qualitative research methods

Several methods of data collection are used in qualitative research. Ethnography, narrative analysis, phenomenological method, grounded theory, interview, focus groups and case studies are important methods used in qualitative research. Other methods are available for qualitative research including document analysis, conversation analysis and thematic analysis.

3.11.1 Ethnography and participant observation

Ethnography is a systematic study to gather observations to produce comprehensive accounts of people, culture and social phenomena. The goal of ethnography is to give an analytical description of other cultures an exploration of emerging phenomenon. The data consist unstructured accounts which are interpreted by researchers according meaning on the basis of observation, description and explanation.

Ethnography comprises the lived experiences and attempts to provide meaning to the culture under study. The process of collecting data in ethnographic research may involve collecting data through field notes, audiovisual sources and cultural and historical facts which can be analyzed later with the help of codes and references. The ethnographer's field work includes a cultural holistic perspective, symbols, emic and etic perspectives and context sensitivity. Cultural aspects occupy paramount importance in ethnographic research. The holistic orientation allows the researcher to look beyond the immediate cultural scene and take into account surrounding cultural factors. Participant observation is a technique employed by researchers to actively participate in the research process along with participants of research.

3.11.1.1 Field notes

Ethnographers take notes based on their observations. The field notes should be brief and noted as soon as possible. Researchers should mention the location, date, time and kind of exchange as early as possible. Field notes must be mentioned with clarity as why certain observations were noted. Nowadays people do digital voice recording of fieldnotes apart from notepad and pen.

3.11.1.2 Visual ethnography

Visual images are taken by researchers and photographers, and visual ethnography is becoming increasingly popular these days. Visual ethnographers have used this technique to discover a variety of subjects of research interest, and this technique of interviewing – asking people to discuss photographs and their meanings and significance for them – is known as technique of photo-elicitation. Visual materials can be analyzed through research reflexive approaches.

3.11.2 Observational research

Observational research involves observation of phenomena in natural settings. Observational research is divided into participant observation and nonparticipant observation. Case studies are a type of observational research involving a thorough descriptive analysis of single individual, event or group. This is an unobtrusive method of research in which the researcher tries to find out "what is going on here" with the understanding of context.

Observational research can be semi-structured, and premature attempts of theoretical concepts are avoided. Ethnography involves observation, but not all observations are necessarily ethnographic. Observational research is also a holistic approach in which the researcher observes the people in the context of their activities, record them as it is happening and try to find a pattern emerging from the data.

3.11.2.1 Participant observation

Participant observation was used by Bronislaw Malinowski in the 1920s. It includes direct observation of human behavior in the field with the help of field notes and interviews. In some of the situations, participants also work as co-researchers acting as contributors and collaborators in the process of gathering and interacting data.

3.11.2.2 Nonparticipant observation

Sometimes researchers are present with the participants, and sometimes they may not be present owing to various limitations of limited access of a phenomenon. Nonparticipant methods are often suitable for the groups or institutions which are not approachable for various reasons. Nonparticipant observation may be covert or overt. The advantage of this approach is that it allows for an objective view to study the phenomena. The disadvantage is that people can modify behavior when they are being observed.

3.11.3 Grounded theory research (Glaser et al., 1968)

Grounded theory was derived from theoretical contributions from pragmatism (Dewey, 1925; Mead, 1934) and symbolic interactionism (Blumer, 1969; Hughes, 1971; Park & Burgess, 1921). In the method of grounded theory, data collection and analysis are interrelated processes or simultaneous work. As compared to other qualitative methods, in grounded theory the researcher collects the data and analyzes them for further cues in research; hence, the research process becomes a guiding factor for further research. The incidents, events and happenings in the course of data collection process are labeled with some concepts. After the finding of concepts, categories are developed. A sampling of the concepts is done according to their dimensions and characteristics, patterns and variations.

Writing theoretical memos is an integral aspect of doing grounded theory. Memos are not related to the formulation of the theory and not limited to the ideas only. Coding is the basic interpretative process by which data are broken down analytically. The preconceived notions and ideas are done through the fracturing of the data. Some of the important characteristics need to be confirmed in order to get a positive outcome from grounded theory.

First and foremost is the generation of concepts and systematic linkages. A grounded theory should be properly linked to categories and subcategories. The density of the categories in relation to paradigm features provide explanatory power.

3.11.4 Thematic and narrative analysis

Thematic analysis is a method to identify, organize and provide insight and themes (meaning) to the data. The thematic analysis allows the researcher to make sense of collective and shared meanings within a data. The thematic analysis allows the researcher to establish interconnections between a particular topic and research question being explored.

Thematic analysis is theoretically a flexible approach, and it can be used in a variety of situations. It can be related to people's perception, experiences and views about certain topics. For example, how does advertisement affect the mobile buying behavior of adolescents, or how do common people understand the concept of cleanliness in India? Thematic analysis can be conducted on three basic types of premises, inducting/deductive, experiential/critical orientation and essentialist/constructionist orientation, which may not be very rigid while doing the analysis.

Cohen et al. (2011) described that data analysis in qualitative research is distinguished by "merging of analysis and interpretation and often by the merging of data collection with data analysis". Grounded theory analysis and thematic analysis are very similar as both focus on interpreting the data. Thematic analysis provides the researcher with tools to uncover some issues more deeply in its meanings from implicit and explicit perspectives. Codes developed for ideas or themes are then applied or linked to raw data as summary markers for later analysis, which may include comparing the relative frequencies of themes or topics within a dataset looking for code occurrences or graphically displaying old relationships.

In the process of thematic analysis, participants' interpretations are important for the explanations of behavior and thought. Diversity of attitude and reflections expressed by participants can lead to the emergence of common themes or the occurrence of statements and can be coded accordingly.

Data reduction is a form of analysis that sharpens, sorts, focuses, discards and organizes data in such a way that final conclusion can be drawn and verified. The researcher may involve outside experts to review the themes emerging from the data in order to validate the themes. In the process of thematic analysis, samples are determined before the start of the study.

3.11.4.1 Narrative analysis

According to narrative theory (e.g. Murray, 1999; Sarbin, 1986), we are born into a storied world, and we live our lives through the creation and exchange of narratives. A narrative is described as an organized interpretation of events with a beginning, middle and end. There are many types of narratives that can be broadly divided into two categories, imaginary and factual. Narrative forms may include various genres such as fantasy, folktale, autobiography, memoir, novels, fiction and so on.

Subjects recognize themselves in the stories they tell about themselves (Ricoeur, 1981). A narrative enumerated by a person also conveys the aspects of selfhood and identity of that person. A well-informed narrative has a value endpoint in which the narrator has a goal to establish which is pre-dominant in its value point; for example, a moral story, a story about criminal behavior, a pleasant story about social reforms, a story of economic plight and many other such constructs. The story should be relevant to the plot, and the sequence of events should hold interconnectivity to each other. The ideal narrative also intends to provide a sense of explanation to make it more coherent.

As Paul Ricoeur (1981) puts it, "explanation must be woven into the narrative tissue" (p. 278). We dream, hope, believe, remember, love, hate and anything worth doing or imagining by narrative. A story appearing truer and apparently well-woven events are closely related to each other and the explanation of a person's life appears as a story of ups and downs, achievements and failures, luck and hard times, and finally, the end result of life of a person appears in a storied form. The stories may take the forms of the achievement spectrum, failure spectrum, heroic saga ultimately conveying and establishing a value point in all such stories.

The primary source of narrative data used by researchers is the interview. The basic aim of this approach is to get a detailed account of one's life from everyday

experiences and important ups and downs. It is important for the researcher to convince the participants that the researcher is genuinely interested in their narrative
accounts. It is important for the researcher to discern the basic framework of the
beginning, middle and end of the story. The researchers should also try to connect
with the theoretical framework being used to interpret the story. There can be a
personal or interpersonal context of narrative accounts.

3.11.5 Phenomenological research

A phenomenology is a research approach aimed at the study of human experiences of phenomena from the first-person point of view. The emergence of
phenomenology took place with the works of Husserl, Heidegger, Sartre and
others. Phenomenological research studies the experiences of perception, thinking, emotionality, social activity, linguistic activity, imagination and embodied
action. Conscious experience is the starting point of phenomenological studies,
but it also comprises the art of interpreting life experience and intentionality.
The intentionality of experience begins from conveying a particular activity
such as perception, thought or imagination. There are several phenomenological
streams of thought which emerged under the umbrella of phenomenological
philosophy.

3.11.5.1 Transcendental phenomenology

Edmund Husserl (1900/2001) formulated this perspective in his "Ideas"; he
described the key distinction between the act of consciousness (noesis) and the
phenomena at which it is directed (the noemata). The intentional process of consciousness is called noesis, while its ideal content is called noemata.

3.11.5.2 Existential phenomenology

Its studies concrete human existence, including our expression of the free
choice. This philosophy is associated with Heidegger, Jean-Paul Sartre and
Simone de Beauvoir. In *Being and Time*, Heidegger (1962) defined phenomenology as the art or practice of "letting things show themselves". In the novel
Nausea (originally published in 1938), Jean-Paul Sartre (1969) described a
bizarre recourse of experience in which the protagonist writing in the first
person describes how ordinary objects lose their meaning until he encounters
pure being at the foot of a chestnut tree and in that moment recovers his sense
of own freedom.

In *Being and Nothingness* (1943), written partly while being a prisoner of war)
Sartre emphasized the experience of freedom of choice, especially the project of
choosing one's self, the defining pattern of one's past actions. Sartre also provided
a vivid description of the "look" of the other which became a significant concept
in later times.

Simone de Beauvoir, a strong companion of Sartre, launched contemporary feminism with her book *The Second Sex* (1952), a detailed description of the perceived role of woman as others. Hermeneutic phenomenology is associated with the works of Hans-Georg Gadamer and Paul Ricoeur. The main focus of this approach is that phenomenology acquires an hermeneutical approach when its methods are transformed into an interpretive mode.

In a classic study of women's romance reading, Radway (1984) summed up that one attraction in this activity is that it creates time and space within which a woman can entirely on her own remain preoccupied with her personal needs, desires and pleasure. Media discourses are not as simplistic as it appears and conveys different meanings in a latent manner.

Communication researchers have also done research is evaluating the role of parenting mediation to mitigate negative effects on children. There have been numerous studies that parental role modeling was an important aspect of child socialization into media use.

THINK BOX

- Describe the advantages of qualitative research in mass-media related subjects.
- Do you think narrative analysis is a good qualitative research method to understand the media effects?

3.12 Media and research interface

Mass media researchers have become important in influencing audience behavior, and media is a very sensitive tool as it is connected to the masses. The increased demand for information has created a need for more researchers both public and private. Earlier theories of media research focused that mass communicators need only "short" messages at an audience resulting into desired effects. Advertising researchers encouraged studies of message effectiveness, audience demographics and placement of advertising to achieve the highest level of persuading effect on customers. Investigating the role of mass media in the development of pro-social and violent effects have been researched extensively. The media research team includes information about consumers' changing values and attitudes, shifts in demographic patterns and developing trends in lifestyles. Large research organizations study trends (new behavior patterns), images (people's perception of media environment) and segmentation (explanation of behavior by types or group people). The packaging strategy of media research involves understanding of audience thinking, use of language in their time-spending behavior and other activities. The method of positioning is applied to get information from the audience and interpret the data for marketing purposes. Modern mass media research includes a variety of psychological and social investigations aimed at understanding the physiological and emotional responses of the media-message users. A more conceptual framework of media research also analyzes political and social context consequences of media-learned frames. The most common finding of framing research perspective is that exposure to news coverage results in learning that is consistent with the frames that structure the coverage. Empirical findings received through the use of content analysis and survey research provide important insights to understand media effects on behavior.

Mass media research has also focused upon analyzing its effect on children's violent behavior. Media scholars agree that media research is evolving to embrace the domains of persuasion, propaganda, cognition and social influence, with human communication expanding its horizons. In the Indian context also, use of mass media research is carried out at a large scale during the time of elections for exit polls and opinion polls.

Cognitive and social psychologists have used priming paradigms for useful explanation of media effects on people's thoughts, beliefs, judgements and behavior. The majority of published experiments have been consistent with the priming explanations of media violence.

3.13 Research methods: applications in media and communication

Media research is the study of psychological, social and cultural effects of mass media at individual and group levels. For example, does watching violence on television lead to aggression among children? Do our interaction and engagement with media gadgets and their messages lead to changes in our attitudes, perception and behavior? Is our environment of technology leading to growth of anxiety, depression and isolation among adolescents and youth? How much time duration in the daily use may be considered as internet dependence leading to withdrawal symptoms? Are there differences in its impact on viewers of various media platforms like radio, television and internet? What is the role of mass media in creating awareness about social and health issues? Does media create artificial needs, wants and attitudes of consumerism among its users? Media researches tend to explore the variation of media effects depending upon the age, education and culture of media users.

Media researches have also investigated the presence of mass media in the family and its impact on psychological well-being. The nature of medium audiovisual can affect the attitudes and behavior in different ways.

Media researches explore and investigate the role of media on children's aggression. Media's role in the development of altruism among people can enable persons to engage in prosocial behavior patterns. The distinction between education, information and entertainment can be investigated and understood with the help of media researches. Research in media reflects the capacity of audiences to influence media representations. Media research uses both quantitative and qualitative methods, and at times mixed methods, to investigate issues of psycho-social relevance. It also makes use of scientific methods of research by identifying the objectives.

Pioneering research in the field of mass media began with studying the nature of propaganda and its influence on their audiences. Media messages through films and other modes of advertisements perpetuate gender stereotypes. Explicit and implicit messages of mass media can depict certain social groups in adverse and unrealistic manners exerting great influence on people's attitudes. Pictorial stereotypes in media that we do not notice can be more harmful because we are not even aware of the negative, false ideas they perpetuate. Stereotypical body images portrayed through media can lead to anorexia and eating disorders among children and adolescents. Media messages of both types of news media and entertainment fiction may trigger emotions of fear among children through long exposure of violent media watching. Crime news has been a staple of journalism for decades. Sensational and even erotic aspects of homicides and brutal assaults and sex crimes create a symbolic awareness of fear and risk in the day-to-day lives of users.

The realm of media research subsequently delved into the area of advertising, audience demography mapping and evaluating the socio-cultural impact of media. Media researchers study the new trends in fashion, new behavior patterns, people's perceptions and attitude of media environment. Media strategists tend to produce a medium as a packaged image rather than a product. Modern mass media research involves investigations from psychological and sociological points of view, determining the why and how of audience thinking and behavior.

Media effects research looks at the ways in which media messages can influence the audiences. Media researches also indicate that messages do not mean the same thing to every person, and the active nature of the audience negotiates and ignores media messages differently.

Lazarsfeld's "two step flow" model posited that certain individuals are not directly influenced by media messages. Instead, they form their opinions based on interpretation of opinion leaders who put them in context.

Empirical research in media also highlights the effect of heavy usage of violence and danger issues in everyday life. People become hyperconscious of such issues as mentioned in Gerbner's cultivation analysis studies. Media researches also discuss the widespread effect popular media plays in setting the agenda for discussion among its users.

Deconstructionism as a research method studies the media messages and tries to search for themes based upon coding processes. Researchers use critical reflexivity and meaningful insights to decode and deconstruct the latent meanings associated with manifest surface images and meanings. They tend to explore manifest dimensions with the interpretation of multiple hidden meanings.

A deconstructive reading of a text calls on the researcher to constantly reflect, question and interpret the understanding of what is actually happening with the text through the processes of manifest expression and hidden suppression. Therefore, deconstructionist researchers question the presumption of a unified, coherent text as single ultimate reality highlighting its implicit assumptions and plausible interpretations.

Media messages projected as simplified ideas are questioned to understand the meanings of a text. Researchers of media following this approach may question the storyline, understanding the dichotomies revealing disruptions in the projected meaning.

Popular music songs are influenced by creation of hegemonic legitimacy in which media consumers interpret media texts from a negotiated position, meaning that the decoding part of the text is more in accordance with industry code and less with personal preference.

Many choices of popular media products are a product of dominant conventions without providing multiple readings of the text from different individuals. Media messages also adopt strategic ambiguity to craft a vague, semantically rich text that is intentionally open to multiple interpretations. The meaning of a film, serial or piece of music cannot be the same for all sections of people. Watching or listening to a dominant interpretational logic is often presented to claim a homogenized meaning of a media message which may not be true in reality.

The careful designing of surveys, extensive interviewing and attention to micro aspects with the help of coding/decoding and polysemy give rise to multiple interpretations of media texts. *Ethnographic* researchers focus on understanding a cultural phenomenon from the perspective of the members of that culture. Ethnographic researchers in the field of communication look at the interaction patterns and power differentials and try to understand the beliefs and behavior of the people.

For example, a media ethnographer may enter a film screening center for days and weeks to understand what film means to the members of the group. How members of media message users make sense through dominant ideological meanings are studied by ethnographic researchers using methods of participation, observation and interviewing.

How do audiences negotiate the meaning making of media texts help the researchers to investigate the subtle and otherwise invisible meanings that a layperson can't understand easily. Media researchers carry out case studies of individual productions who are makers of entertainment content. One of the most influential studies of television industry was carried out by Cantor (1988 [1971]), and in her work she argued about the fundamental structure of media industries rooted in the ideals of capitalism, advertising in which oligopolistic organization prevents creative potential from being realized. Such studies include interviews and surveys with producers and their decision-making processes.

The term "prosumers" was coined by Alvin Toffler (1980), and this new term indicates a mixing of production and consumption in media industry and society, audiences for which one may not be downgraded to simply consuming commercial goods. In a situation when fans and often consumers actively participate in the creation of new content, the term "produsage" (Bruns, 2008) is used to describe participatory forms of production in a digital media environment.

Media researches are also carried out to understand how the media engages in order to produce news. The news media are influenced by four markets: advertisers, audience, source and owners. These various markets are dependent on each other for its success. For example, from a quantitative point of view, audience size, level of investment from the owners and powerful news sources can add potential journalistic value to its products. From a qualitative point of view, quality of news will influence the social and cultural background of its audience. Economic considerations, cognitive aspects and emotional aspects also contribute to the production of stories in newspapers and television channels. Some news stories have low entertainment content and high academic content, whereas others have high entertainment and sensational content, such as the Watergate scandal, but low academic content. Content analysis is extensively used in media researches.

Certain well-defined characteristics in newspapers and television channels, such as the percentage of domains of issues (political, sports, crime, celebrity, business), can be easily identified and measured in quantifiable terms.

Leo Lowenthal, in his Mass Idol (1961) studies about the declining representation of scientists, businessmen and political leaders with a shift in focus on film actors, entertainers and athletes in popular US magazines, described this shift from "idols of production" to "idols to consumption". Survey techniques are often used to gather information about people's attitudes on a specified issue. Interviews and questionnaires including electronic questionnaires are used by the researchers to know about the views of respondents. It is essential that each individual in a survey should be representative of the total population, hence sampling constitutes a key element of quantitative research. A sample of viewers of programs, users of products or citizens for their preferences can be surveyed through questionnaires and interviews which can indicate the opinion of the people at mass level. Longitudinal research and cross-sectional research are procedures to investigate the plausibility of different types of casual hypothesis. In the trend studies of longitudinal research, a given population is surveyed at different points in time which is helpful in gaining information about the changing opinions of people over-time.

Cohort studies are conducted on the basis of age groups of the people. For example, children, adolescents and adults can be included to monitor the changes in attitudes and behavior which are associated with maturation. Content analysis can be used to gather trends of media portrayals such as sensationalism, fiction or real issues. How certain categories of people are included or excluded by the lens of media can also be studied through the representation and quality of representation they get in media.

However, it is difficult to reveal the ideological and stereotypical biases with the use of quantitative research methods. Many experiments conducted on a small sample can't be representative of the entire population. The difficulty of controlling totally extraneous factors that can affect dependent variables can't be ruled out. Laboratory conditions for examining media effects on attitudes and behavior may be different from their behavior in the real world. Media campaign of certain topics or issues such as the Nirbhaya case in India generated a large public impact through organized and sustained focus on a single issue. Media campaigns with issue-specific objectives play a powerful role in forming, persuading and mobilizing a large group of people.

All the leading organizations in the world and in India have a special department of corporate communication or public relations departments whose main objective is to pursue the plans and policies of the organizations with the help of strategic media communication. In case something wrong happens in the functioning, the officials engage in damage control through mass media platforms of social media and press conferences.

Many new programs and policies of the government and private organizations are highlighted through media platforms to improve its reach and impact on the masses.

Research organizations conduct surveys and research to improve the image-building work by knowing the preferences of the audience and suggest measures to create emotional connect with the target audiences. The services of human resource consultancy and public relations firms are engaged to do the job of brand positioning and ideas positioning among the target audiences.

Media researches can establish the impact of media messages at individual and group levels. A great level of researches in the area of digital media platforms has become relevant in the contemporary time period.

3.14 Critical evaluation and summary

This chapter initially addressed basic research concepts used in qualitative and quantitative researches. It dealt with important concepts like theory, deduction, induction, empiricisms, epistemology, ontology and praxis. It further described the processes of constructionism and deconstructionism which is used in various research practices.

In the next major description, the chapter covered quantitative research methods and measurement. It also looked at reliability validity, types of measurement, survey research and sampling techniques which are widely used in the realm of media studies. Content analysis and factorial designs are very relevant to media researches.

Another section described the characteristics of qualitative research methods. The theoretical assumptions related to qualitative researches have been described in detail. It included symbolic interactionism, ethnomethodology and the structuralist perspective. The feminist perspective of research and its importance to media psychology have been well explained for a better understanding of media behavior and society.

In the last section, qualitative research data collection and data analytic methods were described. Ethnography, observation method, grounded theory, thematic and narrative analysis and phenomenological approaches were covered in detail. All the aforementioned methods are used by media psychology researches to understand the relationship and impact of mass media on human behavior. Researchers may use a single method, mixed-method and multimethod depending upon the need of the situation and the context of research objectives. Several other methods, like case studies, focus group discussion and online research, can be applied while doing media research. A lot of authenticity of the research outcome is dependent on the quality and process of data collection and various factors. The sample size and literature review play a vital role in the process of doing quality research. Several other problems of bias, lack of training, lack of rapport formation with the participants and absence of code of conduct may also adversely affect the research outcome.

Mass media is an emerging field, and the application of research methods with a meaningful approach can bring positive outcomes from the research perspective and for the society at large. Researches should not be carried out for creating cognitive illusions; instead, it should amplify and widen our perspectives of understanding the subject of mass media with greater clarity and effectiveness.

Key points

- Key concepts of a good research are induction, deduction, empiricism, epistemology, ontology, positivism and interpretation.
- The general framework of research includes a theory, hypothesis, research design, data collection, data analysis and findings.
- Important statistical strategies used to eliminate confounding variables are stratification, multivariate models, logistic regression, linear regression and analysis of covariance.
- The term reliability in psychological research refers to the consistency of a research study or measuring test. For example, if a person weighs themselves during the course of a day they would expect a similar reading.
- Validity of the measurement tool is the degree to which the tool measures what it purports to measure.
- Measures to represent numerically the degree of attributes under study in a systematic and controlled measure are called levels of measurement.
- Survey research is the process of researching data collection from respondents about their knowledge, beliefs, opinions, attitudes and behaviors.

- Longitudinal research is a type of research method in which data is gathered for the same group of subjects over a period of time.
- Qualitative research involves an introspective and naturalistic approach.
- Ethnomethodology studies and analyzes everyday activities.

Key terms

epistemology, ontology, praxis, Cronbach's alpha, ecological validity, ethnography, field notes, thematic analysis, transcendental phenomenology, existential phenomenology

References

Beauvoir, S. de. (1952). *The Second Sex* (H.M. Parshley, Trans.). Vintage Press.

Berelson, B. (1952). *Content Analysis in Communication Research* (p. 18). Glencoe, IL: The Free Press.

Bergen, L.A., & Weaver, D. (1988). Job satisfaction of daily newspaper journalists and organization size. *Newspaper Research Journal*, 9(2), 1–14.

Blumer, H. (1938). Social psychology. In E.P. Schmidt (Ed.), *Man and Society: A Substantive Introduction to the Social Science* (pp. 144–98). New York: Prentice-Hall.

Blumer, H. (1969). *Symbolic interactionism: Perspective and method.* Berkeley, CA: University of California Press.

Bruns, A. (2008). *Blogs, Wikipedia, Second Life and Beyond: From Production to Produsage.* New York: Peter Lang.

Bryman, A. (2008). *The End of the Paradigm Wars?* In P. Alasuutari, J. Brannen, & L. Buckman (Eds.), *Handbook of Social Research.* London: Sage.

Cantor, M. (1988 [1971]). *The Hollywood Television Producer: His Work and His Audience* (Rev. ed.). New Brunswick, NJ: Transaction Books.

Cicourel, A.V. (1982). Language and belief in a medical setting. In Heidi Byrnes (Ed.), *Contemporary Perceptions of Language: Interdisciplinary Dimensions* (pp. 1–41). Washington, DC: Georgetown University Press.

Cohen, L., Minion, L., & Morrison, K. (2011). *Research Methods in Education* (7th ed., p. 537). London: Routledge.

Davis, D. (2005). *Business Research for Decision Making.* Australia: Thomson South-Western.

Demers, D.P., & Wackman, D.B. (1988). Effect of chain ownership on newspaper management goals. *Newspaper Research Journal*, 9(2), 59–68.

Denzin, N.K. & Lincoln, Y.S. (2000). Introduction: The discipline and practices of qualitative research. In N.K. Denzin & Y.S. Lincoln (Eds), *Handbook of Qualitative Research* (pp. 1–29). London: Sage.

Denzin, N.K. & Lincoln, Y.S. (2011). *The Sage Handbook of Qualitative Research.* Newbury Park, CA: Sage.

Derrida, J. (1976) *Of Grammatology*, Baltimore, MD: Johns Hopkins University Press. (Originally published 1967).

Dewey, J. (1925). *Experience and Nature.* Chicago, IL: Open Court.

Fielding, N., & Fielding J. (1986). *Linking Data.* Beverly Hills, CA: Sage.

Friedan, B. (1963). *The Feminine Mystique.* New York: W.W. Norton & Co.

Garfinkel, H. (1967) *Studies in Ethnomethodology*, Englewood Cliffs, NJ: Prentice-Hall.

Garfinkel, H., & Sacks, H. (1970). On formal structures of practical actions. In J.D. McKinney & E.A. Tiryakian (Eds.), *Theoretical Sociology* (pp. 337–66). New York: AppletonCentury Crofts.. Republished in H. Garfinkel (Ed.) (1986), *Ethnomethodological Studies of Work* (London: Routledge & Kegan Paul), pp. 157–89.

Geertz, C. (1993). *The Interpretation of Cultures: Selected Essays*. New York: Basic Books.

Gerbner, G., Gross, L., Morgan, M., & Signorielli, N. (1986). Living with television: The dynamics of the cultivation process. In J. Bryant & D. Zillmann (Eds.), *Perspectives on Media Effects*. Hillsdale, NJ: Lawrence Erlbaum

Glaser, B.G., Strauss, A.L., & Strutzel, E. (1968). The discovery of grounded theory: Strategies for qualitative research. *Nursing Research*, 17(4), 364.

Goode, W.J., & Hatt, P.K. (1952) *Methods in Social Research*. New York: McGraw-Hill.

Habermas, J. (1971). *Knowledge and Human Interests*. Boston, MA: Beacon Press. (Originally published 1968)

Heidegger, M. (1962). *Being and Time*. New York: Harper and Row. (Originally published 1927)

Hong, Y.Y., Chao, M.M., Yang, Y.J., & Rosner, J.L. (2010). Building and testing theories: Experiences from conducting social identity research. *Acta Psychologica Sinica*, 42(1), 22–36.

Hughes, E. 1971. Going concerns: The study of American institutions. In E. Hughes (Ed.), *The Sociological Eye* (pp. 52–64). Chicago: Aldine-Atherton.

Husserl, E. (1900/2001). *Logical Investigations* (J.N. Findlay, Trans.). London: Routledge.

Katz, E., & Lazarsfeld, P.F. (1955) *Personal Influence*. Glencoe, IL: Free Press.

Kelley, T.L. (1927). *Interpretation of Educational Measurements* (p. 14). New York: Macmillan

Kuhn, T.S. (1962). *The Structure of Scientific Revolutions*. Chicago, IL: University of Chicago Press.

Larson, G.J., Bhattacharya, R.S., & Potter, K.H. (2014). *The Encyclopedia of Indian Philosophies, Vol. 4: Samkhya, a Dualist Tradition in Indian Philosophy*. Princeton Legacy Library.

Lasorsa, D., & Reese, S. (1990). News source use in the Crash of 1987: A study of four national media. *Journalism Quarterly*, 167, 60–71.

Lazarsfeld, P.F., Berelson, B., & Gaudet, H. (1944). *The People's Choice: How the Voter Makes Up His Mind in a Presidential Campaign*. New York: Columbia University Press.

Lowenthal, L. (1961). The triumph of mass idols. In L. Lowenthal (Ed.), *Literature, Popular Culture, and Society*. Englewood Cliffs, NJ: Prentice-Hall. (Originally published 1941)

Lyotard, J.-F. (1984). *The Postmodern Condition: A Report on Knowledge* (G. Bennington & B. Massumi, Trans.). Minneapolis: University of Minnesota Press.

Maynard, M. (1994). Methods, practice and epistemology: The debate about feminism and research. In Mary Maynard & Jane Purvis (Eds.), *Researching Women's Lives from a Feminist Perspective* (pp. 10–27). London: Taylor and Francis.

McLaren, P. & Farahmandpur, R. (2000). Reconsidering Marx in post-Marxist times: A requiem for postmodernism? *Educational Researcher*, 29(3), 25–33.

Mead, G.H. (1934). *Mind, self, and society*. Chicago, IL: University of Chicago Press.

Mohler, B.J., Bülthoff, H.H., Thompson, W.B., & Creem-Regehr, S.H. (2008). A full-body avatar improves distance judgments in virtual environments. In *Proceedings of the 5th Symposium on Applied Perception in Graphics and Visualization*, August.

Montgomery, K. (1989) *Target: Prime Time: Advocacy Groups and the Struggle Over Entertainment Television*, New York: Oxford University Press.

Murray, S. (1999). Saving our so-called lives: Girl fandom, adolescent subjectivity, and *My So-Called Life*. In M. Kinder (Ed.), *Kids' Media Culture* (pp. 221–35). Durham, NC: Duke University Press.

Park, R.E., & Burgess, E.W. (1921), *Introduction to the Science of Sociology*, Chicago, University of Chicago Press.

Radway, J. (1984). *Reading the Romance*. Chapel Hill: University of North Carolina Press.

Rentz, J., Reynolds, F., & Stout, R. (1983). Analysing Changing Consumption Patterns with Cohort Analysis. *Journal of Marketing Research*, 20, 12–20.

Ricoeur, P. (1981) *Hermeneutics and the Human Sciences: Essays on Language, Action and Interpretation*, Cambridge: Cambridge University Press.

Rosengren, K.E., & Windahl, S. (1989) *Media Matter: TV Use in Childhood and Adolescence*, Norwood, NJ: Ablex.

Ross, S.S. (1998). Journalists' use of on-line technology and sources. In D.L. Borden and K. Harvey (Eds.), *The Electronic Grapevine: Rumor, Reputation, and Reporting in the New On-Line Environment*. Mahwah, NJ: Lawrence Erlbaum.

Sarbin, T.R. (1986). The narrative as a root metaphor for psychology. In: T.R. Sarbin, (Ed.), *Narrative Psychology: The Storied Nature of Human Conduct* (pp. 3–21). New York: Praeger.

Sartre, J.P. (1943). *Being and Nothingness* (H. Barnes, Trans.). New York: Philosophical Library.

Sartre, J.P. (1962 [1936]). *Imagination: A Psychological Critique* (F. Williams, Trans.). Ann Arbor, MI: University of Michigan Press.

Sartre, J.P. (1969). *Nausea* (L. Alexander, Trans.). New York: New Directions Books. (Originally published 1938)

Schutz, A. (1962). *Collected Papers* (Vols. I–II). The Hague: Nijhoff.

Sellitz, C., Jahoda, M., Deutsch, M., & Cook, S. (1976). *Research Methods in Social Relations*. New York: Holt, Rinehart & Winston.

Shank, G. (2002). *Qualitative Research: A Personal Skills Approach*. New Jersey: Merrill Prentice Hall.

Siegel, P.M., & Hodge, R.W. (1968). A Causal Approach to the Study of Measurement Error. In H.M. Blalock, Jr. and A.B. Blalock (Eds.), *Methodology in Social Research*. New York: McGraw-Hill.

Stevens, S.S. (1946). On the theory of scales of measurement. *Science*, 103(2684), 677–80.

Studtmann, P. (2007). Aristotle's categories. In E.N. Zalta (Ed.), *The Stanford Encyclopedia of Philosophy* (Fall 2008 edition). Retrieved 11 October 2020 from https://plato.stanford.edu/entries/aristotle-categories/

Toffler, A. (1980). *Third Wave*. New York: William Morrow.

Toulmin, S. (1990). *Cosmopolis: The Hidden Agenda of Modernity*. New York: Free Press.

Wimmer, R.D., & Dominick, J.R. (1994). *Mass Media Research: An Introduction* (4th ed.). Belmont, CA: Wadsworth.

Wittgenstein, L. (1958). *Philosophical Investigations*, Oxford: Blackwell.

Wober, M., & Gunter, B. (1988). *Television and Social Control*. Aldershot, Hants: Avebury.

Zuckerman, M. (1994). *Behavioural Expressions and Biosocial Bases of Sensation Seeking*, Cambridge: Cambridge University Press.

4

MEDIA AND SOCIETY

Learning objectives

After reading this chapter, you will be able to understand:

- Media and society interaction
- The dominant paradigms of media sociology
- The role of media and its implications for children
- The role of media and its implication for youth
- Implications of media for family
- Critical evaluation in the Indian context

4.1 Mass media and society

In the contemporary period, the developing technology of mass media has a strong impact on the lives of people and society. Most of our assumptions are based upon exposure, access or attention to media messages. Media contents and its portrayal are shaping beliefs, attitudes, perception, thinking and the minds of people. Mass media research suggests strong links of people's behavior at the individual and group levels. The rising rates of violence, crime and aggressive behavior in the society are also partly influenced by exposure to media messages.

Media depicts the functioning of our society. Media sociology studies suggested that sociological resources should focus on the institution of journalism and try to understand its ownership and operations. Media representation and its content constructs a version of its own reality rather than mirroring the reality of society. Media content provides collective shared meaning and in turn supports societal homogeneity. The influence of mass media on society covers a wide spectrum of activities, changing our belief attitudes and behavior. Each one of us is affected by the presence of mass media in various degrees. Mass media and society concept are concerned with how content of mass communication persuades or affects attitudes, behavior and emotion of the people on both a short-term and long-term basis. Different modes of mass communication such as advertising, journalism, public relations, social media, audio media and convergence film and television and interactive media has far-reaching implications for the receivers and users. In the book, *The Lonely Crowd* (Reisman et al., 2001), David Reisman identified three main cultural types: tradition directed,

FIGURE 4.1 Social media faces social networks.
Source: *Needpix*. https://www.needpix.com/photo/277304/social-media-faces-social-networks-media-system-network-news-personal-connection

inner-directed and other-directed. Those of tradition-directed types of people believed in rules and norms and acted accordingly and had difficulty adapting to the changes of modernity. The inner-directed believed in themselves and not much according to the norms which were caused due to increased ability to consume goods and material abundance. Gradually the third type as other-directed emerged, which involves comparing how others are living, what they consumed, and these people wanted to be loved rather than esteemed. The focus of other-directed people was on being in tune with others.

Garfinkel (1967) suggested that we are socialized not simply by ideas, but by the way ideas are structured, related to authority and pertinent to our needs and interests by complying with rules. We forge patterns of "daily life (that are) known in common with others and with others taken for granted".

To behave strictly according to literal rules carries the risk of becoming a "judgmental dope" rather than a "competent rule user" (Garfinkel, 1967). Paul Bouissac (1976) argues that rule-breaking is at the heart of why people enjoy the circus. Many a time rule-breaking can also produce heroes. Electronic media contributes to shape and maintains rule and ideological predispositions through powerful media imagery in the construction of interpersonal discourses that people follow in social life. Mass media-promoted messages traverse not only to graphic frontiers but also to the boundaries of role, class and gender.

We can always notice sufficient levels of transmission of rules and behaviors across macro-social and micro-social environments. The public sphere has been mediated and reconstituted in the electronic age (Thompson, 1995), both technologically and socially.

According to Katz and Sugiyama (2005), mobiles like other fashion items are used as a device to project a sense of identity and self into public arenas, and it can become an aesthetic object that people adapt and modify according to their sense of self and group affiliations.

Fundamentally, all communication technologies have effects on opinions, attitudes and behaviors. Media is considered as the fourth pillar of democracy, the other three being legislative, executive and judiciary. However, there are also different types of media, and "media" is not a uniform concept.

Denis McQuail, in the sixth edition of his canonic textbook (2010) based on normative approaches to the media, described four models:

1. The liberal pluralist or market model
2. The social responsibility or public interest model
3. The "professional model
4. The alternative media model

Media in its monitoring role acquires institutional power and informational power. It largely remains in the hands of people owning such institutions. Media's facilitative role includes civic and public journalism, where people can express their views. In the radical approach of media, liberation movements are noteworthy.

From an economic point of view, the nature of society has become more materialistic and consumeristic. The opportunities for business activities have emerged,

FIGURE 4.2 Network society social community.
Source: Retrieved 18 June 2020 from https://pixabay.com/illustrations/network-society-social-community-1019842/

and the whole world has become a market. Large-scale growth of multinational corporations has a major share of market activities, and large-scale automation has also led to unemployment in the formal as well as informal sectors. Traditional businesses have suffered huge setbacks owing to the lack of infrastructure and resources for advertisements. Large-scale migration of people has taken place particularly from developing to the developed countries in the field of IT professionals. In general, the level of competition has also grown, and people from rural India, where a strong network of IT infrastructure is still not well established, are lacking adequate progress and development.

There have been awareness activities with the help of mass media. The general level of awareness has increased in the minds of common citizens, and the demand for transparency in government programs and policies have increased. So many offices which took several months to years to process routine activities related to citizens are either becoming paperless or a hassle-free activity. The use of RTI (Right to Information) has become a powerful tool to enforce transparency in government offices. Public awareness has increased many times, and people at high and mighty places also hesitate to do anything unethical due to the sudden upsurge of criticism on social media platforms.

In the case of entertainment and lifestyle-related products, strong use of social media platforms is being utilized for the popularity of such products. A huge variety of music with technology has become part and parcel of the youth generation. Similarly, there is an abundance of products related to fitness and health improvement, and advertisements pertaining to them have penetrated both urban and rural places.

An important development in social media is related to reports of crime against women. Though the percentage of crime against women has not decreased much, electronic evidences have helped to achieve a better conviction rate for the perpetrators of the crime. Women groups, also with the support of like-minded law-abiding citizens, can raise the awareness voice on social media platforms.

The young and old generations of people share different value patterns. This explains conflicts and intergenerational trust deficits. In particular, spending lots of time using mass media mediated activities including chatting, video sharing, educational purposes and entertainment by the younger people is leading to conflict.

There is also a significant reduction in community-related activities of voluntary participation for social welfare, and the tendency for exhibitionism and symbolism has risen in recent times. There had been a significant decline in the use of physical and sports activities of children due to their increased involvement in media-dependent activities. Bedroom culture has risen in recent times, and people who are more dependent on media activities are also reporting mental health problems of depression and sleeplessness.

Education has also become more accessible through the popularity of online courses. Mass media has also contributed to the promotion of self and self-representations, and attention to self-management has gathered momentum in recent years. A significant trend with media-mediated communication has been the area of the private and public sphere.

Mass media as a process is typified as predominantly impersonal and individualistic, leading to the diminished interpersonal identity and sense of community. The media are seen as a significant contribution to this process due to the remoteness of institutions, isolation of individuals and lack of strong local or group integration.

4.2 Dominant paradigms in media sociology

Thomas Kuhn (1970) defined a scientific paradigm as "accepted examples of actual scientific practice, examples which include law, theory, application and instrumentation together (that) provide models from which spring particular coherent tradition of scientific research . . . men whose research is based on shared paradigms are committed to the same rules and standards for scientific practice". Harman (1970) defined a paradigm as "the basic way of perceiving, thinking, valuing and doing associated with a particular vision of reality".

The dominant paradigm of mass media played a vital role in the digital era. Nowadays media has not remained a one-way flow of communication from source to the audience. It has become more interactive, and the new environment of media has become more user-centric. The agenda-setting role of media has also changed with the changing times, and every user of media networks can play the role of an editor.

The conflict paradigm prescribes the process of socialization as coercive and the values and norms are forced to be accepted by ordinary citizens. The conflict paradigm further suggests a lack of consensus among groups or individual members of society. There are conflicts over wealth, power and status. Also, there are status gaps in the family in terms of gender roles, and a high level of inequality exists between men and women.

The functionalist paradigm describes society as stable and social structure attempts to maintain balance among different components of the society. The structural-functionalist paradigm attempts to serve the needs of society through consensus. People follow legitimate authority for their safety as well as maintaining social order. In this paradigm, the families are well integrated and cultural transmission is passed from one generation to the next.

From a symbolic interactionist paradigm, society is based upon interpretation of culture, perceptions, belief systems and media images. The values and norms of society are in a state of change depending on situations and circumstances. The structure of the society is subjective, abstract and in a state of constant change. Negotiated meanings of interaction determine the quality of relationships among people. The dominant paradigm of mass media is essentially normative. The purpose of mass media is integration, continuity and order in the society.

THINK BOX

- In your views, is the news coverage by TV news channels good enough to portray social reality?
- How authentic are stories being told in Televisions and Newspapers regarding various sensitive issues?

4.3 Media and children

How children spend time on media gadgets like mobile phones, the internet and television have emerged as a major concern for the policymakers, caregivers and parents. Life events unfold over time. Media use studies suggest that 8- to 18-year-old youth spend several hours a day with various media (for example, television, computers and video games) in the home. In the words of Spigel (1992), television was a "panacea for the broken homes and hearts of wartime life as well as the object that could destroy family relationships and can cause massive disruptions to the smooth functioning of households" (p. 2).

FIGURE 4.3   Children and technology.
Source: Retrieved 18 June 2020 from https://www.pikist.com/free-photo-vnpem

Television became a sure source of entertainment in the 1980s and 1990s, and this new medium impacted children and families. More hours of television viewing in the family did not contribute to the increased interaction among family members except physical togetherness. The nature of the family social life during a program could be described as "parallel" rather than interactive. The leisure time of children is occupied by television, computers and other interactive video games. Children are using various media platforms in a day contributing to a larger number of hours spending time on media gadgets.

4.3.1 Role of advertisements

There has been a phenomenal rise in advertising catering to the interests of children and selling them a distant set of values. With the advent and blossoming of digital technology, the specialized television channels, video games and the dot-com boom, the value of children as a market for selling products has risen by enormous proportions. As Montgomery (2007) has noted:

> All the ingredients were in place to create a highly commercial digital media culture with unprecedented access to the child consumer. The dramatic crash of the over-hyped online market did little to stop the flow of the new media into young people's lives. As a consequence, the digital generation has become the most heavily researched demographic group in the history of marketing.

4.3.2 Economics of the children's advertisement market

It is important to mention that the economics of developing and producing a children's series requires huge financial investment even in a per-hour program. The famous producers from the USA include PBS Kids, Cartoon Network and Playhouse Disney. Another giant in this business of children's TV program is Animation Collective, one of the largest animation studios in New York City with multiple original series in production. France, Canada and Japan are also major players in this field of producing programs dedicated to children.

The emotional aspects related to the power of children to influence parents' behavior have increased in recent times. Advertisers spot toys, games and food products for marketing products to children, who are considered a safe future market for goods and services. Marketing tactics respond to them from present and future perspectives for becoming future consumers. A variety of techniques and channels are used to influence children, beginning when they are toddlers, to foster brand loyalty and product purchase behavior.

4.3.3 Children as consumers

Children have become an important target of marketers and big advertisement organizations due to changes in the dynamics of the family system. Advertisers target children intending to target the parents. Children can't very easily distinguish between fiction and facts, and children respond positively to the products which appear in a dream-like world. Once a child is persuaded and hypnotized by the power of constant advertisement, they will start pressuring the parents to buy the product, good or bad. This may include an exaggerated world of cartoons or any other food products. Brand loyalty is developed in the minds of children at a very young age, and it is further reinforced by peer pressure.

Orientation in brands cultivated at an early age becomes a part of the social environment. Children in this age live their everyday lives in an environment dominated by commercial communications. The parents do not perform the proper role for emotional, intellectual and social development of children due to lack of time owing to professional engagements. Parents have greatly reduced the time spent put into raising children owing to fulfill the job requirements fueled with economic anxieties. Nuclear families have become a norm in the metropolitan cities, and children do not get sufficient time from the parents.

There are different types of parenting styles, such as "child-centered, expert-guided, emotionally absorbing, labor-intensive and financially expensive". Hays wrote in her book *The Cultural Contradictions of Motherhood* (1998) that nowadays more women have joined the workforce and child care has become a joint initiative by both mothers and fathers, a new trend among working-class couples. There are also differences in raising the children of different socio-economic groups. The marital lives of people around the globe and in India have become short-lived due to adjustment problems resulting in divorce having short-term and long-term psycho-social implications for children. It has been observed that children experience healthy outcomes when they live with two married biological parents rather than with a single parent. Along with the rising use of technological gadgets, children have access to media gadgets from an early age. The proliferation of internet access in households and lack of parental control allows children to spend hours a day on media activities. Long-term exposure to media platforms influences the highly impressionable minds of children through various products. There has been a significant increase in the use of tools and gadgets by the younger generation, and their immersion in digital technology also exposes them to greater influences.

4.3.4 Technology effects

There is much stimulation available to children which is not required at an early age and over-pre-occupation with technological gadgets interferes with children's routine physical activities. Nowadays children do not spend enough time in parks and playgrounds; most of the time is spent surfing on the internet, glued to television programs, playing video games and other related activities.

A Kaiser Foundation study in 2010 showed that children between the ages of 8 and 18 spent an average of 7 hours and 38 minutes a day with digital media. When the use of more than one digital device at a time is taken into account, they spend more than 10.5 hours a day with digital technologies.

Results of a 2016 Common Sense media report found that 50% of teens "feel addicted" to mobile devices, while 59% of parents surveyed believed that kids are addicted to their devices. There are various patterns of usage adopted by children owing to socio-economic differences and parental mediation factors. Even children in parks and playgrounds play along with the use of some form of technology. Experts suggest the use of screens for long durations can affect the quality of sleep due to the overstimulation of the brain. Children listen to music, surf the web and contact their friends as they simultaneously do their studies. Roberts (2000) distinguishes between media exposure and media use, with media exposure defined as "the sum of the amount of time youth spend with each medium to obtain an estimate of total exposure" and media use defined as the number of "person-hours" devoted to media. It is important to highlight that those hours of exposure can be more than hours of use owing to children engaging in two or three activities at the same time.

There are several techniques through which a tentative estimate of children's media use patterns can be estimated. Time use diaries require individuals to describe their activities or the activities of their child, sequentially for 24 hours. Diaries are more accurate than the self-reported time estimates that are often used in surveys.

Home video observation uses video equipment to record what is on television, who is in the room and what is happening when the set is turned on. Parental behavior of media usage patterns also plays an important role in determining the media usage pattern of children.

Parents influence children's viewing by setting an example of media use and habits by co-viewing with their children, by discussing their values and attitudes about television and by regulating or encouraging viewing of different types of content. Many parents watch a lot of television with children; it has become a dominant aspect of leisure utilization. Rideout and Hamel's (2006) findings revealed that parents (the sample consisting of primary mothers) not only encourage their children to use media for educational reasons but encouraged media use to keep their children occupied; this then provided parents with uninterrupted time to do chores and tasks within the home setting.

There are not significant and notable differences in the time spent on media by boys and girls. However, some references in the choice of programs can be noticed. Some variations can be noticed in media use patterns getting affected by the number of siblings in the family, the family type (joint/nuclear) and background (rural/urban) factors. Television does affect children's intellectual development through observational learning which is not very high in entertainment activities.

4.3.5 Media effects on children

Bandura's (2001) social cognitive theory proposes that the mass media contributes to acquiring value systems and rules of conduct for society by providing models from which children can learn. In the famous "Bobo doll" experiments, Bandura had shown that children, when exposed to aggression and violence, exhibited aggressive behavior by hitting, kicking and using hostile language. Such aggressive scripts are learned by children as they copy styles from television viewing which weakens the general restraint against violence through desensitized reactions to cruelty.

The majority of the crimes taking place in society are non-violent, but on television the frequency of major crimes are violent. According to Bandura, the fear of violence increases due to unpredictability of its happening, the gravity of its consequences from murder to rape and its nature of uncontrollability or perceived helplessness to control it. The tendency of sensationalism and wide coverage attributed to violent crimes tends to encourage these behaviors. According to Bandura, prosocial modeling or positive behavior modeling can foster traits of co-cooperativeness, empathy and sharing.

Bandura's social cognitive theory highlighted the agent perspective in which people are not considered just reactive but proactive, self-regulating and reflective. Plasticity is considered as a core quality of human nature which is largely governed by neural and cognitive processes mediation. Moral aspects have a dual role to play in our functioning: inhibitive and proactive. The inhibitive aspect is manifested through our tendency to refrain from inhuman activity, and proactive morality is manifested with our tendency to behave humanely.

Most of the activities, including behavioral, cognitive and affective, can be learned vicariously by observing others actions and its consequences. Observational learning is governed by attention, retention, modeling and motivational processes. Modeling is not a process of blind imitation; rather, it is also governed by generative and innovative processes known as abstract modeling. Heavy exposure to media programs may influence the children to internalize the beliefs as authentic representation of social reality.

4.3.6 Gender role beliefs

Stereotypes of men being strong and women being represented as weak and subservient are often portrayed by media programs. In television programs, cartoons, music videos and commercials, males are depicted as more adventurous, aggressive, violent and dominant in interpretation; females as more subservient, nurturing, affectionate and the object of implicit, explicit and aggressive sexual advances. Age and sex are the main principles of an Indian family hierarchy. M.S. Gore (1965) notes that men have more decisive authority in the traditional Indian family as compared with women.

Cultivation theory assumes that television is the primary storyteller in the culture and that televised stories are consistent over programming and time (Gerbner et al., 1994). In the media occupational preferences are also stereo-typed some professions like scientists, athletes, army, police and engineering are portrayed as more suitable for men and professions like nursing, teaching and household activities are portrayed as soft jobs more suitable for women. Most of the children who are excessively dependent on media usage can face certain health risks; however, there are some advantages also associated with media usage. According to Karve (1953), a wife in all her relations with her husband should adhere to the scriptural ideas of being a Pativrata, one who follows her husband's will and authority in all respects.

Loss of time: children addicted to social media and other media gadgets end up spending hours ignoring important activities related to growth and development.

Loss of emotional well-being: children spending long hours on media platforms also experience emotional strain due to lack of physical activities and lack of relational activities sharing their feelings. The prolonged usage may also result in becoming irritable, moody, anxious and in some cases suffering from depression. They do not learn real-life situations and lack the adequate ability to grasp non-verbal cues, sense of empathy and lack of adequate verbal communication.

Obesity: due to individual and sedentary style of engagements, children do not pay sufficient attention to eating at designated intervals; instead, they overeat ready-made food items. A large number of children face the problem of obesity, which also turns into serious health problems at later stages. Children who are overly busy using the internet and other media may experience loneliness and dissatisfaction with themselves.

Advantages: There are some advantages related to children's media usage. By the use of certain educational and simulation-based video games, problem-solving and critical thinking are facilitated. An increasing number of learners on social media also acquire the capability to question incorrect data and information. They also acquire the ability to learn faster technical skills through peer learning.

Different forms of creativity can be expressed with the help of mass media platforms. The drive to stay connected and updated about realities and innovations of science, the need for curiosity and innovativeness are all nurtured with the help of media technology.

Information related to the environment, human rights, respect for women, advancements in science and literature, music and arts also help children's cognitive and social development. It will be wise to analyze and explore the influences of mass media on children through critical evaluation of its impact. A deeper look at the functioning of mass media and its impact on children can help shape the future of our educators and learners.

THINK BOX

- How can media influence the way children think?
- The youth are using Technology or the technology is using Youth... In which direction are we heading?
- Children today live more in virtual reality with a total disconnection from the real world. Do you agree? Why/Why not?

4.4 Mass media and youth

The concept of youth helps in understanding the "growing up" stages in the life course. Eisenstadt (1964) summarized the main features of youth as follows: the transition from childhood and adolescence to adulthood, the development of personal identity, psychological autonomy and self-regulation, the attempt to link personal temporal transition to general cultural images – and to link psychological maturity to the emulation of definite role models.

There are certain similarities among youth across cultures, and some differences also exist. In modern industrial societies, social roles are not delineated according to age. Due to lack of employment, youth are often exposed to uncertainty and risk factors.

The youth of the contemporary period does not easily fit into established categories of class, caste or social-economic category definition, and they tend to stick to their individual decisions as to how to proceed with their journey. The transition of youth to adulthood is also marked by features like school to work, moving from family of origin to the family destination and having a house of their own. Several youth cultures display distinctive features. The established signifiers conveyed through languages were modified by making a different standard in the society for their evaluation. Skinheads, mods and punks, disrupted the conventional clothing, and unconventional dresses are to reflect their separate identity. The ideology of romance, feminine culture, bedroom culture and club culture are some of the types that evolved due to different lifestyles and identity manifestations by youth in contemporary times.

According to Erikson (1902–94), concepts of identity and identity crisis are very important in the course of human development. He described eight stages from infancy to late adulthood that a healthy developing individual must undergo. Identity crisis as described by Erikson (1963) is more pronounced in the stage of adolescence which is a synthesis of an earlier stage of childhood and preparation and anticipation for entering a state of adulthood.

During the youth stage, particularly during the early 20s, predominant conflicts are that of intimacy and isolation as described by Erikson. Thus the stage of adolescence marks the formation of fidelity and which is marked by identity and role confusion, and by the stage of youth, people are more capable of intimate relationships. The changing trend of commitments at the stage of adolescence is converted into the firmness of commitment by the youth stage. James E. Marcia, a clinical and developmental psychologist, developed four identity statuses of identity foreclosure, identity diffusion, moratorium and identity achievement taking place from 13 to 35 years of age. Identity diffusion is one of the four identity statuses.

A positive relationship of self-esteem and locus of control with identity achievement has been suggested in psychological studies. Attachment styles (e.g. Bartholomew & Horowitz, 1991) suggest a stronger positive link between secure attachment and the committed identity status. Hazan and Shaver (1990) suggested that exploration in adult attachment theory generally refers to social, intellectual and environmental exploration such as developing new interests, working towards new goals and traveling.

Kohlberg (1984) developed a stage sequence in the complexity of reasoning surrounding questions of justice in moral decision-making. Jesperson, Kroger and Martin Ussen (2010) studied the relationship between identity status and moral reasoning and found the identity achieved was significantly more likely to be reasoning at post-conventional levels of moral reasoning than non-post-conventional levels and a moderate correlation between identity status and moral reasoning.

Loevinger (1976) has assessed different levels of complexity in how we make meaning of one's life and life experiences. The low end of the continuum indicated the pre-conformist stage which is determined by the organization of self in individual terms. The conformist stage is marked by interpretation of the world in the opinion of others, and post conformist is a complex of the balance of inner- and outer-world interpretations and tolerance for ambiguity.

Identity is a core question that affects the questions "Who am I?" and defines oneself, by which one is defined by others. At the individual level, "I" (self as known) and "me" (self as known/object), and at the societal/cultural level, self-identification with collective identities highlights the reciprocity of societal factors in the formation of "I" and "me". Higgins's (1987) self-discrepancy theory focuses on the discrepancies between three self domains – actual self, ideal self and ought self – which are how a person or others see the attributes that the person possesses but attributes that a person or others would like the person to possess, the attributes that the person or others think the person should possess.

The nature and varieties of discrepancies occurring in these three selves can affect a person's emotional vulnerabilities. In the case of mass media usage, the person's construal of these three selves is dynamic and uncertain, leading to a lot of difficulties in the identification of oneself. The theory of possible selves for understanding human behavior represents those elements of the self-concept that individuals could become, would like to become or are afraid of becoming (also known as fear possible selves).

   The identity of adolescents and youth is also affected by internationalizing symbols of conformity propagated by media resulting in stress and anxiety.

4.4.1 Youth and media culture

Youth are growing up in a technological and digital landscape that was not experienced by previous generations of people. The expanding social networks have its impact on youth's interpersonal relationships with family, friends and work settings. The constant interaction of youth with media technologies has produced multiple choices drawing their attention as consumers. The youth of today have become media multitasking, consuming more than one medium at a time. Youth cultures are being mediated and shaped by the effects of mass media production and proliferation of images and in which consumerism has emerged as the normative conditions of everyday life.

   Horkheimer and Adorno (1972) had argued that the culture industries (the artifacts and experiences produced by the corporations who sold or transmitted film, popular music, magazines and radio) threatened to undermine rich and autonomous forms of cultural life. They pointed out that movies, advertisements and television were signs of the commodification of culture, and the culture itself, epitomized by the rich European traditions of classical music, painting and literature, was being reduced to a saleable commodity, just like any other commodity in a capitalist society. Culture no longer promotes critical and autonomous

FIGURE 4.4   Boy clicking selfie.
Source: Retrieved 18 June 2020 from https://www.pxfuel.com/en/free-photo-xhojw

thought; rather, culture industries promote sameness, uniformity of experiences and a standard way of living that distract people from the relevant issues of real-life situations.

Most often characterized by creating a media panic, youth in industrial societies are positioned as a source of fear and misplaced anxiety. Media panics are a special kind of moral frenzy over the influence of the vulnerable population. Some of the recent examples of media panics include cyberbullying, sexting and fears of stranger danger. It is not to say that such problems do not exist in society, but these are not the problems of the same magnitude, as much attention and highlight is drawn by the media. Chun (2016) described databases and identifiers enable algorithms to target, engage and integrate a diverse range of youth into the global imaginary of consumer's celebrity cultures and the archives of surveillance states.

4.4.2 Media and youth empowerment

Since the mid-1990s online media worlds have emerged as counter environments that afford teenagers a rich and inviting sphere of digitally mediated experiences to explore their imaginations, hopes, desires and innovativeness. The internet, social media and other digital resources have become central to new kinds of participatory politics and shared civic spaces that are emerging as an outgrowth and extension of young people's cultural experiences and activities.

There are numerous instances when youth from social media platforms participate and protest political power. Media also plays a vital role in deciding what young people should wear and eat. Media projects a lifestyle and a fashion style through the help of advertisements, and use of certain products by film stars in the movies has also greatly influenced the minds of the youth generation. Dresses are also produced in a gendered way to create a special attraction among youth.

Mass media's role in the generation of digital-based employment has been phenomenal in the Indian context. So many youth are selling online products and services through online platforms. Social networking sites and related delivery of products have provided numerous jobs to Indian youth. Social media can reach large audiences around the globe. Many people such as artists and educators have become famous personalities, creating their own blogs to promote their activities. Nowadays even youth staying in remote and rural localities can make unlimited friends worldwide and chat with them at no cost. The idea of e-learning has helped in the awareness level of our youth. Youth can connect to expert lectures, online courses required for becoming empowered individuals. People can also remain healthy by using e-resources from credible institutions. Youth can also obtain advantages of learning by associating themselves with the e-libraries of the world.

Mass media influences youth behavior: it is an axiom that is ingrained in the popular imagination. Media promotes idealistic paradigms of social-political-economic behavior and also shapes popular youth choices.

The tendency of contemporary youth to turn to the social media for entertainment and education can transform the awareness levels of our youth. Sociologists refer to this as a mediated culture wherein the media both reflects and creates a definitive way of life. Social networking sites have also resulted in increased voter participation.

4.4.3 Does beauty sell?

Chaiken (1979) found clear support that physically attractive communicators were more persuasive than unattractive communicators. However, attractive communicators may also be perceived as warmer, more confident or more likable, even in the absence of real differences due to the "what is beautiful is good" stereotype (Dion, Berscheid & Walster, 1972).

Consumer behavior research suggests that a model's physical attractiveness has a positive effect on consumers' attitudes towards the product, their willingness to buy the product and their actual purchasing behavior. This tendency of undue importance assigned to physical attractiveness, which is determined mostly by genetic factors, also leads those trying to imitate a superlative beautiful model and their resultant frustration in not achieving it. There is an increased demand among youth for weight loss, hair care and cosmetic surgery under the influence of media-mediated advertisements.

In his social-cultural norm theory, Thompson, Heinberg, Altabe and Tantleff-Dunn (1999) suggest that social and cultural factors have a great deal of influence on the attitudes people hold towards their bodies. In India's situation and social-cultural context, a favorable premium is attached for females being fair and tall, which is also advertised very frequently in the matrimonial columns advertisements, making the stereotypes even stronger. In the majority of situations, these rigid body images of men and women are compared with the culturally idealized images from media sources.

The thin-ideal internalization also results in body dissatisfaction and negative mood. Youth also start underestimating their self-worth fearing reflection from the peer group and opposite-sex partners. Sanchez and Crocker (2005) found that individuals who wanted to resemble gender's ideal appearances reported created external contingencies of self-esteem, which led to lower global self-esteem and more eating disorder symptomatology. Fredrickson and Roberts (1997) argue that media depiction of women as objects contribute to woman's feelings of objectification. It is a very common feature among adolescents and youth to consume less food to lose weight, and many a time it results in eating disorders.

However, not everything can be generalized so simply while describing the effect of mass media on youth. Several liberation movements, social activities and educational programs are also bringing enormous opportunities for youth. Within the broader category of youth culture also various constantly changing youth subcultures continue to emerge, and this dynamic relationship between media technology and youth development can't be objectively evaluated. Youth culture has also helped in the preservation of superior human values and awareness through social media. Youth are also adaptive to multicultural contexts in search of jobs, and they try to be more independent in their outlook. Young people can be a powerful force for bringing change in society if their energy is handled in the right direction.

4.5 Mass media and family

A family is a social group characterized by common residence, economic corporation and reproduction. It includes adults of both sexes, at least two of whom maintain a socially approved sexual relationship and one or more children, own or adopted, of the sexually cohabiting adults (Murdock, 1949). Family as an integral social unity has existed for ages with so many changes over the periods performing basic functions of reproduction, economic and educational in almost all the known societies of the world. Other important functions of the family include socialization of the children and the shaping of adult personalities. The breakdown of the joint family in India is attributed to modern economic organizations and changes in perceptions and attitudes of different generations of people. The proportions of nuclear households have increased among many groups, more because of economic factors than because of any spurring of joint family obligations (Kapadia, 1958; Desai, 1964). The values of the joint family ideal still have a powerful influence on individual behavior. The sharp rise in mass media messages has led to changes in the values and attitudes of the people. A society flooded with information requires greater rationality, punctuality and discipline than an agricultural society.

Media claims a significant portion of leisure time and family well-being can be improved or reduced with varying consumption patterns of its messages in the family set-ups. In the context of family, White and Klein (2008) suggests families are greater than just a collection of individuals and its critical components consist of the relations, boundaries and the equilibrium among the members.

Members of the family are embedded in a web of kinship relationships, and these kinship groups are involved in the production of goods and services. The structure and function of family varied in preindustrial and postindustrial societies. The smallest unit of the family is known as a nuclear family which consists of husband and wife and their immature offspring. Units larger than nuclear families are known as extended family or joint-family in which people of three generations live together. Families headed by males are known as patriarchal, and family headed by females are known as matriarchal or matrifocal families.

There has been a lot of research, and it is continuing, regarding the dominance of males and the subjugation of females in the patriarchal system of family. The male head of the household had a greater role in the decision-making on family resources, and the head of the household provides maintenance for other family members. We see the familial basis of domestic groups as an important element in continuing the patriarchal nature of our society, i.e. in the continuance of men's dominance over women and children (Delphy & Leonard, 1992).

4.5.1 Changes in the family system

There has been a massive change in lifestyles resulting in an increase in marital breakdowns and a big rise in dual-earner households. Blanden et al. (2002) noted that many multi-generational families are now long and thin and typically described as beanpole families; they have fewer intergenerational ties because of high divorce rates, falling fertility and smaller size, but more vertical intra-generational ties because of increased longevity.

Indeed, family systems across cultures have diversified existence and domestic arrangements have undergone a sea change. Being parents outside of marriage, cohabitation outside marriage, lack of following social norms, surrogate mother-hood, and lesbian and gay families are important forms of diversification in the family system. Consequently, the modern family system has lost a number of its functions in modern industrial society.

THINK BOX

- Due to technological advancements, the cultural boundaries are getting blurred day by day. What influence can it have on the youth today?
- Does media mirror reality or it constructs reality? How do youth respond to it?
- What should be the contribution of media in youth development?

4.5.2 Family interaction

Family is also constituted through the communication system existing in a par-ticular socio-cultural context. Fitzpatrick and Caughlin (2002) argued that family relationships are defined by the way people act and interact. Now media technolo-gies have a strong presence in families. The structure and functions of the family system have been transformed in a variety of ways. The prevalence of comput-ers, the internet, mobile phones, the time spent interacting with family mem-bers and time spent with media gadgets have been affected in significant ways. Naturally, children will be exposed to different forms of media in an environ-ment of media ecology, but in the majority of situations, children are first intro-duced to media by parents. In the Indian context, dinner and lunch used to be a collective process, but with the presence of individual media, this habit is gradually decaying. In rural India also, earlier it was a strict ritual to have dinner with all the members of the family, but now this has changed due to interference by media engagements.

Roles are the behavior patterns family members engage in to preserve and fulfill family functions.

Family leisure time being replaced with media activities reduces the opportunity for families to explore and strengthen intra-family interaction. Families have mainly three types of media effects: cognitive, affective and behavioral. Media increasingly claim the leisure and recreation time of family members and a realistic understanding of family dynamics also needed to include family time and family-plus-media time. The nature of media interaction can starve the family of learning and modeling with each other's social cues, interpersonal relationship skills, communication skills and bonding.

Sometimes elderly can make use of internet related platforms for spiritual recreation and health benefits.

4.5.3 Media and leisure

Media claims a significant portion of leisure time in urban areas, and it has micro- and macro-level outcomes on family health and well-being. Leisure research has established a positive relationship between leisure's positive outcomes

Nowadays, children, adolescents and youth do not get sufficient quality time to resolve the conflicts they are faced with due to higher media involvement and lesser face-to-face interaction with the family members. Many personal emotional issues faced by children and adolescents are not accorded sufficient attention which may result in negative outcomes for them. Family leisure is positively correlated with a greater degree of cohesiveness, open communication between parents and children and collective negotiations of the challenges and opportunities in family dynamics. Consuming a high dosage of media has become synonymous with people of all ages, with adolescents and youth becoming heavy consumers spending long hours in a day. Mediated communication has become the predominant pattern of communication among family members. Television and internet activities are replacing other previously engaged at-home activities. Spending more time together watching television may not translate into an increase in quality family interactions. Television is a fundamentally solitary activity.

With increasing variety and growth of mass media, many children, adults, youth and families rely more on media for leisure and recreation. Parental media monitoring helps in reducing the harmful effects on children. The family communication climate may act as a deterrent for children and adolescents getting drawn to moral deviant behavior. Parental monitoring is influenced by the awareness and attitude of parents, understanding the usage of particular media content by children of young age and balancing of outdoor/indoor activities.

4.5.4 Cultivation effects

According to Gerbner et al. (1994), repeated exposure to messages over time cultivates views of the world that are consonant with television content. The portrayal of the family by media and its continuous consumption alters people's perception and views. Children who are heavy viewers of television report more homogeneous viewpoints about families that are consistent with what is portrayed on the screen then do light viewers.

Gerbner et al. (1994) cultivation theorists suggest that the powerful storytelling ability of television creates a social reality for heavy viewers that can be at odds with the real world. Media portrayals can strongly influence the perceptions of children as they are not mature enough to distinguish the real-world reality and media-world portrayals. The socialization of children is influenced by the parental monitoring and mediation of media activities in the family. Other factors of socialization, like peer groups, school environment and social context, play important roles in the socialization of children.

Engaging in certain types of media-based activities and balancing them with a variety of leisure activities can improve the quality of family interaction and satisfaction. Individual-level effects are overpowered by the larger social-cultural milieu, and this can be at variance with each other.

Social media has far-reaching implications in terms of emotional bonding among the family members. Virtual social interaction can't replace traditional face-to-face social interaction. Most of the prosocial activities that families used to take part in are being ignored with excessive social media usage. Social media facilitates families to connect and share information on a large network. Geographic mobility and advantages in business and education can be achieved through online interactions. Researches also indicate that people are communicating more often with family due to media technology advancements, but the quality and impact potential of such communications are not very strong.

THINK BOX

- "Family? What is it? Is it a new App?" What are your views on this statement?
- Families are shrinking so do our thinking abilities. Is it True? Is it because of media?
- Families can benefit from media only when used with critical understanding. Comment.

4.6 Critical evaluation and the Indian perspective

Indian society has also emerged as a huge platform for media mediated technologies. The use of media-mediated communication has permeated various sections of our country. There has been a gradual disintegration of the joint family system and an emergence of the nuclear family system. The process of industrialization, migration and urbanization has resulted in the weakening of the joint family system in India. The rise of individualism and the impact of Western culture have also contributed to the decline of the joint family system in India.

The media technology revolution has brought cultural and social changes that may not be synchronized with our traditions and values. There are visible differences in the patterns of communication leading to poor intergenerational bonding. There are also stark differences in the lifestyles adopted by the digital generation and the old generation, leading to problems of conflicting co-existence. In traditional families which used to adopt a basic normative guideline of functioning and fulfillment of roles, one can easily notice the changes with the emergence of the new media climate. Value conflicts regarding dress, eating preferences, recreational activities and community activities are becoming very common in Indian families. Children's participation in outdoor activities has come down significantly due to excessive involvement and dependence on media platforms such as Facebook, Instagram, Twitter, video games and television programs. Interconnectedness with neighbors and relatives have reduced significantly in the past few years with the growth of urbanization and media-mediated lifestyle activities. Youth are socializing through online platforms and are also taking the form of dependence. The opportunities are emerging from local to global platforms, opening the possibilities for jobs and education with the help of social media. Nowadays youth have also emerged as a potent pressure group influencing the future of political parties. Digital commerce has created an abundance of opportunities in every field of business, and a lot of diversification of careers has taken place in India also. Social media and other media platforms constitute a new ecology, with multiple pathways, enormous possibilities and challenges on the social-cultural, economic and political fronts, that needs a careful examination of its positive and harmful influences.

Media messages also play a powerful role in shaping the attitudes and behavior of people. The rate of juvenile crimes is a matter of concern among policymakers, and on many occasions cues for enacting aggressive acts have been drawn from media sources. The violent scenes portrayed in media are imitated by children. The teachers and counselors in schools sometimes report deviant behavior patterns among children of young age. The rising trend of internet-related dependence is a matter of great concern among parents and school teachers. There is a need to carry out good research studies for evaluating and analyzing the implications of media usage among users of media content. It is better to raise the awareness level of our citizens so that media messages' negative effects can be reduced and people start utilizing the positive aspects of media technology.

THINK BOX

- What role can media play in mediating education at different levels?
- Media usage without proper awareness can be dangerous. Comment.
- India is a country with diversity. What role does media play in celebrating or stereotyping diversity in Indian Context?

4.7 Summary

By reading this chapter, one can understand the relationship between media and society. Our day-to-day interactions with media messages shape beliefs, attitudes, perceptions, thoughts and behavior. The norms and socialization patterns of people interacting with mass media are partly influenced which leads to internalization of behaviors portrayed through the lens of media. Powerful media imagery also plays a role in identity formation and ideological predispositions towards a wide range of topics. Mass media also plays a facilitative role, allowing ordinary citizens to express their views and adding to the process of civic participation in democracy. So, many relevant issues like the right to information, crimes against women and environmental issues can be highlighted through social media platforms which can bring social changes in a positive direction.

There are intergenerational differences of values among the users of media across generations on many occasions. Lack of media literacy results in the misuse of media propaganda for promoting hate and prejudice in society. At the same time, mass media can be used to promote prosocial behavior and volunteerism on a large scale. The dominant paradigm approach in media sociology advocated the role of technology to achieve developmental goals.

Media plays a crucial role in the development of thoughts and behavior of the children as they spend considerable amounts of time watching television. It is difficult for children to understand the difference between reality and fiction. In India also, children are using media gadgets in a big way, which affects their outdoor activities, academic activities as well as their sleep patterns.

Mass media also plays a differentiating role in the formation of gender stereotypes. Youth identity is also influenced by the dominant media messages and so many behavior patterns are imitated by interaction with media. Youth culture all over the world is shaped through media portrayal and a variety of marketing products and services are highlighted which are subsequently adopted by them.

Beauty is also a socio-cultural construct, and a particular brand of beauty is highlighted through media. Adolescent girls form an identity with media-mediated images of beauty. In the Indian context also, a preference for being thin and having a white complexion is glorified as a sought-after goal which is imitated by these girls. The media's presence also affects the quality of interaction among family members. Nowadays family members struggle to find quality interaction time with their children in rural and urban parts of India.

It can be concluded that the role of mass media and society has become far more complex, influencing each other in a variety of ways, good as well as bad, which needs further scientific investigation.

Key points

- Mass media has strong influence on people's behavior at individual and group levels.
- In the contemporary period the nature of society has become more materialistic and consumeristic with the influence of mass media.
- Mass media messages play a crucial role in the development of awareness levels for the members in a society.
- Paradigm is the basic way of perceiving, thinking, valuing and doing with a particular vision of reality.
- Mass media messages target children as potential consumers as they have difficulty differentiating fiction and reality.
- Mass media gadgets and related activities by children affect their well-being and creates health-related problems.
- Mass media and its expanding social networks have led to the emergence of a distinct youth culture.
- Mass media strategies tend to promote stereotypes related to beauty to attract more consumers to its advertised products.
- Socio-cultural norm theory suggests that social and cultural factors have a great deal of influence on people's attitudes.
- The interaction pattern and quality of relationship in a family is strongly affected by the usage pattern within the family.

Key terms

judgmental dope, public sphere, paradigm, symbolic-interactionism, gender-role beliefs, identity diffusion, media panic, objectification, matriarchal, parental monitoring

References

Bandura, A. (2001). Social cognitive theory: An agentic perspective. In S.T. Fiske (Ed.), *Annual Review of psychology* (Vol. 52, pp. 1–26). Palo Alto: Annual Reviews, Inc.

Bartholomew, K., & Horowitz, L.M. (1991). Attachment styles among young adults: A test of a four-category model. *Journal of Personality and Social Psychology*, 61, 226–44. doi:10.1037/0022-3514.61.2.226

Blanden, J., Goodman, A., & Gregg, P. (2002) *Changes in Intergenerational Mobility*. London: Centre for the Economics of Education and School of Economics & Political Science.

Bouissac, P. (1976). *Circus and Culture: A Semiotic Approach*. Bloomington: Indiana University Press.

Chaiken, S. (1979). Communicator physical attractiveness and persuasion, *Journal of Personality and Social Psychology*, 37 (August), 1387–97.

Chun, W.H.K. (2016). *In Updating to Remain the Same: Habitual New Media.* Cambridge, MA: MIT Press.

Delphy, C., & Leonard, D. (1992). *Familiar Exploitation*, Cambridge: Polity Press.

Desai, I.P. (1964). *Some Aspects of Family in Mahuva.* Bombay: Asia Publishing House.

Dion, K.K., Berscheid & Walster 1972. What is beautiful is good. *Journal of Personality and Social Psychology, 24–285–290.*

Eisenstadt, S.N. (1964). *From Generation to Generation.* New York: The Free Press.

Erikson, E.H. (1963). *Childhood and Society* (2nd ed.). New York: Norton.

Fitzpatrick, M.A., & Caughlin, J.P. (2002). Interpersonal communication in family relationships. In M.L. Knapp & J.A. Daly (Eds.), *Handbook of Interpersonal Communication* (Vol. 3, pp. 726–77). Thousand Oaks, CA: Sage.

Fredrickson, B.L., & Roberts, T. (1997). Objectification theory: Toward understanding women's lived experiences and mental health risks. *Psychology of Women Quarterly*, 21, 173–206.

Garfinkel, H. (1967). *Studies in Ethnomethodology.* Englewood Cliffs, NJ: Prentice-Hall.

Gerbner, G., & Gross, L. (1976). Living with television: The violence profile. *Journal of Communication*, 26, 172–99.

Gerbner, G., Gross, L., Morgan, M., & Signorielli, N. (1994). Growing up with television: The cultivation perspective. In J. Bryant & D. Zillman (Eds.), *Media effects* (pp. 17–40). Hillsdale, NJ: Lawrence Erlbaum Associates.

Gore, M.S. (1965). The traditional Indian family. In M.F. Nimkoff (Ed.), *Comparative Family Systems.* Boston, MA: Houghton Mifflin.

Harman, W. (1970). *An Incomplete Guide to the Future.* New York: W.W. Norton.

Hays, S. (1998) *The Cultural Contradictions of Motherhood.* New Haven: Yale University Press.

Hazan, C., & Shaver, P.R. (1990). Love and work: An attachment-theoretical perspective. *Journal of Personality and Social Psychology*, 59, 270–80.

Higgins, E.T. (1987). Self-discrepancy: A theory relating self and affect. *Psychological Review*, 94(3), 319–40.

Horkheimer, M., & Adorno, T.W. (1972). The culture industry: Enlightenment as mass deception. In M. Horkheimer & T.W. Adorno (Eds.), *The Dialectic of Enlightenment.* New York: Herder and Herder.

Kapadia, K.M. (1958). *Marriages and Family in India.* Bombay: Oxford University Press.

Karve, I. (1953). *Kinship Organisation in India.* Poona: Deccan College Post-Graduate Research Institute.

Katz, J.E., & Sugiyama, S. (2005). Mobile phones as fashion statements: Evidence from student surveys in the US and Japan. *New Media and Society*, 8(2), 321–37.

Kohlberg, L. (1984). *Essays on Moral Development, Vol. 2: The Psychology of Moral Development.* San Francisco, CA: Harper & Row.

Kuhn, T.S. (1970). *The Structure of Scientific Revolutions* (Rev. ed.). Chicago, IL: University of Chicago Press. (Originally published 1962)

Loevinger, J. (1976). *Ego Development: Conceptions and Theories.* San Francisco, CA: Jossey-Bass.

McQuail, D. (2010). *Mass Communication Theory* (6th ed.). London: Sage Publications.

Montgomery, K. (2007). *Generation Digital.* Cambridge, MA: MIT Press.

Murdock, G. (1949). *Social Structure.* New York: The MacMillan Company.

Reisman, D., Catazer, N., & Denney, R. (2001). *The Lonely Crowd.* New Haven, CT: Yale University Press.

Rideout, V.J., & Hamel, E. (2006). *The Media Family: Electronic Media in the Lives of Infants, Toddlers, Preschoolers and Their Parents.* Menlo Park, CA: Henry J. Kaiser Family Foundation.

Roberts, D.F. (2000) Media and youth: Access, exposure, and privatization. *Journal of Adolescent Health*, 27(2 Suppl.), 8–14.

Sanchez, D.T., & Crocker, J. (2005). How investment in gender ideals affects well-being: The role of external contingencies of self-worth. *Psychology of Women Quarterly*, 29, 63–77.

Spigel, L. (1992) *Make Room for TV: Television and the Family Ideal in Postwar America*. Chicago, IL: University of Chicago Press.

Thompson, J.B. (1995). *The Media and Modernity*. Cambridge: Polity Press.

Thompson, J.K., Heinberg, L.J., Altabe, M., & Tantleff-Dunn, S. (1999). *Exacting Beauty: Theory, Assessment and Treatment of Body Image Disturbance*. Washington, DC: American Psychological Association.

White, J., & Klein, D. (2008). *Family Theories*. Thousand Oaks, CA: Sage.

5

MEDIA AND CULTURE

Learning objectives

After reading this chapter, you will be able to understand:

- Mass media and culture
- Mass and media
- Mass society, mass culture and popular culture
- Psychology of entertainment media
- Critical evaluation of mass media and culture
- Indian context of media and culture

5.1 Mass media and culture

According to sociologist Michael Richardson, "culture is produced and preserved by human beings". There are several definitions of culture which highlight the characteristics of a culture. Culture can be represented through artifacts, physical symbols, social customs and practices including attitudinal components.

Culture has characteristics of sharing, making it a collective process of rhetorical functioning of symbolic, historical and ideological constituents. Hofstede's Cultural Dimension theory proposed initially four, and later two more, dimensions along which cultural values could be analyzed:

- Individualism–collectivism
- Uncertainty avoidance
- Power distance
- Masculinity and femininity

These dimensions refer to long-term orientation indulgence versus self-restraint (Hofstede, 1991). Geert Hofstede proposed four dimensions for cross-cultural communication. Four dimensions along with cultural values can be analyzed. Later on, Hofstede added two more dimensions, namely long-term orientation and indulgence versus self-restraint. Uncertainty avoidance index is described as society's tolerance for ambiguity. Societies scoring high on this dimension will have people with strict rules and codes of behavior, whereas societies will have lesser rules and regulations indicating a free-flowing environment in terms of social codes.

FIGURE 5.1 Man making video of concert.
Source: Retrieved 20 June 2020 from https://pixabay.com/photos/recital-music-entertainment-media-4051735/

Power distance is an index where strict divisions in the society are based on power structure. Lower-strata people perceive the inequal distribution of power by powerful people. For example, in a feudal society, the behavior of the dominant class has different standards as compared to the disadvantaged class members. Masculinity and femininity dimensions are described through preference in society assigned to masculine traits of heroism or feminine traits of care and cooperation. Long-term orientation versus short-term orientation dimension refers to connection of the past with current and future challenges. Indulgence versus restraint dimension indicates the degree of freedom enjoyed by citizens in terms of societal norms.

5.1.1 Functions of ideology

Ideology is a system, a manner or the content of thinking which forms the basis of social/economic and political theory. From a sociological point of view, ideology is considered as cultural beliefs and social arrangements in society. It provides a window for people to see the world and act as justifications for the act. Examples of ideologies can be socialism, capitalism, communism, liberalism, Gandhism or fascism.

An ideology prevalent in a socio-cultural context limits the range of acceptable ideas that a person may consider at a given point in time. Some ideologies are manifested in its meaning, while other ideologies are not very easily decoded by the people. Also, some elements of inequality are justified in the realm of social relations, and it appears normal. For example, authority for deciding matters related to health is easily assigned to doctors, and teachers are considered to be the natural educators of students which is a result of ideological value hierarchies. In some societies like India, elders' views are considered supreme, and this power of superiority is inextricably tied up with the ideological constructs of a particular culture.

In a capitalistic economy, the laborer and workers do a lot of hard work, but it is the powerful owners and management that reap the maximum benefit from such works. Louis Althuser, an Algerian Marxist, held that ideology is so infused into a social structure that it serves as the force to interpellate us or the force that calls us into existence as social subjects.

People's identity is closely related to the idea of culture, which is strongly influenced by ideology. Durkheim (1947) argued that collective conscience of the society is formed by the totality of sentiments and beliefs shared by its citizens. Multiple ideologies are existing in culture, and small subcultures have powerful ideologies.

5.1.2 Myth, Doxa and hegemony

Barthes described the theory of ideological dominance in which myth is integrated in the form of a sacred story representing ideology in relation to an object. For example, the video game Super Mario Brothers relates to the classic story of a hero who rescued the princess from evil, thus conveying a meaning of bravery and masculinity which is also part of American culture.

5.1.3 Doxa

Bourdieu introduced the concept of Doxa, treated as common sense, which is in fact a constructed process but treated as knowledge beyond question. The process of social rules remains unquestioned despite critical facts existing contrary to its existence.

5.1.4 Hegemony

For Italian Marxist theorist Antonio Gramsci, consent and force nearly always co-exist, though one or the other predominates. Among paramilitary regimes, only the weakest are forced to rely on domination; normally they rule through hegemony, even though the threat of officially sanctioned force always remains implicit. The ruling groups do not maintain their hegemony merely by giving the world domination an aura of moral authority through the creation and perpetuation of legitimating symbols; they must also seek the consent of subordinate groups to the existing social order.

Gramsci argues that cultural hegemony indicates who has the power which includes cultural, economic and political power having the ability to define boundaries either by common-sense reality or by ignoring those outside boundaries by labeling as deviant, tasteless and irresponsible text, sermons, advertisements, folklore and popular ritual. This needs to be examined to understand the process of acculturation.

Russian critic Mikhail Bakhtin described culture as a multilayered, multi-voiced conversation and argued that language is not a neutral medium. It is overpopulated with the intentions of others. Language is dialogical, marked by a plurality of value-laden perspectives. In a hegemonic culture, language is used by speakers to win the popular consent of the people.

Raymond Williams, in his book *The Long Revolution* (1961), recognized the importance of viewing the culture from idea and documentary (anthropological) standpoints but also proposed a social view which treats "culture" as "a description of a particular way of life, which expresses certain meanings and values are not only in art and learning but also in institutions and ordinary behavior".

5.1.5 Ideology and media representation

Cultural studies indicate a strong interplay between popular media texts and hegemonic ideologies creation which compels an ordinary citizen to realize that capitalism and class immobility are natural forms of social existence. The capitalist dreams turn individuals into complaining workers and ignore the real stories of success and failure at a mass level. An effort of tokenism is adopted to provide legitimacy to exception as a general rule of success. Media texts operate across ideological lines through psychological processes to create hierarchies providing privilege to some at the cost of significant others.

Exclusion: this is a process by which various cultural groups are symbolically annihilated or "written out of history" through under-representation or distorted representation in media. The mainstream media that we consume every day over-represents the interests of dominant groups and the symbolic exclusion of marginal groups.

Stereotyping: the term stereotype was first introduced by Walter Lippmann (1922). Stereotyping is the process of constructing a set of convictions or beliefs about members of a particular group. Media stereotypes make value judgments about the worth and mobility of another culture, influencing our attitude, behavior and actions towards members of that culture. The repeated portrayal of a singular event as representative of a particular group identity is also constructed as a stereotype by media processes of categorization, comparison and social perception.

Assimilation: according to Jean Piaget (1963 [1936]), assimilation refers to the process through which we take in new information or experiences and incorporate them into our existing ideas. Assimilation is attained through socio-economic status, geography distribution, language attainment and intermarriage, particularly in the case of immigrants. Assimilation and tokenism techniques adopted by media representations help to create and sustain the privileged status of the dominant class.

Othering: the concept of self requires the existence of the other as the counterpart entity required for the definition of the self. Hegel (1772–1831) introduced the concept of the other as a part of self-consciousness. Jacques LaCan associated others with language and with the symbolic order of things. Philosopher of ethics Emmanuel Levinas associated the other with the ethical metaphysics of scripture and tradition. The ethical proposition is that the other is superior and before self.

Othering is a process of discrimination that encompasses the many expressions of prejudice based on group identities and promotes a set of conditions that propagate the group's inequality and marginalization. Group position theory suggests that race and other categories are socially constructed. Our sociocultural context and environments prime us to observe stereotypical differences among different groups and also instruct us that these differences are relevant. The social cognitive researches have two fundamental dimensions that locate group positions in society, which are warmth and competence. It is observed in the social context that people rated low on warmth and competence are treated as outgroups.

5.1.6 Communication as culture

Communication and culture are related to each other, as communication practices do not happen in a vacuum and its continuous transaction across space, time and social collectives have complex implications for culture. Whatever reality we experience at different points of time is a product of construction using technology-mediated symbolic communication. In this way, mass media acts as a significant force in deciding the character of social order.

Technology is a product of human imagination and communication technologies create a huge impact on the social and cultural organization. As Carey and Quirk (1989) have argued in "The Mythos of the Electronic Revolution", expansionist tendencies of modern technological organizations can be controlled by political classes, allowing space for democratic discussion.

In the last few years, there has been multiplication in the means and forms of various types of communication. People possess aims, beliefs and knowledge which cannot be transported physically and they require communication for consensus or disagreements. The very medium that forms its ambience also supports its existence. Similarly, when we perform a variety of our mundane activities like sharing ideas, imparting knowledge or being entertained, we hardly pay attention to the process of communication.

The reality, as perceived by us, is not a natural product; rather, it acquires its existence by the process of construction, communication, apprehension and utilization of symbolic forms. Our activities to construct, maintain and transform reality are enacted through a variety of symbol systems of art, science, common sense or mythology. Earlier models of communication were rooted in religious and cultural traditions, but these days, science and technology are guiding mass and inter-personal human interaction, and many forms of communication models take the form of social institutions which prescribe certain styles and forms with powerful social effects.

5.1.7 Mass and media

The realities of the world are continuously adopted and remade to suit human purposes which is a new suburb of the language. Science is also a point of view among other points of view in the conversation and communication for mankind. There are central concepts of objectification and expressivism that bring in the core divide among communication scholars.

According to Lippmann, public opinion is merely a statistical aggregation of private opinions informed by the news media. Albert Camus described that dialogue and personal relations have been replaced by propaganda and polemic in modern times. It is also argued that truth-revealing functions language has declined with the pervasive use of media messages, and public institutions are not guided by authentic opinions of the public.

There is a larger possibility of divorce of truth from discourse and action owing to the institutionalization of communication which has increased the incidence of propaganda and the sense by which it takes place; the perspectives of the world are compromised. Their communication does not remain a mere reflection but takes the form of deliberate action. Therefore, to apply Wittgenstein's term, changing the communication forms also means changing our way of life associated with it seems relevant.

The language used through communication is a form of action and interaction that does not merely describe the world but constitutes it. Of the essence of communication, Heidegger (1968) described that being "of man" (human) is found in language which is continually created and contemplated by humankind. Through the symbols that are conveyed through linguistic practices and the practices that organize communication, actors of these practices have a vital role to play in the production of communication.

Techniques are a vectoral process that is even applied in building; a building's precise structure anticipates and imagines certain forms of relations and permits and desires, and so is the case with the television signal. The reality created through the social process of communication is a product of work and action, sustained, transformed and celebrated in our day-to-day existence. There are various actors where artists paint, writers write, speakers speak and filmmakers film, and simultaneously the site of social conflict negotiation over the real. Communication is a simultaneous site for co-determination of ideas, techniques and social relations. Conflict over communication occurs over the determination of real as well as thought, techniques and social realities are cast for exclusion, denial and dominance. There is always a strong bias in the access of machinery for reality production in the hands of few by which miracles of communication are controlled. Reality is determined through the medium handled by few experts, and public life of mass and the media technology rarely co-determine the aspects of reality.

5.1.8 Communities and subcultures

Some communities are held together at a particular location in history with its self-conceived identity. Communities of interest refer to cultural formations that are united across space by some perceived objectives or identity. Examples of subcultures include hippies, goths, bikers and jazz.

Subcultures are cultural collectivities that have sufficient distinctiveness. They are also heterogeneous with reference to the outside world or at times alien to the identity of the mainstream culture.

Ferdinand Tönnies (1957) outlined a distinction between two forms of social organization:

1. Geminschaft: Homogenous, communitarian and non contractually governed social formations and
2. Geisellschaft: Heterogeneous, individualistic and contractually governed social formations.

These two categories represent both infrastructural and imagined aspects and pose the question as to what type of community different social groups aspire to promote.

In media studies theories, it is argued that communication acts as an instrument for social transformation through various mediums of mass communication like press, radio and television. Everyday theory of media accords importance to citizens and consumers at the local level, who participate and produce communication and community which is aimed at the empowerment of local communities. This also led to the growth and rise of local radio and television. An important approach for subculture studies has been associated with the "Birmingham School of Cultural Studies" (Hall, 1980). They celebrated its authenticity and legitimacy among particular groups, especially youth who developed the identities through social interactions around music and other forms of verbal, visual and auditory techniques.

5.1.9 Intercultural communication

Intragroup communication includes interactions between people of different ages, genders, socio-economic backgrounds and cultural backgrounds. The objective of intercultural communication is to overcome the barriers of good

FIGURE 5.2 Oral communication.
Source: Retrieved 20 June 2020 from https://commons.wikimedia.org/wiki/File:Oral_communication.jpg

communication when communicating with people of different cultures. There are both verbal and non-verbal codes embedded in the people of different cultures, and intercultural communication helps to manage conflict by providing a model of the intercultural person promoting the common good. In a situation where large-scale migration and diaspora have become characteristic of modern times, the role of electronic communication in shifting the relations between space, place and culture becomes very important.

5.1.10 Mass media and cultural imperialism

Modern mass media which is dominant is perceived as invading and even displacing local cultures. On empirical grounds, the imperialistic nature of media has been highlighted which considers developing countries as cultural dumping for its markets.

Throughout most of the twentieth century, the trend in culture industry ownership was towards concentration in the hands of a few multinational corporations (Bagdikian, 1997). The social and cultural implications of mass media ownership patterns were dramatic and long-lasting. The human community willingly started to harbor non-religious agents in the form of mass media to deal with the affairs of social and cultural life.

American popular music, TV serials and computer software industries in Silicon Valley made their markets all over the world. The popularity of corporate culture became possible with the expansion of communication technologies and the creation of a marketing ideological atmosphere.

With the growing industrialization and coming of modern institutions of mass media, individuals and small group settings find themselves relatively powerless to escape from their surroundings and social circumstances. Media infrastructure combines with the interests of capitalists to dominate artisans and artists, depersonalizing their work and exploiting work and creativity in their terms.

THINK BOX

• Should cultural representations be made a compulsory part of media portrayals? What are your views?
• Culture is getting transformed slowly with the advent of media and technology. Comment.
• Media facilitates cultural exchanges but in the process, it also transforms it. Think.

5.2 Mass society, mass culture and popular culture

In the new order, humans have become incorporated into a society of digital territory. Mass society membership has reduced the sacredness of authority, loosening of the power of tradition has been achieved through an elaborate network of technology and communication. However, there are numerous disparities also co-existing in mass society in terms of prejudice, stereotypes, class inequality, disordered personal relation and growth of individualism. Cultures also categorized themselves in superior, mediocre and brutal forms by highlighting a different set of characteristics representing each culture style. Mass production technologies of standardized goods wanted mass consumption by mass consumers. Techniques and strategies were devised by the marketing experts to engineer consumers' desires and to translate wishes and wants into purchases. How media technologies influence the beliefs and behavior of the masses became a dominant objective of modern institutions, including the government. The popular media and commercial broadcasting organizations adopt several mechanisms and strategies to influence the mass society for its products and votes necessary for public support of the government. The concepts of mass society, mass consumption and mass culture become interrelated to each other for its survival, growth and dominance. The strategies adopted by advertisers help to promote the mass society.

According to Jhally and Livant (1986, p. 125), "the viewing of advertising is productive because it helps" speed up the selling of commodities, their circulation from production to consumption. Through advertising, the rapid consumption of commodities cuts down on circulation and storage costs of industrial capital. Through the process of watching and interacting with informational commodities products create values in the minds of consumers.

5.2.1 Mass culture

It is debated in public and private spheres that the development of mass media is debasing the culture of ordinary citizens. Dwight McDonald's (1957) theory of mass culture distinguished between folk art, high culture and mass culture.

- Folk art: this was the culture of the "common people". It grew from below, which was a spontaneous expression of people by themselves, pretty much without the benefit of high culture to suit their own needs
- High culture: McDonald (1957) considered high culture as the product of great individuals who are capable of producing work that appeals to the minority who can appreciate the work of this caliber.
- Mass culture: it lacks the originality of its own and a form of standardized commercial Kitsch imposed by businesses in the masses for profit objective. (*Kitsch* is a German word for popular culture.) Mass culture is imposed from above. It is fabricated by technicians, hired by businessmen; its audiences are passive consumers, their participation limited to the choice between buying and not buying.

McDonald (1957) highlighted several problems related to mass culture. According to him, mass culture threatens the high culture by the sheer game of numbers. High cultures can be vulgarized and homogenized in single mass culture and this could alienate the persons who created such cultural products. McDonald also talked about the creation of infantile adults unable to cope with adult life without turning to escapist mass culture for leisure and overstimulated children who grew up too fast. McDonald believed that mass culture was creating a mass society with atomized individuals.

5.2.2 Plurality of taste cultures

Gans (1974) proposed that "all people have a right to the culture they prefer" and described that America had a large number of different taste cultures. He identified five main taste cultures which include high culture (more creative), upper-middle (professional and managers), lower-middle (followers of high culture), low culture (believers and masculinity; depends on luck and fate) and quasi-folk low culture (a simpler version of low culture). He described about cultures based on age and ethnic criteria which included total cultures (drug and music culture, religions cultures such as Jesus freaks), partial cultures (part-time version of total culture), ethnic cultures, globalization-like mass culture and global culture to be the result of mass communication technologies.

As John Storey (2003) has stated, globalization as "the name given to the complex relations which characterize the world in the 21st Century" (p. 107). It refers to the relentless global flows of capital, commodities and communications across increasingly porous borders. Globalization has shrunk the boundaries of different geographical regions through advance technology of communication and the internet. In every aspect of our daily lives, we can find the presence of globalization – in clothes, music, films, education and healthcare. Coca-Cola, Microsoft software, iPhones, Adidas shoes and Levi's jeans can be found in almost every part of the world resulting in homogenization that is the reduction of the world into a global village.

Mass communication imposes an ideology on the mass audience, but the response of the local people varies from place to place. Hybridization is a process of mixing different cultures which gives rise to a new culture. Globalization enables individuals to connect the world and exchange new ideas, commodities, belief systems and voluntary group memberships. Syncretism has resulted in the growth of globalization which refers to the combination of different beliefs into a new harmonious belief.

Anthropologist Arjun Appadurai (1991) has discussed five specific "scapes", or flows of globalization, which can be termed as:

- Ethnoscapes
- Mediascapes
- Technoscapes
- Finance scapes
- Ideoscapes

These landscapes work as building blocks of the "Imagined Worlds", i.e. the multiple worlds which are constituted by the historically situated imaginations of persons and groups spread around the globe. By ethnoscapes, he means the landscape of persons who constitute the shifting world in which we live: tourists, immigrants and refugees, and these moving groups can never afford to let their imagination rest for too long.

By technoscapes, Appadurai meant the fluid nature of technological establishments crossing its boundaries. Examples include a cement factory in South Africa owned by an Indian, and a steel complex in Libya owned by the Chinese. According to Appadurai, mediascapes tend to be image-centered, through which scripts can be formed for imagined lives of their own and other people.

The term financescapes describes how disposition of global capital flow is a more mysterious, rapid and difficult landscape to follow owing to volatility of market conditions. It is also highlighted that the global relationship between ethnoscapes, technoscapes and financescapes is deeply disjunctive and profoundly unpredictable, since each of these "scapes" is subject to its own constraints and incentives.

Ideoscapes are linkages of images frequently related to the ideology of states and counterideology of movements. Ideoscapes provide the role of presenting a picture of the worldview which consists of cementation of ideas, terms and images.

5.2.3 Deterritorialization

Giddens (1990) defined deterritorialization as "the moment by which we leave a territory". Considered an essential feature of globalization, it implies the growing presence of social forms of contact and involvement which go beyond the limits of a specific territory, a kind of "weighing of anchors" of social relations.

Mediatization is an essential aspect of contemporary cultural experience and works as an important source of deterritorialization. Paradoxically, deterritorialization also includes reterritorialized manifestations which García Canclini (1990) defined as "certain partial territorial re-localization of old and new symbolic productions (p. 288). It speaks of the loss of natural relations between culture, and the very experience of spatial experience changes due to joining of proximity and distances in a peculiar way.

5.2.4 Globalization

Globalization and technological advancement are transforming the architecture of buildings. The universal and the particular concepts converge where locals are adopting cosmopolitan culture. The local is not counterposed to global with diminishing national borders mediated by information technology mediation. One of the pertinent aspects of contemporary diversity is the complexities it poses for traditional notions of culture. Lila Abu-Lughod (1991) calls "halfies" with mixing of cultures, of poly-ethnicity, who combine in themselves as individuals several cultural, ethnic and general features (Tsing, 1993), a closely related theme to hybridization. The processes related to globalization and glocalization, Deterritorialization and different types of landscapes also contribute to the development of mass culture. People's identities and imaginations are now highly influenced by commercial media, and cultural products are more suited to consumer expectations of the users.

5.2.5 Popular culture

The powerful mechanisms of commercial media dominate the discourse with ample diversion and distraction techniques employed by advertisers. Mass communications tend to colonize our intimate and personal aspects of life, highlighting serious flaws in our bodies and minds through inducing anxieties and fears. Contemporary mass media distorts culture, trivializes art by turning them into commodities and creates a hostile environment that is against empathy, critical inquiry and historical thinking. The emergence of the amusement park, the personal motion picture halls, music halls and dance halls carved out a new kind of social space for working-class people to enjoy leisure activities in this age of commercialization of leisure.

Literary scholar Michael Bristol points out the culture crisis posed by the theatre in Elizabethan England. An actor is not just someone whose speech is "dissembling"; the deeper problem is that he is most valued for its ability to disseminate convincingly.

The theatrical stage allowed individuals to escape from routine social responsibilities to pursue personal desires through fictive representation. Theatregoers in modern society started sharing an audience with no shared history and no reciprocal obligations. The unfamiliarity of the crowd provided a platform for the participants to express personal emotions and feelings without any explanation to anyone. Theatre becomes relatively a reliable source for fulfillment of unfulfilled desires, unfulfilled lusts in the form of images represented in the theatre. People's sexual desires and impulses received symbolic manifestation in theatres. This increased the number of people going to the theatre to see a performance of happiness and pleasure missing from one's day-to-day activities. Theatres also provided space for the imagination and means to escape from parental surveillance. Motion pictures' model of the commodification of culture also served as ingredients for purchasing other commodities.

Williams (1980) describes four meanings for the term "popular": well-liked by many people, interior kind of work, work deliberately done to win favor with the people, culture made by people themselves. There is no strict definition of popular culture, but it can be identified through prominent characteristics that it possesses. Popular culture is a commercial culture with no fixed forms. The reception and appropriation by the masses make it popular culture. Popular culture is often equated with a highly romanticized concept of working-class culture construed as the major source of symbolic protest within contemporary capitalism (Bennett, 1980), but this view does not take into account the commercial nature of resources which constitute popular culture.

Sociologists Pierre Bourdieu's categories of participation and investment accurately characterize audience expectations from American popular culture since World War II. Another way to describe popular culture focuses on the residue of high culture as popular culture, which is based on the premise that popular culture is this result of mass-produced commercial culture. Gramsci (1971, 1996) used the term "hegemony" in which dominant groups win the consent of subordinate groups through a process of intellectual and moral leadership. Popular culture is also constructed with a political motive by the people in power. Popular culture is a site where everyday life activities are determined through political interest.

Melodrama emerged as a prominent subtext of the popular culture. Carnival traditions also supplemented themselves as important factors for the promotion of popular culture by ignoring conventions and traditions.

Popular culture strongly influences the attitudes of the people towards consumer products. Popular culture products may be classified as entertainment, sports, news, politics, fashion and technology. Sources of popular culture from a mass media perspective include films, radio, music, television, video games and internet, which may be fictional or non-fictional as well. It involves the aspects of children, youth's and adults' social life through everyday interactions, rituals, eateries and varying styles of dresses that are generally agreed upon by the majority of the population. For example, in Indian sports, cricket is part of popular culture, and a large section of people show allegiance and identification with this game. Popular culture has high accessibility to people. Urbanization has also strengthened the formation of popular culture in cities of the world, which has given rise to ideals of individualistic aspirations or individualism, the postmodernist view of modernity, the processes of differentiation, rationalization and commodification are suppressed by hyper-differentiation, hyper-rationalization and hyper-commodification.

Sources of one's identity are invaded by commodities, creating differences of lifestyles even within the families. Media mediated images often obscure the differences between authentic and inauthentic culture. Media-mediated realities become powerful sources of our sense of reality, and style acquires more substance than the substance.

Fast-food restaurants, burgers and pizza have become popular all over the world, which undermines the idea of family meals in which there is a time for conversation. Toys and other entertainment products being produced mechanically have replaced the businesses and livelihood of local artisans.

Consumption patterns have become more predictable with excessive use of technology, which even the most skilled workers cannot achieve. Popular culture dehumanizes people by getting them to act in standardized ways and not allowing them to be creative and imaginative.

Musicians always rely on a network of people to be heard and flourish in its business. Consumers have multiple choices to purchase individual tracks from digital music sites. Internet and digital technologies are bringing a variety of techniques for emerging musicians. Online social platforms produce multicultural interactions of people and personal media has acquired greater importance in the recent past. It is suggested that in the interaction of consumption and style, the practical actors of everyday life formulate their versions of cultural diversity. The sensation-seeking tendency of digital media does not necessarily take into account the rational assumptions of a culture.

Popular culture stimulates a sensory experience and creates sociality that lacks intimacy and accountability. Popular culture manifests itself as a community of consumers who share pleasures not necessarily in binding aspects of culture.

THINK BOX

- How popular cultures influence the way we think and behave?
- Globalization has given rise to many new cultures that cut across national boundaries. Do you agree? Think of some examples to support your views.
- Can Mass Culture be the mirror reflection of popular culture?

5.3 Psychology of entertainment media

Entertainment is an activity that holds the attention of the person to provide delight or happiness. Numerous varieties of entertainment are available for the masses in the form of music, movies, sports, television, digital platforms, comedy and so on. The world "entertain" comes from the medieval Latin *intertenere* which means "to hold inside". The prefix "inter" means "inside" and the suffix "tenere" means "to hold". Entertainment is a multidimensional concept that primarily describes the pleasant experiences of users and keeps their attention engaged. Never before in the history of humankind has so much entertainment been readily accessible to a large number of people due to the immense capacity of media technology for compression, transmission and exhibition of massive amounts of information.

Several forms of media entertainment catch the attention of people who seek diversion, excitement, relaxation, amusement, satisfaction of other aesthetic experiences. The entertainment needs of the people vary with varied intellectual, aesthetic and emotional interests.

The role of humor, comedy and laughter in entertainment and enjoyment has certain advantages. There are credible indications for enjoyment derived from conflict-laden stories real and fictional. The entertainment concept also relates to the conditions under which displays of violence hold appeal for consumers and issues related to adolescents' desensitization from the mastery of entertainment-elicited distress. Another relevant concern related to media entertainment is on excessive erotic displays on television soap operas and digital music sites. Entertainment media products also need to be analyzed in terms of identifying the distinction between fantasy and reality with its consequences of usage on children. Adolescents and young people's fascination for popular music is mediated through vital aspects of appeals for favorable emotional reactions.

People spent their leisure activities by doing things like animal hunting, swimming, sports, dance, horse riding, gambling, gardening and many such activities for entertainment in previous times. Poetry, music, dance, magic and wrestling were activities enjoyed by the people during festivities and other occasions. Ancient cultures offered entertainments within a well-defined format for the rich and for the poor (masses). Animal fighting was also a very popular mode of entertainment in the medieval period. Christianity also used moral plays and allegories to entertain parishioners. In medieval Europe, animal beating was popular among commoners, the nobility and kings.

With the onset of media communication and technology, entertainment and its various forms gathered considerable support from policymakers. Recreation became the motive of entertainment activities, and audiences could be reached through technologies traveling to a large number of the population. Around 1920, radio had reached the maximum number of households in American society. Later on, television and the internet quickly reached the majority of households in developed nations and a significant number of households in the developing nations. Media users' freedom to choose their heart's content from among the wealth of offerings ensures that democratization does not lead to massification, as some have feared. The trend towards more leisure time for the masses increased in quantity and quality of entertainment extravaganza with newer forms of mass media.

5.3.1 Personality and entertainment preferences

It will be erroneous to perceive the presence of media and its effect in a simplistic cause-and-effect relation mode rather than personality dimensions, and consumption of media entertainment varies a lot from person to person. An individual's personality attributes strongly influence media use and gratification.

Media preferences are usually conceptualized as reflecting an individual's beliefs and expectations of both the media and their various content themes. Personality characteristics also indicate the attitude and behavior of the people's interaction with the media. They are seen as influencing perceptions of the media via cognitive, affective and physiological mechanisms, though there are variations also that can be noticed in the psychological orientation of a person and his/her media viewing pattern owing to various other external factors. A great variety of personality characteristics such as sensation seeking (Litle & Zuckerman, 1986), the Machiavellian trait of deceit (Tamborini, Stiff & Zillmann, 1987) and coping styles (Sparks & Spirek, 1988) have been shown to influence cognitive and affective responses to contemporary horror films.

Psychological traits of loneliness and shyness are found positively correlated with the social compensation viewing motive of television. The personality factors of extroversion, neuroticism and psychoticism have also some linkages for having preferences of various prime-time television programs and popular music. It is reasonable to understand that psychological factors, in particular personality factors, play a potential mediating role in determining peoples' attitudes, beliefs and behaviors towards media technologies.

5.3.2 Role of narrative in mass media

Narrative transportation is the concept where a person is placed into and immersed in the world of the story. The characters in the story allow spectators or listeners to immerse themselves in the realm of imagination with the potential for emotional involvement. Narrative transportation requires consumers to receive and interpret the story with empathy and mental imagery. Once transported into stories, the receiver loses the track of reality, temporality and physiological awareness.

Greig's (1993) description of a story "someone" (the traveler) is transported by the same means of transportation as a result of performing certain actions.

The traveler goes some distance the same distance from his or her world of origin which makes some aspects of the world of origin inaccessible. The traveler is changed by the journey undertaken for the same distance.

In the experience of feeling lost in a story, transported readers might experience strong emotions and motivations, even knowing that stories are not real. Transportation meets the enhancement of beliefs resulting in persuasiveness. Character is the driving force in fiction, and therefore attachment to characters may play a critical role in narrative-based belief change.

Cultivation theorists suggest that media messages shown on television present a systematic distortion of reality which results in internalization by viewers. Heavy television viewing is associated with greater anxiety and fearfulness and greater interpersonal mistrust (Gerbner et al., 1980; Shrum, 1999). Gerbner et al. (1980) argued that television cultivates primary dispositions from infancy that can be acquired from religion or education, and the mass-produced messages and images forms the mainstream of a common symbolic environment. According to Gerbner et al., television has become the central cultural arm of our society.

5.3.3 Accessibility and media effects

The accessibility model suggests that media viewing increases the accessibility of information in memory which subsequently relates to our cultivation of judgments. The accessibility model assumes that people apply the availability heuristic (Tversky & Kahneman, 1973) and base their judgments on the ease with which relevant information can be recalled.

The Elaboration Likelihood Model (Petty & Cacioppo, 1986) proposes that motivation to process information increases persuasion especially if the message arguments are strong ones. Narrative transportation of an individual is also determined by emotional involvement. Surprisingly, a fictional narrative can often be just as powerful as a factual one in changing beliefs (Green et al., 2006).

It has been suggested through researches that messages from purely fictional worlds can affect real attitudes and actions of the people. Authors of transportation theory suggested that (Green et al., 2004) we are persuaded by the fictional narrative in part due to low elaborative scrutiny. Social psychological theories help understand media imagery and social learning. Coercive behavior theory (Tedeschis & Felson, 1994) has suggested aggression as a social influence behavior and its goal includes coercion, power, dominance and impression management.

5.3.4 Realistic conflict theory

Sherif's robbers cave experiment (Sherif, 1958/2001; Sherif et al., 1954/1961) proposed a realistic conflict theory which suggests that when people compete for scarce resources (e.g. jobs, land, etc.), there is a rise in hostility between groups due to negative prejudices and stereotypes. A proposed mechanism of harm is the notion that media ideals distract women by concentrating their energy on so-called beautification and also by damaging women's self-esteem (Kilbourne & Pipher, 2000; Wolf, 2002).

There is an intentional process to highlight the portrayal of an unattainable ideal that becomes socially acceptable due to continuous presentation by media. The derogatory portrayals of women in the media also discourage them to take part in traditionally male-dominated professions. Learning theories of perceptual learning, association learning, cognitive learning and emotional learning also play an important role in attention, memory and behavior of the people using media messages.

THINK BOX

- The masses are becoming the puppets in the hands of the entertainment industry. Can you think of some examples to support this?
- Who are the targets of the entertainment business? And how are they being lured to spend their luxury time in entertainment from various media sources?

5.4 Critical evaluation

Mass communication does not exist in a vacuum. Rather, it operates in a structured process through which symbolic forms are produced, transmitted and received. The institutions of mass communication have extended the boundaries of society into a global society. The development of institutions of newspapers, book publishers, broadcasting organizations and the digital landscape marked the emergence of new forms of information diffusion and cultural transmission.

Culture consists of ideas and thought made public through various forms of externalization and internalization through the powerful medium of mass communication. Our day-to-day social life, everyday life activities and long-term orientation are strongly influenced by the cultural themes produced with the help of mass media. Cultural domains influenced by the realm of mass media include religion, spirituality, family, friendship, sex and romance, social festivals, rituals, arts and music, literature, theatre, etc.

Culture also influences our emotions and motives through various media representations, constructing personal and collective meanings. Language is one of the primary symbol systems of cultural representation that we encounter through our sense organs. It also produces class consciousness by commodifying habits and lifestyles as a superior culture and an inferior culture. Cultural orientations are intentionally created, reinforced through various actors and agencies of mass communication which forms the basis of habits as consumers.

All cultural forms have dominant symbolic space for developing cultural identity through which different cultural identity groups express themselves through distinctive styles.

Mass media representations also produce stereotypes, prejudices by creating dominant images and status differentials. Carnival culture, for example, is a kind of sensation a cultural ritual that became mediated, commercialized and globalized by the entertainment industry and mass media organizations. Symbolic power and popular culture constitute and reinforce each other through various social and marketing strategies that become the basis of everyday life.

The differences between reality and fantasies are getting blurred, and people start believing and acting based on imagery created on the basis of fictional narratives. Audience behavior is thoroughly researched and the activities are programmed for their leisure time utilization in such a way that media-represented symbols strongly influence their attitudes, beliefs and behaviors. Social media platforms also make the commodity orientation of the people through commercial exploitation of mass culture symbols. Advertisers do the emotional branding works to influence the dreams and fantasies of poor and middle-class people of achieving the status of becoming rich. Various scientific and psychological methods of persuasion are applied by the advertisers to stimulate the imagination of a better life through the consumption of goods propagated by them.

Beauty, youth, good health and affluent lifestyle are weaved into the stories of media-represented realities which ultimately contribute to the making of consumers in large numbers in expectation of the fulfillment of their aspirations and goals. The culture of mass media fuses places, persons and styles of everyday life which keeps changing itself into new ways for the construction of self and collectivities. It is worthwhile to maintain mass media-produced images are not capable of creating universal effects on people, and a considerable amount of individual differences may exist owing to parental mediation and social-cultural context variation. Culture of a society is not a fixed set of the undifferentiated block; instead, it keeps changing its ideas and practices according to changing demands of the situation and people.

Our microscopic realities of food, dress, education and health to macroscopic realities of social and political orientation, choice of music, sports and a whole range of life activities are influenced, reproduced and invented by the mass media-produced realities, which give a structure of predictability to the practice of community life. Cultures produced through mass media provide the framework to interpret ourselves and others and provide grounds through which we form our personal, collective and social identities. People always have a strong desire to recognize and belong to the symbolic power of culture and have strong tendencies to relate to the mainstream culture of the time.

5.5 Indian perspective of culture

According to Indian culture, the identity of the person is developed around "we" rather than "I". A person is conceptualized as a microcosm, reflecting the whole cosmos (Kakar, 1982). Lapierre (1986) observed that "every individual in India is always linked to the rest of the social body by a network of credibly diversified ties with the result no one in this gigantic country of inhabitants could ever be completely abandoned".

The strives for the collective's achievement are appreciated (Mehta & Belk, 1991), for achievement in Indian culture implies being a good person, thinking about the well-being of others fulfills one's duties helping others and being able to get the affection and blessings of others (Agarwal & Misra, 1989; Misra & Agarwal, 1985). Compared to the people in the West, Indians are found to be high on helping behavior (Levine et al., 2001). A strong emotional connection with others and helping people in times of difficulty constitutes the sense of *we-ness* in Indian society. Striving to earn money (artha) has been recognized as a cardinal motive from ancient days, as it is the basis for indulging in earthly pleasures as well as taking care of one's loved ones (Arthashashtra of Kautilya; Rangarajan, 1992, p. 145).

Indian mythologies are full of stories that emphasize various modes to acquire divine qualities, and a substantial part of this includes participation in ceremonies, sacrifices, collective prayer and collective feasts (Langar), and throughout the year some religious festivals take place. The traditional values for group embeddedness personalized and dependency relationships tolerance and duty that Indian employees hold are enshrined in family dynamics (Sinha & Sinha, 1990). While Westernized self is centered on "I-ness", the conception of the Indian self is centered on "we-ness" which is also characterized by reciprocity and mutual dependence.

Indian society has also undergone significant changes with the introduction of mass media into people's day-to-day lives. The traditional social structure of people living in villages and cities has been influenced by the westernization culture. Folk music, traveling singers, "Nautanki" shows, Ram Leela, Krishna Leela type of shows, hand weaving and many other practices which used to be a major activity of the people have either diminished or neglected into oblivion with the technological advancement of mass media.

Traditional theatre-like folk dance, folksong and puppetry are also on the decline. Folk theatre in the oral tradition was prominent in the different parts of India. Notable among these are various regional forms – Rajasthan has Bhavai and Khayal, Orissa has Daskathia, Maharashtra has Gondhal, Nautanki is famous in North India, Maanch in MP and many more – that are no longer visible in Indian society. The major source of evidence for Sanskrit theatre is a treatise on theatre (Natyashastra, 200 BC to 200 AD) whose authorship is attributed to Bharata. The Natyashastra addresses acting, dance, music, dramatic construction, architecture, costuming, makeup, props, etc., and offers a complete account of dramaturgy. During the 4th and 5th centuries AD, three famous romantic plays were written by Kalidas Malvikagnimitram, Vikramuurvashiya and Abhijanana Sakuntala. In the modern period, Rabindranath Tagore was an internationally famed playwright who wrote *Chitrangdha* (1892), *The King of the Dark Chamber* (*Raja*, 1910), *The Post Office* (*Dakghar*, 1913) and *Red Oleander* (*Raktakarabi*, 1924).

Mushayra, Kawali and Yakshagana are examples of the popular semi-classical theatre art form from coastal Karnataka. They too are declining. Dance is considered an important form of expression of emotions. The Indian classical dance has eight prominent forms of dance: Bharatanatyam, Kathak, Kuchi Puddi, Odissi, Kathakali, Sattriya, ManiPuri and Mohiniattam. They are expressive dance forms of religious performance. Art forms related to Vaishnavism, Shaivism, Shaktism, pan-Hindu epics and the Vedic literature include storytelling in Sanskrit or regional language plays (Brown, 2013).

The Indian classical dances have also spread to various parts of India. Folk dances are also in large numbers. Some of the most famous include Bihu, Garba, Dandiya, Theyyam, Bhangra and Choliya dance from different states or regions of India. The plight of artists does not indicate a sound support system from either the government or private organizations. Several tribal dance forms are depicting the life of forest people, but they do not occupy the limelight of mass media and remain in a state of ignorance. These tribal dance forms have their diversity with high-quality aesthetics and depiction of minute details of tribal life. There are more than a hundred tribal dance forms but they very rarely catch the attention of the public at large. Modern Bollywood Hindi cinema dance styles, often blending with Western dance styles and high-intensity sound music with disc jolly, have become popular all over India. The continuous and repeated representation by mass media and famous music industry organizations supported music and dance has become popular, creating a huge consumer demand throughout the country. Traditional Indian arts like Tanjore paintings, Mysore paintings, Ravi Varma paintings and Madhubani paintings are a thousand years old in their origin, but their perception among the common masses is very weak. Some of the paintings of Indian painters become of world fame in the international market but face difficulties for survival in their homeland.

The implications of mass media and culture are short term to long term for individuals and society at large. Several actors are involved in the production of mass media images as well as a complex network of economic, political and institutional influences. The production of reality through fantasy, myths do not have a simple cause-and-effect relationship from one source to another. Instead, it follows a complex pattern of symbolic manifestation at manifest and tacit levels. The mass media-produced culture also brings autonomy and freedom to the people on the periphery. At the same time, it has enormous potential to create public images that influence the attitudes and beliefs with long-term consequences.

Not every individual and society is influenced with the same impact. They respond differently to media messages. But to deny its gigantic influence on shaping the opinion and cultures will also amount to doing away with the real picture. Researchers of media culture and academics must pay sincere attention to understand and evaluate its impact on society.

THINK BOX

- The traditional entertainment sources have taken a back seat, giving way to technology. What influence can it have on the development of a society?
- It is not just about entertainment, it is also about the ethics, the values and the emotions that are learned and taught. Comment.

5.6 Summary

The present chapter highlights the interaction between media and culture. Culture is considered a collective process that functions symbolically and it changes, evolves and even disappears over time. Cultures that are portrayed through media teach people using it to see the world in particular ways. Our regular interaction with media messages influences our attitudes and behaviors according to the frameworks of ideology portrayed through media. Media can impose certain ideas practices by limiting possible perceptions and interpretations of the world. Ideological value hierarchies assign unequal powers because all social relations exist in a web of ideologies. In this process, the media plays the role of normalizing relations of power by socially parenting groups. Antonio Gramsci's concept of the hegemony ruling class maintains their domination of subordinate class through the creation and perpetuation of legitimate symbols.

Media also plays a crucial role in the creation and maintenance of stereotypes about certain groups. Mass media acts as a significant force in deciding the culture through communication. Communication is suggestive of a form of action that does not merely describe the world but contributes to it. Communication by different types of exports becomes a site for co-determination of ideas, techniques and social relations.

Communities that are held together by a perceived unity of identity are cultural formations. With the rapid pace of industrialization and growth of powerful mass media institutions, small-group identities are rendered powerless. The emergence of mass culture that is followed by a large number of people can lead to the elimination of alternative culture with the dominating presence of its numbers. Anthropologists have highlighted the phenomenon of globalization which alters the social configuration of identities. Mediatization is an essential aspect of contemporary cultural experience and works as an important source of deterritorialization.

Deterritorialization means the growing presence of social contact that goes beyond the limits of a geographical territory. Popular culture is created through mass media by trivializing the serious aspects of commodities. Popular culture is used by a large number of people and has more commercial characteristics.

Entertainment media is a multidimensional concept whose primary objective is to keep the attention of the audience engaged in pleasant experiences. Personality factors of individuals play an important role in the choice of entertainment media. Narrative transportation of the audience being lost in the story is presented by the media. Different theories of learning contribute to the attention, memory and behavior of the people using media messages.

Indian culture is also being influenced by the all-round presence of media in day-to-day life. So many creative arts and paintings are on the verge of decline, and Western music has occupied a dominant role in our cultural space. Several traditional dances, theatre and architecture are losing their existence due to the continuous influx of Western influences. The implications of mass media and culture have short-term as well as long-term consequences that need to be analyzed and understood in a scientific manner.

Key points

- People's identity is closely related to the idea of culture which is strongly influenced by ideology.
- The theory of ideological dominance is based on myth, which is a sacred story or type of speech that reproduces ideology in relation to an object.
- Cultural hegemony argues that people having power can manufacture consent of its masses.
- Stereotyping is the process of constructing a set of convictions or beliefs about members of a particular group.
- Othering is a process of discrimination that encompasses the many expressions of prejudice based on group identities and promotes a set of conditions that propagates the group's inequality and marginalization.
- Mass culture creates a mass society with atomized individuals.
- Hybridization is a process of mixing different cultures which gives rise to a new culture.
- Technoscapes means the fluid nature of technological establishments crossing its boundaries.
- Deterritorialization is the moment by which we leave a territory and is considered an essential element of globalization.
- Narrative transportation is an important method for emotional involvement of audience in the plot of stories.

Key terms

Doxa, hegemony, othering, Geminschaft, Gesellschaft, ethnoscapes, deterritorialization, *narrative transportation, cultivation, fictional narrative*

References

Abu-Lughod, L. (1991). Writing against culture. In R. Fox (Ed.), *Recapturing Anthropology: Working in the Present.* Santa Fe, NM: School of American Research Press.

Agarwal, R., & Misra, G. (1989). Variations in achievement cognitions: Role of ecology, age, and gender. *International Journal of Intercultural Relations,* 13, 93–107.

Appadurai, A. (1991). Global ethnoscapes: Notes and queries for a transnational anthropology. In R.G. Fox (Ed.), *Interventions: Anthropology of the Present.* Santa Fe, NM: School of American Research.

Bagdikian, B. (1997). *The Media Monopoly* (5th ed.). Boston, MA: Beacon.

Bennett, T. (1980). *Popular Culture: Themes and Issues.* Milton Keynes: Open University Press.

Brown, F.B. (2013). *The Oxford Handbook of Religion and the Arts.* Oxford: Oxford University Press.

Carey, J., & Quirk, J. (1989). The mythos of the electronic revolution. In J. Carey, *Communication as Culture: Essays on Media and Society* (pp. 113–41). Boston, MA: Unwin Hyman.

Durkheim, E. (1947). *Suicide: A Study in Sociology* (G. Simpson, Trans.). New York: Macmillan.

Gans, H.J. (1974). *Popular Culture and High Culture.* New York: Basic Books.

García Canclini, N. (1990). *Culturas Híbridas.* Buenos Aires: Editorial Grijalbo.

Gerbner, G., Gross, L., Morgan, M., & Signorielli, N. (1980). The "mainstreaming" of America: Violence profile no. 11. *Journal of Communication,* pp. 10–29.

Giddens, A. (1990). *The Consequences of Modernity.* Cambridge: Cambridge Polity Press.

Gramsci, A. (1971). *Selections from the Prison Notebooks* (Q. Hoare & G.N. Smith, Trans. & Eds.). New York: International Publishers.

Gramsci, A. (1996). *Prison Notebooks* (Vol. 2) (J. Buttigieg, Trans. & Ed.). New York: Columbia University Press.

Green, M.C., Garst, J., & Brock, T.C. (2004). The power of fiction: Determinants and boundaries. In L.J. Shrum (Ed.) *Blurring the Lines: The Psychology of Entertainment Media* (pp. 161–76). Mahwah, NJ: Erlbaum.

Green, M.C., Garst, J., Brock, T.C., & Chung, S. (2006). Fact versus fiction labeling: Persuasion parity despite heightened scrutiny of fact. *Media Psychology,* 8(3), 267–85.

Greig, D. (1993). Internal exile. *Theatre Scotland,* 3(11), 8–10.

Hall, S. (1980). Cultural studies and the centre: Some problematics and problems. In S. Hall et al. (Eds.), *Culture, Media, Language* (Chap. 1). London: Hutchison.

Heidegger, M. (1968). *What Is Called Thinking?* (J.G. Gray, Trans.). New York: Harper & Row.

Hofstede, G.H. (1991). *Cultures and Organizations: Software of the Mind.* London: McGraw-Hill.

Jhally, S., & Livant, B. (1986). "Watching as working": The valorisation of audience consciousness. *Journal of Communication,* pp. 124–43.

Kakar, S. (1982). *Shamans, Mystics and Doctors.* Delhi: Oxford University Press.

Kilbourne, J., & Pipher, M. (2000). *Can't Buy My Love.* New York: The Free Press.

Lapierre, D. (1986). *The City of Joy.* London: Arrow Books.

Levine, R.V., Norenzayan, A., & Philbrick, K. (2001). Cross-cultural differences in helping strangers. *Journal of Cross-Cultural Psychology,* 32, 543–60.

Lippmann, W. (1922). *Public Opinion.* New York: Free Press.

Litle, P., & Zuckerman, M. (1986). Sensation seeking and music preferences. *Personality and Individual Difftrences,* 7(4), 575–77.

McDonald, D. (1957). A theory of mass culture. In B. Rosenberg & D.M. White (Eds.), *Mass Culture: The Popular Arts in America*. New York: The Free Press.

Mehta, R., & Belk, R.W. (1991). Artifacts, identity and transition: Favorite possessions of Indians and Indian immigrants to the United States. *Journal of Consumer Research*, 17 (March), 398–411.

Misra, G., & Agarwal, R. (1985). The meaning of achievement: Implication for a cross-cultural theory of achievement motivation. In I.R. Lagunes & Y.H. Poortinga (Eds.), *From a Different Perspective: Studies of Behaviour across Cultures* (pp. 250–66). Lisse: Swets & Zeitlinger.

Petty, R., & Cacioppo, J. (1986). *Communication and Persuasion: Central and Peripheral Routes to Attitude Change*. New York: Springer-Verlag.

Piaget, J. (1963 [1936]). *The Origins of Intelligence in Children*. New York: W.W. Norton & Company, Inc.

Rangarajan, L.N. (1992). *Kautilya: The Arthashastra*. New Delhi: Penguin Books India.

Sherif, M. (1958/2001). Superordinate goals in the reduction of intergroup conflict. In M.A. Hogg & D. Abrams (Eds.), *Intergroup Relations: Essential Readings* (pp. 64–70). Philadelphia, PA: Psychology Press.

Sherif, M., Harvey, O.J., White, B.J., Hood, W.R., & Sherif, C.W. (1954/1961). *Intergroup Conflict and Cooperation: The Robbers Cave Experiment*. University of Oklahoma Book Exchange, 1961. Reprint edition, Wesleyan University Press, 1988.

Shrum, L.J. (1999). Television and persuasion: Effects of the programs between the ads. *Psychology and Marketing*, 16(2), 119–40.

Sinha, J.A., & Sinha, D. (1990). Role of social values in Indian organizations. *International Journal of Psychology*, 25, 705–15.

Sparks, G.G., & Spirek, M.M. (1988). Individual differences in coping with stressful mass media: An activation-arousal view. *Human Communication Research*, 15(2), 195–216.

Storey, J. (2003), *Inventing Popular Culture: From Folklore to Globalisation*. Oxford: Blackwell.

Tamborini, R., Stiff, J., & Zillmann, D. (1987). Preference for graphic horror featuring male versus female victimization: Personality and past film viewing experiences. *Human Communication Research*, 13(4), 529–52.

Tedeschi, J.T., & Felson, R.B. (1994) *Violence, Aggression and Coercive Actions*. Washington, DC: American Psychological Association.

Tönnies, F. (1957). *Community and Society* [Gemeinschaft und Gesellschaft]. East Lansing, MI: Michigan State University Press.

Tsing, A.L. (1993). *In the Realm of the Diamond Queen: Marginality in an Out-of-the-Way Place*. Princeton: Princeton University Press.

Tversky, A., & Kahneman, D. (1973). Availability: A heuristic for judging frequency and probability. *Cognitive Psychology*, 5, 207–32.

Williams, R. (1961). *The Long Revolution*. New York: Columbia University Press.

Williams, R. (1980). *Problems in Materialism and Culture*. Great Britian: Redwood Burn Ltd.

Wolf, N. (2002). *The Beauty Myth: How Images Are Used against Women*. New York. Perennial.

6

MEDIA AND ADVERTISING

Learning objectives

After reading this chapter, you will be able to understand:

- Field of media and advertising
- Psychological factors in advertising
- Consumer advertising
- Developing an effective advertisement program
- Critical evaluation of media and advertising
- Indian context of advertising

6.1 Introduction

Today, human needs are fulfilled by the various sources of advertisement. The impact of advertising is so pervasive that it has brought changes in the lifestyles and desires influencing the minds of people through advertisement, creativity and innovation. Advertising is a paid, non-personal communication designed to communicate information about various products, services and ideas. The word "advertise" originates from the Latin *adverte*, which means to turn toward or to take note of. Important functions of advertising also include persuasion, information, communication, attention, attitude formation and decision-making. Some of the advertisements, including Nike's "Just Do It" campaign, Apple's Get a Mac, Pepsi's IS Pepsi Ok? Progressive insurance's Flo, Unilever Dove's Campaign for Real Beauty and Coca-Cola's Share a Coke, proved to be the most successful campaigns in the past few decades.

Similarly in the Indian context, advertisements like Airtel Matic (share the load), Meri Maggi (Me and Meri Maggi), Surf Excel (Daag ache hain, idea cellular – what an idea), Vodafone (Zoo Zoos), Fevikwik (Todo nahi jodo), Fortune oil (Ghar ka khana) and Havells Fan (Hawa badlegi), have been some of the most successful campaigns on the Indian market.

Billions of dollars are spent in the business of advertising globally, and Indian advertising spending is also very large. Some of the most prominent campaigns launched by the government in India in recent years include Digital India, Selfie with daughter, Beti Bachao Beti Padhao, Make in India and Swachh Bharat.

Some of the social media campaigns also become very popular and help to overcome stereotypes and prejudices existing in our society. In order to understand the impact of advertising on the people and society, it is desirable to understand the dynamics of advertisement from economic, social and psychological perspectives.

Mass communication refers to the technology used to communicate to a large group or groups of people in a short time frame (Pavlik & Mcintosh, 2004). Mass media applies the techniques and strategies to produce, promote and spread communication to a large number of audiences. Mass media's role is to provide information about issues and events that relate to members of society. In addition to this, mass media also functions as a model for cultural transmission and entertainment. Mass media originates from a source reaching to the audiences and has an enormous capacity to connect a large number of people. Several sources of media like computers, telecommunications and digital media have widened the scope for media outreach. The emergence of economic interests have led to the convergence of mass media companies. The Gutenberg printing press was established in 1450, the phonograph invented in 1890. Subsequently, radio, television and the internet have opened huge networks of communications around the globe.

Advertising is a form of communication to persuade a large section of the people (goods, services and ideas) through various channels of mass communication. Advertising is any non-personal medium used to target populations through newspapers, radio, television, telemarketing, social media marketing, sponsored events and programs to inform, persuade and satisfy the consumer's

FIGURE 6.1 Digital marketing.
Source: Retrieved 21 June 2020 from https://www.pxfuel.com/en/search?q=advertising

needs. The popular brands have more loyal customers. as compared to less popular brands that have fewer buyers and fewer loyal customers.

Advertising is often the most visible element of a company's overall marketing communication programs. It is used as a primary tool by private and government organizations to reinforce the identity of brands and ideas by promoting them to attract.

6.1.1 Human nature

Emotions, desires, interests and dreams play a key role in an advertising success. The advertisement is considered a process of persuading and creation of desires. The rational mode of cognitive processing is also influenced by the process of advertisements. Changes in the nature of economy driven by principles of capitalism contributed to the need of product differentiation, and emphasis shifted from product to want competition. The ability of the advertiser to become successful is also strongly influenced by the psychological factors of fear of public conformity, competition and comparison, approval from others, recognition and status satisfaction. Apart from appeal to reason, pathos is also considered as an effective selling agent for all people who are interested in tragedy as an interesting component of thrilling experience.

Most of the people are flattered by personal attention, appeals to personal appearance and prestige. Concern for health also plays an important role in the process of advertising. Trillions of advertisements are shown every year to people, and the average person might witness a million advertisements in a year. Advertising agencies take the routes of thinking, feeling and hyper-reality imagination with the help of images, stories and music.

The use of color enhances the attention of a person through images and stories. For instance, Coca-Cola's "Happiness Factory" campaign cultivated a strong connection to arouse the emotions of the customers and link it with joy in living. Google's "Friends forever" campaign was the most shared advertisement in 2015. That year Google had amassed 6,432,921 shares on social media platforms like Twitter and Facebook. Advertisements are considered as the nervous system of the business world. The aim of the advertisement is to call forth activity in the minds of readers to attract attention and to sell goods (Scott, 1903).

Dill Scott wrote, "man has been called the reasoning animal but we could with greater truthfulness be called the creature of suggestion". He is reasonable, but he is to a greater extent suggestible. A person can be appealed to most easily and most effectively through dominating imagery and other classes of images.

According to Scott, consumer suggestibility was based on three factors: emotion, sympathy and sentimentality. Scott proposed attention comprehension and understanding as three stages of advertising.

THINK BOX

- How can advertisement through various sources of media, generate some kind of (desired) response among viewers?
- What can be the possible benefits and harm that advertisement through media can cause for the consumer?

6.2 Psychological factors in advertising

6.2.1 Emotions

Some of the core features of emotions include the appraisal of the situation. It connects with subjective experiences of feelings. The current model of emotion involves person-situation transactions that compel attention, have meaning to an individual in the light of currently active goals and give rise to coordinated yet flexible multisystem responses that modify the ongoing person situation transaction in crucial ways (Barrett et al., 2007; Gross, 2008).

The first core feature of emotion regulation is the activation of a goal to modify the emotion. This is called the generative process (Gross, Sheppes & Urry, 2011). There are two types of emotions: extrinsic emotions and intrinsic emotions. They are related to regulation in self and regulation in others, respectively which may be active simultaneously in some situations.

According to Gross (1998), another core feature of emotion regulation involves the use of implicit or explicit strategies. Depending on the individual's goals, emotion regulation may increase or decrease the latency, magnitude, duration or offset of the emotional response, compared to the emotional response that would have occurred in the absence of emotional regulations.

In the process of emotional regulation, situational and cognitive aspects play an important role. Thus, situation selection is the point in which a person is expected to elicit desirable emotions, positive or negative. Similarly, situation modification requires bringing internal or external changes that can lead to change of cognitive contexts.

One of the most common features of attentional deployment is distraction which focuses upon diversity of situation. Attentional deployment refers to directing attention within a given situation in order to influence an emotional process in a person. Attentional deployment is one of the first emotion regulatory processes to appear during development (Rothbart, Ziaie & O'Boyle, 1992) and it is used from cradle to grave, particularly when it is not possible to modify one's situation. One of the most common forms of attentional deployment is a distraction, which focuses attention on other aspects of the situation or moves attention away from the situation altogether. Distraction also may involve changing internal focus, as when someone calls to mind the thoughts or memories that help to instantiate the desired emotional state. William James (1950 [1890]) argued attention as possession of mind in which localization or concentration of consciousness is its essence.

6.2.2 Attitude-behavior link

The MODE model defines attitude as the association in memory between an object and its summary evaluation (Fazio, 1990; Olson & Fazio, 2006). The main function of attitude is to provide a quick assessment of objects in the environment which automatically facilitates behavior.

The Dual Attitudes model (Wilson et al., 2000) posits that "capacity and motivation" are required to retrieve the newer, explicit attitude effortfully. According to the Dual Attitudes model (Wilson et al., 2000), implicit attitudes are deeply ingrained, and even if attitude representation changes, it is not fully supplanted by new altered attitude, and this may differ from explicit attitudes.

Associative processes activate associated representations from memory, and propositional processes validate information activated by associative processes. Behavior of a person is influenced by attitudes in combination with social factors about what others think we should do. People tend to behave in ways that are consistent with their attitudes when they know the factual aspects. Namasivayam et al. (2006) examined the socio-economic factors that are responsible for purchase of life insurance policies and the preference of policyholders towards various types of policies of LIC.

Biswas and Biswas (1997) examined the impact of culture along with different levels of socio-economic development and caste on pro-economic attitudes and beliefs of individuals from rural areas of Gujarat and Odisha. Results of this study indicated that individuals' pro-economic beliefs and attitudes were significantly affected by their regional cultures. Exploring the impact of TV and television advertising on children, Unni Krishnan and Bajpai suggested the dominant images of TV serials, cartoons and commercials on the impressionable mind of children.

The SEM model and the Dual Attitudes model suggest that implicit attitude is slower both to form and to distinguish while explicit attitudes can be modified relatively quickly. The Iterative Reprocessing model (Cunningham & Zelazo, 2007) considers the role of dynamism in regulating evaluative responses. According to Gross (2002), though the terms attitude and evaluation are often used interchangeably, attitude is considered to be relatively more stable than evaluations because evaluations take the support of pre-existing attitudes as well as the environment and contextual factors. Reframing is the ability to change one's evaluation of an event to alter its emotional significance.

Reframing is used as a communication technique that changes the conceptual and/or emotional setting or viewpoint in relation to how a brand is perceived by placing it in a different frame that fits us better. Message reframing does lead to higher attention, perceived novelty and attitude toward advertisement. The three most common methods of reframing include realistic reappraisal, positive reappraisal and compassionate reappraisal.

6.2.3 Attention

In the process of advertising, capturing consumers' attention has paramount importance. During the 1950s, some inspirational research took place, which Darrell Lucas (1960) described as "probably the finest example of experimental design ever reported on advertising research", when referring to the PARM Study by the Alfred Politz Organization (Helpman & Krugman, 1985). The PARM Study (A study of Printed Advertising Rating methods) was a study to investigate issues regarding the measurement of advertising, in particular, the difference between recognition and recall of advertisements.

Krugman (1986) stated the recognition was more sensitive than recall, and the special virtue of the recognition measure is to elicit information of brief, low-attention exposure to advertising, whereas recall is for advertising that has been more closely attended to. The selective attention theory focuses on how input is transferred from the sensory register to short-term memory.

Broadbent (1979) suggested a "filter" that mechanically screened out the non-attended stimuli. Treisman (1960, 1964), however, suggested an "attenuating" mechanism which may significantly reduce the incoming input but does not necessarily block information. Situational variables also contribute to the process of attention by consumers. According to Belk (1975, p. 157), a situation is a point in time and space, furthermore, all those factors "Observable" that do not follow

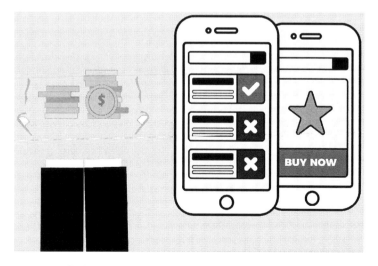

FIGURE 6.2 Digital advertisement.
Source: Retrieved 21 June 2020 from https://pxhere.com/en/photo/1583443

from a Knowledge of personal (intra-individuals) and stimulus (choice alternative) attributes and which have a demonstrable and systematic effect on current behavior. To understand the situational characteristics influencing attention, several factors play a contributing role. To identify what constitutes a situation, Belk (1975, p. 159) puts forward five groups of situational characteristics representing general features.

Physical surroundings – it includes such aspects as geographical and institutional location, decor, sounds, aromas, lighting, a visible configuration of merchandise or other material surrounding the stimulus object.

Social surroundings – this includes other persons presenting their properties, roles and interpersonal interactions.

Temporal perspective – a dimension of situation specified in time units.

Task definition – it refers to the features of a situation, including an intent or requirement to select, shop for or obtain information about a general or specific purchase.

Antecedent states – these are moods or short-termed conditions immediately antecedent to a situation. In order to communicate with the consumer, capturing attention becomes a vital factor in the process of advertisements with an ever-increasing number of advertisements competing for existence, and the consumers' attention has become a scarce resource (Adler & Firestone, 1997; Beck & Davenport, 2001; Pieters & Wedel, 2004). According to Pieters and Wedel (2004), three key elements can be identified in an advertisement: the brand, the picture and the text. Pictorial representation attracts more attention than texts. Researchers report that the pictorial is by far the "most important structural element in magazine advertising" (Rossiter & Percy, 1997, p. 295) and studies (with eye movement tracker) are showing that around 90% of the viewers fixate the main picture in an advertisement before they start focusing on the copy text (Kroeber-Riel, 1984) The enduring effect after viewing the advertisement is the formation of visual memory of the advertisement that enables subsequent recognition (Finn, 1988). Therefore, an advertisement without pictorial images will be less received by the consumers as compared to the advertisement with pictorial elements. Text elements are studied after attraction to the pictures, which are divided into a headline and copy text.

One of the more well-known statements in advertising originates actually from David Ogilvy (1963), saying that "the wickedest of all sins is to run an advertisement without a headline". Increased complexity on websites (Bruner & Kumar, 2000) is created by using more graphic images, more text (even blinking or the like) more hyperlinks, more sound, more animation and also more full-motion video.

William James (1950 [1890]) once wrote: "Everyone knows what attention is. It is the taking possession of the mind in clear and vivid form, of one out of what seem several simultaneously possible objects or trains of thought. Focalisation, Concentration of consciousness are its essence".

Color is considered to be a suitable way to make a stimulus distinct, and differences in colors make it easier to discriminate between targets and the distractions. Size, depth and gloss also contribute to easily identifiable features. It is reasonable to summarize that the phenomenon of attention is extremely important in the process of attention. It is also evident from various studies that the attention of consumers towards the products can be influenced by a variety of factors, and important among them are shape, size, brightness, color, pictorial representation, physical surroundings and situational factors. Pre-attentive processes also contribute to the process of attention. Advertisers make use of attention techniques through generating meaningful frames of reference for the consumers.

6.2.4 Motivation

The behavioral aspect of motivation plays an important role and it differs greatly among individuals. Advertisers make use of several strategies to analyze and understand consumer motivation and accordingly plan their products and services to improve buyer motivation.

Motivation describes the degree of psychological need and drive. If it is very high, the likelihood of buying also increases consumers' perceptions, beliefs, identification with the product. Attitudes shape the favorable or unfavorable evaluation about a product or brand. The social environment in which the consumer is placed also plays an important role in the decision-making developed by the motivation to buy a product. There may be conflicts caused by limited attention to the product, conflicting sources of information received by him or her or conflict between awareness and beliefs which can influence the motivation of the consumer.

6.2.4.1 Instinct theory of motivation

The Instinct Theory of Motivation suggests that all organisms are born with biological tendencies that help them survive. Ethologist Konard Lorenz (1903–89), also called as the father of ethology, developed a psychohydraulic model of the motivation of behavior. His theory of instinctive behavior saw behavior patterns as largely innate but triggered through environmental stimuli; for example, the hawk/goose effect. Lorenz observed that the phenomenon of imprinting allows the goose to learn to recognize members of its species, enabling them to display behavior patterns such as mating. (Tinbergen and Lorenz conjointly received the Nobel Prize in 1973.)

Freud stated that humans have two basic instinctual drives, i.e. life (Eros) and death (thanatos). The life drive eros causes us to engage in behaviors promoting the preservation of life, such as engaging in sex, eating to survive and exercising to good health. The death drive (thanatos) causes us to engage in risky or aggressive behaviors. William James suggested that instincts remain functional and human instincts such as anger, love, play and other instincts can explain much of human behavior.

6.2.4.2 Incentive theory of motivation

This view suggests that a person will be more likely to do an action that is positively received. This theory, proposed by behaviorists, involves the concepts of conditioning, homeostasis and positive reinforcement. Motivations are commonly separated into two categories based on motivator: intrinsic (arising from internal factors) or extrinsic (arising from external factors). According to Deci (1971), intrinsically motivated behaviors are defined as ones for which the reward is the satisfaction of performing the activity itself. Extrinsic motivation is defined as "engaging in an activity to obtain an outcome that is separable from the activity itself".

Extrinsic rewards are used by advertisers to create desires and motivation among consumers. Physical reinforcements such as money, verbal reinforcements such as praise and social reinforcements such as status have a reinforcing effect on the behavior and motivation of people towards certain products and brands. However, the effect of intrinsic and extrinsic motivation also varies due to individual differences in self-esteem, locus of control and neuroticism. Content theories of motivation, which are also called need theories, relate motivation to the fulfillment of our needs. Maslow's needs hierarchy theory, Adderfer's ERG Theory, McClelland's achievement motivation and Herzberg's two-factor theory are prominent need theories of human motivation. Skinner's reinforcement theory, Victor Vroom's expectancy theory, Adams's equity theory and Locke's goal-setting theories are important process theories of motivation. The concept of goal-setting has been incorporated by management theorists into a number of incentive programs including management by objectives. The reinforcement theory based on the operant conditioning principles of Skinner makes use of praise, appreciation status that can increase the rewarded behavior's repetition.

6.2.5 Equity

The concept of equity may be explicitly stated as an even exchange of values such that what is received is presumed to be equal to what is given (Adams, 1965). According to Walster (1975), equity operates within a range, with a lower and upper limit, and inputs ("what is given") are defined as what one perceives as his or her contribution to the exchange for which he or she expects a just return. Equity-based motivational forces are useful in the advertisement as the inequity of seller-buyer relation may give rise to consumer dissatisfaction and the motivation to restore equity.

The functional purchase preference of a product involves not only buying the product but other after-sales services, too. Customer care also plays an important role in the decision-making process. The inputs such as advertising, availability of deals, post satisfaction with the product, referred to as "antecedents" (Jacoby, 1976), may induce the consideration of one brand over another.

Sheth (1976) distinguished between various types of utility needs related to five motivational dimensions:

1. Functional motives
2. Aesthetic-emotional motives
3. Social motives
4. Situational motives
5. Curiosity motives

Social motives are related to the impact that consumption makes on the relevant others. Social motives play a role through an impact on status, prestige and esteem derived from the usage of certain products.

Motives represent "means-end beliefs". Their cognitive dimension relates to buying of products and attainment of satisfaction. This expectation is in the form of subjective probability. Need achievement theory (McClelland, 1961) attributes the strength of motivation to the cognitive expectation that the action will result in the consequence.

6.2.6 Fear

In advertising, an appeal to fear is used to motivate people to purchase a product. The consumer appraises the product in the light of lurking fear in their mind related to safety or prestige, or for social, climatic changes related to the entirety of humanity. For instance, advertisements related to saving water equipment highlight reducing wastage of water. Similarly, the advertisements related to anti-pollution highlight life processes. Fear-based advertising becomes more effective when it clearly depicts the dangerous implications, suggests specific ways to overcome the fear and the process suggested is not very complex. For example, the use of airbags in cars became a popular choice with advertisements like one by Volkswagen, "Safe Happens", promoting customers to buy cars with airbags. Behavioral psychologist Wyatt Woodsmall explains it as follows: "If you can find out what people's worst nightmare is, camp out inside their nightmare (they will) do anything to get out of that situation." Some popular brands which have used fear to grow successfully and some other techniques are L'Oréal using the tagline "Because I am worth it" to aim the insecurities of people regarding their appearance.

FedEx uses the tagline "Absolutely, positively overnight" to make people fear of missing a deadline. The advertising professionals make use of fear appeal to persuade people by creating an appeal in the minds of people that they are inviting a risk if they do not purchase certain products. For example, if some company is selling fire extinguishers and the advertisement strategy achieves to show that buying extinguishers will save them and their family in case of a fire, it will have a positive impact on buying such products. There is always an ethical issue of not highlighting the undue amounts of fear, but in practicality, the grey areas also exist which depend on the persuading skill set a salesman and the person concerned inclined to buy a product for safety and security. The cognitive and emotional aspects are activated with an appeal to fears, and people are motivated to release the emotional tension by compliance to certain messages and recommendations used by advertisers.

The protection motivation is the tendency of the people to avoid threats related to health, safety and security of a person: verbal persuasion, visual imagery perceptions of fear, perceptions of norms, fear strength and other individual differences also play a role in the impact of advertisements on consumers' selling beauty.

Advertising is used for the promotion of cosmetic and beauty products aimed at women wishing to improve their appearances and attractiveness. Beauty advertising often seeks the consumers of the product value or even its necessity for the consumer's well-being and self-image/self-worth by the use of such products. Such advertising also aims at sex appeal in overt, covert or subliminal ways. One of the earliest known uses of sex in advertising is by the Pearl Tobacco brand in 1871, which featured a naked maiden on the package cover. Similarly, Jovan Musk oil, introduced in 1971, was promoted with sexual attraction properties. As a result, Jovan's revenue grew from $1.5 million in 1971 to $77 million by 1978.

Calvin Klein's advertisements became controversial in the mid-1990s. Lintas promoted Kamasutra condoms filled with erotic images of actors and actresses. Famous brands use advertising products with the help of celebrities. Beauty products promise consumers that they will look younger through the use of their products. Several products such as fragrance, eyeliner, soaps lipstick, have permeated in the lives of common and rich people. The size of the beauty industry is huge with enormous multi-billion dollar investments in the beauty business which are ever-growing at the global level.

There are a wide range of products available in the market related to skincare, hair care, health clubs, diet pills and fashion that seek to persuade customers to use them and improve positive feelings of confidence, social acceptance and joy. People have been conditioned by stereotypes that if they are not beautiful, they will not be successful and consumers start aspiring for perfection which advertisements promise.

Cosmeceutical is a combination of cosmetics and pharmaceuticals aimed at propagating anti-aging organics to improve both beauty and health, a perfectly ideal condition to be achieved by prospective consumers. Beauty is a currency in every known society of the world. Researchers (De Casanova, 2004; Hunter, 2002) note that smooth skin, thick hair, and symmetrical body are valued in most cultures. In the USA, people spend more money on personal care and beauty products than on reading materials, education or social services (EtCoff, 2000). In Japan and France, consumers spend over $230 per capita annually, USA and Germany spend $173 and $164 respectively and India spends $4 (Jones, 2012) on beauty products. In fact, L'Oréal (France) and Proctor & Gamble (USA) account for over one-fifth of total world sales of all beauty products (Jones, 2012). The impact of television on the beauty industry had far-reaching consequences that made beauty pageants into international media news events. The USA introduced a Miss Universe pageant in 1958 which was televised to many countries.

The number of women magazines grew, driven by global brands in need of advertising vehicles. Some of the famous women magazines like *Cosmopolitan*, *Vogue* and *Glamour* are also published in other languages to reach a larger audience.

Many researchers have noted a relationship between skin color and beauty that has become a form of "social capital" for women in many cultures (Hunter, 2002; Frith et al., 2005. Advertisements promise skin fairness, which is also related to marital prospects of women in the Indian context. In fact skin color is prescribed as a favorable proposition and the term "milky white" (*Dudhiya Gora*) is used in newspaper ads in the matrimonial columns. In India, the most successful fairness cream is the brand Fair & Lovely, produced by lex Hindustan Lever Ltd (HLL) (Challapalli, 2002) and fair skin is an obsession with women reiterated by extensive advertising for fairness creams (Karan, 2008).

6.2.7 From makeup to makeover

The global players of the beauty industry have made deep inroads in the Indian market with the huge growth of beauty parlors, cosmetic surgery and various types of makeovers supported by continuous advertisements through TV, magazines and other types of advertisements.

Reality television shows like *The Swan, Nip and Tuck, Extreme Makeover, Big Boss* (In India) and several others have become very popular. Marwick (2010) argued that shows like *The Swan* are examples of "Body culture media – a genre of popular culture which positions work on the body as a morally correct solution to personal problems."

Many women continually struggle to measure up to the increasingly mass-mediated pervasive version of what is beautiful, desirable and acceptable. This tendency to acquire beauty has an impact on their lives. These advertisements target children at a very young age through emphasizing looks as a fundamental asset exchangeable for social position, money even, for a loving partner. It is a kind of illusionary state that is almost impossible to satiate, but participation in the stereotypical role for new norms of beauty is ever-growing with psycho-social and health implications.

THINK BOX

- What can be the possible psychological influence of advertisement on consumer behavior?
- How do various companies use an advertisement to play with the psychology of their customers? Is it ethically appropriate?

6.3 Consumer advertising

Consumer advertising is directly related to influence the purchaser or consumer of the products or services. It is a process of making products or services known to the public through different techniques at persuasion to buy them. Consumer advertising takes place through television, radio, print, digital methods and sales promotion schemes to inform and persuade the public to buy.

Persuasive communication is defined as the process through which people attempt to influence the beliefs and actions of others. Persuasion is often used as a tool of personal or positional resources to change consumers' behavior or attitudes. The factors of reciprocation, consistency and commitment and authority influence the minds of consumers.

Reciprocity makes it possible to build a strong relationship through exchanges. According to the sociologist Alvin Gouldner (1960) the norm of reciprocity is nearly universal and only a few members of society – the very young, the sick or the old – are exempted from it. The principle of reciprocity is a powerful method for gaining compliance with consumers through advertising.

6.3.1 Consistency

The social pressure to be consistent is also known as a normative social influence which is frequently used in advertising. Once a person accepts the commitment, they want to be consistent with the decision. There is always an internal pressure to be consistent with our decisions when we know that other people are aware of their decisions. Repeatedly exposing the target by advertisers of a specific image helps to move the images from short-term memory to long-term memory. One of the most effective approaches for visual consistency is to repeat the same tagline, and imagery helps the consumer establish a connection with the brand.

6.3.2 Simplicity

In the process of consumer advertising, simple messages are more useful than complex messages. It is better to identify a single unique selling point as a salient feature of the advertisement. For example, news channel of India Today Group Aaj Tak uses the tagline Sabse Tej ("Fastest of all") to influence its users.

6.3.3 Scarcity

According to the scarcity principle of economics, the price of a good which has low supply and high demand rises to meet the expected demand, and marketers often use this principle to create artificial scarcity for a given product to improve its demand. Consumer disequilibrium is a situation of disruptions caused by internal or external factors that prevent market equilibrium from being reached. From a social psychology perspective, consumers place a higher value on goods that are scarce than on abundant goods. We quite often see advertisements like "super-discount" sale for festivals, "Limited time offer", and sale of few items left in the stock and so on to attract customers.

6.3.4 Authority

The authority principle refers to the human tendency to comply with people in positions of authority with the implicit assumption that people with authority positions have greater wisdom and knowledge. For example, Sachin Tendulkar talking of cricket tips will have a much higher impact on young cricketers as compared to other people talking about cricket on television. Similarly, Roger Federer talking about tennis-related game activity and products related to playing tennis will be easily accepted by the upcoming players of the game.

6.3.5 Advertisement through television

A television advertisement is one of the most popular means of advertisements throughout the world. The viewership of television programming is measured by companies like Nielsen Media Research in the United States on BARB in the UK. A television advertisement is a span of television programming produced and paid by an organization also known as a television commercial.

Television has also become digital, and billions of dollars are spent on TV commercials. Short commercial breaks are routine phenomena in all types of programs being telecast on TV channels. Animations are often used in advertisements and it is also combined with actors. Other techniques used in television advertisements make use of songs or slogans which are easy to remember by the viewers. In 1985 a Burger King advertisement used the original recording of Aretha Franklin's song "Freeway of Love" in a television advertisement for the restaurant, and in 1987 Nike used the original recording of The Beatles' song "Revolution".

In an advertisement for athletic shoes, music licensing agreements with the major artists, especially those that had not previously allowed their recordings to be used for this purpose, such as Microsoft's use of "Start Me Up" by the Rolling Stones and Apple's use of U2's "Vertigo" became very popular advertisements.

The term "Adstock" was coined by Simon Broadbent, and the Adstock theory suggests that exposure to television advertising builds awareness in the minds of consumers which ultimately influences their purchase decisions.

6.3.6 Brand awareness

Through television and other techniques, brand awareness is created through cognitive and affective states. Once activated, they influence the purchase decision of the consumers. Lavidge and Steiner (1961) proposed a six-stage model from brand awareness to the purchase of a product.

Stage I: Awareness: consumer becomes aware of the brand.

Stage II: Knowledge: consumer learns about the product.

Stage III: Liking: consumer develops a disposition.

Stage IV: Preference: consumer starts rating brands.

Stage V: Conviction: consumer demonstrates a desire.

Stage VI: Purchase: consumer acquires the product.

Brand awareness through recognition and recall processes can increase the probability that a consumer will include a given brand in his/her consideration. Repeated exposure to a brand can facilitate consumer processing by developing an attitude towards the brand.

Intensive advertisement programs are used by advertisers to expose people multiple times to a particular brand. The phenomenal growth of social media networks has added to the opportunities for opinion leaders to play a significant role in creating brand awareness. Bloggers, Twitter users and Facebook users have become dominant influencers in the advertising of consumer goods, services and ideas. The awareness of a product on social media sites leads to the spread of the brand and more people are exposed to the messages. Some advertisements like "Share a Coke" received multiple "Creative Effectiveness" awards at the Cannes Lions international festival of creativity, and this campaign led to huge sales in Australia.

6.3.7 Consumer advertising management

Advertising management is a complex process of developing strategies, planning, targeting the market, developing a message and evaluating the feedback of the advertising efforts and effectiveness. Advertising principles can't be employed in every situation. Rather, it is built to achieve a particular adjective. An integrated media and advertising campaign involves proper planning and execution of plans to establish brand awareness and its conversion into sales. The promotional mix is a method which comprises a variety of tools such as branded entertainment, public relations, personal selling, promotional items, event marketing and (sports music festival) exhibitions with a broad range of activities aimed at creating a single voice in favor of a product

The integrated attempt of communication tries to inculcate image integration with the relationship integration of consumers. Consumer advertising is an evolved technique involving huge expenditures on the part of organizations. There are several pre-test and post-test methods employed before launching a consumer advertisement program, as cost implications are involved in it. Qualitative and quantitative methods of research are applied to evaluate the effectiveness of consumer advertisement programs.

Choosing the right media channel or a combination of channels is decided to gain maximum advantage and cost-efficiency. Media planning is done to determine appropriate platforms to convey a message to the target audience, other demographic and geographical areas are also taken into account according to the objectives of the advertisement.

THINK BOX

- Is it just about earning more profit or there is something else that the companies aim to do while advertising their product? From the perspective of the customer, how do various advertisement tactics influence buying behaviour?
- In your views, what are the important things about consumer behaviour that a company might be taking into consideration while advertising its products?

6.4 Developing an effective advertisement

The basic premise of an advertising plan requires attention to some key considerations such as, what is the objective of advertising? For whom is the advertising related? What should be the message? And, what advertising medium needs to be adopted? A good advertising plan should mention the goals of advertising – for example, to attract current customers or potential future customers, improve the number of sales or simply improve the brand value of the product.

Another important aspect of a good advertising program is to specify the demographic characteristics of target customers and a close look at the needs and desires of the target customers. Selection of the right people and assigning them appropriate responsibilities are also important factors.

The message or central theme of the advertising needs to be finalized while keeping in view the profile of consumers. There are traditional mediums of the advertisement, but nowadays people spend considerable time on airports, railway stations and metro stations, and advertisers should prefer a place where the maximum number of the target audience may visit. Traditional media like television, radio, magazines, direct mail and telemarketing, and social media networks in recent times have become an influential media for advertisement.

6.4.1 Creativity

Creativity plays an important role by presenting ideas in a novel way so that it becomes artistic and attractive for the consumers. The novelty in a product by offering something that no one else has done so far at a low cost as compared to other competitions of the same product. Creativity is all about finding new ways to do things to obtain a strategic advantage.

The five M's of advertising include: Mission, Money, Message, Media and Measure (measuring effectiveness). They are prescribed as an effective way for advertising, but in today's era of global networks, innovativeness has to play a big role in the success of developing an effective advertising program.

6.4.2 Innovation

In 1934, Schumpeter added a definition of "innovation" or "development" as "new combinations" of new or existing knowledge resources, equipment and other factors (Schumpeter, 2008). According to Schumpeter's model, the trade cycle consists of two stages. The first stage deals with the initial impact of innovation which entrepreneurs introduce in their production process, and the second stage follows as a result of the reactions of competitors to the initial impact of the innovation.

According to Schumpeter, "creative destruction" is the essence of capitalism. Innovations are essential to facilitate economic growth and the entrepreneur is the central innovator. Tidd and Bessant (2013) described 4 P's of innovation as product, process, position and paradigm. Paradigm innovation is the change in the underlying mental models which frame what the organization does or how the company frames what it does.

6.4.3 Segmenting consumer markets

It is important to understand that strategy for consumers of airlines and the strategy for consumers of toothpaste should be different. Many purchasing decisions involve low risk or no risk, and the consumer also spends least efforts in decision-making for buying these products. In a situation of high-level involvement of buying at a high cost, buyers spend considerable effort before arriving at a decision.

Customers need to be segmented based on their knowledge, purchasing power, experience and need involved in the buying of a product. The most common basis of business segmentation is by the benefits customers derive from the product and process as service. Customers' requirements, existing needs to emerging expectations, need to be mapped while applying for an advertisement program.

6.5 Critical evaluation

Advertising has become an integral method to inform the people about products and services available in the market. Advertising plays an imperative role for both manufacturers and consumers. Advertising also helps business organizations to earn profits through influencing people by adopting various means and strategies. Advertising generates brand loyalty, attracts new customers and helps a business to compete with other businesses in the market. Advertising is necessary to popularize good products to the masses and provides information for comparison with other products and services.

Goods produced on a mass scale are marketed through advertising. Luxuries of life have acquired a significant place in the lives of people, and they work hard to achieve such intangible status by the use of luxurious products. Advertising is a well-developed field employing psychological, sociological and economic theories to persuade a large section of society. Advertising is completed through various channels of communication, and other innovative and unconventional approaches are used to do the advertising. The use of technology, television, internet, radio, newspapers and other methods is to ensure the commitment and loyalty of the consumers. Social media has also become a powerful tool in the world of advertising. A target audience is selected by the advertisers, and they accordingly design the strategy to identify customer needs with a differentiated and segmental approach. Communication platforms such as Twitter, Instagram and Facebook have become a wider stage as people are also influenced by the behavior of others. Nowadays, consumers also look at reviews forums before purchasing a product. The concept of the four P's of the marketing mix (product, price, place, promotion) proposed by McCarthy (1960), the four P's extended by 7 P's made up of original four P's and extended by three other P's – process, people and physical evidence (Booms & Bitner, 1980); the model of 4 C's – consumer, cost, convenience and communication) by Lauterborn's (1990) 7 M's of marketing (market, message, mission, message design, media strategy, money, measurement). The concept by David Bell and several other concepts have added to the diversity of ideas and complexity about the field of advertising.

In a far more complex world of advertisement theories and practitioners with an abundant surplus of products and services, it is difficult to prescribe a singular approach to an advertisement. But the fundamental principles related to emotions, credibility, novelty, attention and fear still hold importance in the techniques applied for persuasion.

There are numerous side effects also that advertising poses for society. Advertising creates a sense of discontent and negative stereotypes. Advertising also promotes materialistic desires exploiting our vulnerabilities to spend more and more, which seems endless. The selling of beauty and projecting masculinity breed discontentment among a large number of people. So many unhealthy lifestyles, like workaholism, unrealistic views of body image in advertisements and a faulty picture of reality impact the social and psychological satisfaction depletion among the masses, and children, in particular, are most vulnerable to advertisement effects owing to difficulty in distinguishing reality and fantasy. Political campaigns also acquire a vicious cycle through accusatory mud-slinging on their opponents. Smaller firms and businesses also face survival threats due to the over-dominance of products with a tremendous economic support base and global outreach with an excess of advertisements.

New challenges of coping with media in day-to-day life have been aggravated with advertisements on social media. The phenomenal increase in online marketing has also eroded the livelihood of people doing small street vendors' job. Emotional awareness and decision-making spread through innovative advertisement techniques also confuse people regarding the authenticity of products. The volume of media and popularity of the digital landscape has put many newspaper businesses redundant.

THINK BOX

- What are the things that you think, influence you in an advertisement and motivates to you buy a product or service?
- Do you think, it is ethical to highlight certain features of the products while hiding its possible negative effects, just to increase the sale of the product through advertisement?

6.6 Indian context

Ideally and ethically, advertisements' role is to inform and educate the society in general. But in a country like India where poverty and illiteracy are major problems, it becomes easier for the advertisers to highlight the lopsided view of products through mentioning the words of caution in small letters that they are unable to differentiate. It is no wonder that beauty products and services have created huge markets not only in urbanized places but also in smaller cities and villages

TV commercials often portray fast-food and frozen-food options as more fresh and natural, hence appealing to the consumers in remote areas of villages. The advertising of educational institutions promising a bright future when actually they are not in many situations is a very common practice due to lack of awareness of the uneducated parents. Advertisements of insurance companies, automobile companies, housing companies through aggressive marketing tactics provide loans to the consumers promising zero percent interest and several terms and conditions not properly highlighted while explaining it to the consumers. India has been turning into a major player of the EMI (equated monthly installments) scheme of business, a nation with a large number of its people adopting it. A large number of items available on EMI include cell phones, house maintenance, medical plans, gym memberships, airline tickets, cars, homes, televisions and refrigerators. The saving attitude of Indians has changed in the last few years, and now many things aspired by them are available at the EMI scheme. Tier II and Tier III cities constitute a majority of the Indian population, and this EMI scheme is a huge success by financial companies operating in such areas. There are many instances of fraud being committed upon innocent citizens that are reported by the media. Claiming to make the customers millionaires by paying a certain amount for some years is also the result of the negative effects of advertising.

The role of advertising is twofold of having positive and negative effects as consumers, and when the awareness level is low, chances are very high of harmful effects of advertising. So many consumer products become part of identity and status due to the dominance of advertising. Now the people in villages also treat the guests with items like pastries, cakes and soft drinks, ignoring their traditional way of providing treating guests. Similarly, people buy in village areas many products which are not needed, due to the effect of advertisement.

Finally, it can be said that consumers need to be made aware of the propaganda by advertisement companies and, in many cases, they need to be protected so that their hard earning to sustain their livelihoods is not blown with the wind of advertisement. At the same time, the positive aspect of advertisement of knowing credible products also can't be underestimated.

6.7 Summary

Media advertising requires an intricate understanding of the efficient media selection for an advertising campaign. Media advertising can involve various options such as television, radio, print advertising, internet and other out-of-home options such as billboards, signage, holographic images and mobile device advertising. Detailed research and evaluation of the targeted audience is an essential requirement for planning and advertisement campaigns.

A demographic variable like socio-economic status, educational backgrounds or gender also needs to be taken into account while formulating an advertisement campaign. An integrated communication strategy also needs to be selected highlighting the central messages to be promoted through promotional activities. Advertisement campaigns are designed to achieve a particular objective.

Establishing a brand and raising awareness for an advertisement campaign needs to integrate communication, marketing strategies and positioning of the messages to have clarity and impact on the audiences. Psychological factors play a major role in the overall design and success of the advertisement. The emotions play an important role in generating persuasion and favorable responses. Basic emotions like fear, pleasure and love appeal to vanity and is frequently used by the advertisers in making effective programs.

The attitude-behavior link proposition also inevitably influences consumer behavior. The creative strategy of preparing the message content plays a helpful role in the decision-making intent of the consumers. Several studies suggest a positive attitude-behavior link between advertisement campaigns and consumers' receptivity to the products.

Attentional processes also play a significant role in capturing consumers' attraction towards advertising products. Motivational theory suggests that people are motivated to buy certain products due to intrinsic and extrinsic factors of reward and satisfaction. Consumer psychology focuses more on the emotional aspects of the advertisement. The theory of social pressure, simplicity of messages and scarcity principles are used in developing successful consumer attraction strategies. Theorists like Harlow Gale in 1895 (Eighmey & Sar, 2007) describe the effects of advertising and attention on memory.

Walter Dill Scott (1903) described that people were highly suggestible and obedient. Harry Hollingworth wrote about the crucial role of attention in consumers' behavior. Brand positioning and brand architecture have acquired complex dimensions in the modern age of capitalism. Several theorists argue about the role of innovativeness (Schumpeter) in the process of effective advertising. Online advertising also has huge potential, and creating trustworthiness of brands will require more innovative ideas and strategies in the future times.

Key points

- Psychological factors of emotions play a crucial role in the process of advertising.
- The recognition is more sensitive than recall.
- Attention plays a paramount role in capturing the consumer's attention to the products.
- Pictorial representation attracts more attention than texts.
- Advertisers use several strategies to analyze and understand consumer motivation.
- Extrinsic motivation is defined as engaging in an activity to obtain an outcome that is separate from the activity itself.
- The concept of equity is stated as an event exchange of values such that what is received is presumed to be equal to what is given.
- The protection motivation is the tendency of the people to avoid threats related to health.
- Persuasive communication is the process through which people attempt to influence the beliefs and actions of others.
- Brand awareness through recognition and recall processes can increase the probability that a consumer will include a given brand in his consideration.

Key terms

emotion regulation, attentional deployment, antecedent states, equity, reciprocity, brand awareness, creative destruction, promotional mix, media strategy and paradigm innovation

References

Adams, J.S. (1965). Inequity in social exchange. In L. Berkowitz (Ed.), *Advances in Experimental Psychology* (pp. 267–99). New York: Academic Press.

Adler, R.P., & Firestone, C.M. (1997). *The Future of Advertising: New Approaches to the Attention Economy*. Washington, DC: The Aspen Institute.

Barrett, L.F., Ochsner, K.N., & Gross, J.J. (2007). On the automaticity of emotion. In J. Bargh (Ed.), *Social Psychology and the Unconscious: The Automaticity of Higher Mental Processes* (pp. 173–217). New York: Psychology Press.

Beck, J.C., & Davenport, T.H. (2001). *The Attention Economy: Understanding the New Currency of Business*. Boston, MA: Harvard Business Review Press.

Belk, R.W. (1975). The objective situation as a determinant of consumer behavior. In M.J. Schlinger (Ed.), *Advances in Consumer Research* (Vol. 2). Chicago, IL: Association for Consumer Research.

Biswas, U.N., & Biswas, S.N. (1997). Pro-economic attitudes and development: A cross-cultural study, *Psychology and Developing Societies*, 9(2), 225–43.

Booms, B.H., & Bitner, B.J. (1980). Marketing strategies and organisation structures for service firms. In J. Donnelly & W.R. George (Eds.), *Marketing of Services* (pp. 47–51). Chicago: American Marketing Association.

Broadbent, S. (1979). One way TV advertisements work. *Journal of the Market Research Society*, 23(3).

Bruner, G.C., II, & Kumar, A. (2000). Web commercials and advertising hierarchy-of-effects. *Journal of Advertising Research*, 40(1/2), 35–42.

Challapalli, S. (2002). All's fair in this market. *The Hindu Business Line*.

Cunningham, W., & Zelazo, P. (2007). Attitudes and evaluations: A social cognitive neuroscience perspective. *Trends Cognitive Science*, 11(3), 97–104.

De Casanova, E.M. (2004). No ugly women: Concepts of race and beauty among adolescent women in Ecuador. *Gender and Society*, 18(3), 287–308.

Deci, E.L. (1971). Effects of externally mediated rewards on intrinsic motivation. *Journal of Personality and Social Psychology*, 18, 105–15.

Eighmey, J., & Sar, S. (2007). Harlow Gale and the origins of the psychology of advertising. *Journal of Advertising*, 36(4), 147–58.

EtCoff, N.. (2000). *Survival of the Prettiest: The Science of Beauty*. Cambridge, MA: Harvard University Press.

Fazio, R.H. (1990). Multiple processes by which attitudes guide behavior: The MODE model as an integrative framework. In M.P. Zanna (Ed.), *Advances in Experimental Social Psychology* (Vol. 23, pp. 75–109). New York: Academic Press.

Finn, A. (1988). Print ad recognition readership scores: An information processing perspective. *Journal of Marketing Research*, 25(2), 168–78.

Frith, K.T., Shaw, P., & Cheng, H. (2005). The construction of beauty: A cross-cultural analysis of women's magazine advertisements, *Journal of Communication*, 55(1), 56–70.

Gouldner, A.W. (1960). The norm of reciprocity: A preliminary statement. *American Sociological Review*, 25, 161–78.

Gross, J.J. (1998). Antecedent- and response-focused emotion regulation: Divergent consequences for experience, expression, and physiology. *Journal of Personality and Social Psychology*, 74, 224–37.

Gross, J.J. (2002). Emotion regulation: Affective, cognitive, and social consequences. *Psychophysiology*, 39, 281–91.

Gross, J.J. (2008). Emotion regulation. In M. Lewis, J.M. Haviland-Jones, & L.F. Barrett (Eds.), *Handbook of Emotions* (3rd ed., pp. 497–512). New York, Guilford Press.

Gross, J.J., Sheppes, G., & Urry, H.L. (2011). Emotion generation and emotion regulation: A distinction we should make (carefully). *Cognition and Emotion*, 25, 765–81.

Helpman, E., & Krugman, P. (1985). *Market Structure and Foreign Trade*. Cambridge, MA: MIT Press.

Hunter, M.L. (2002). "If you're light you're alright": Light skin color as social capital for women of color. *Gender and Society* 16(2), 175–93.

Jacoby, J. (1976). *Consumer Psychology: An Octennium*. West Lafayette, IN: Purdue University.

James, W. (1950 [1890]). *The Principles of Psychology* (G. Miller, Ed.). New York: Dover Publications.

Jones, G. (2012). *Beauty Imagined: A History of the Global Beauty Industry*. New York: Oxford University Press.

Karan, K. (2008). Obsessions with fair skin: Color discourses in Indian advertising. *Advertising nd Society Review*, 9(2), 1–13.

Kroeber-Riel, W. (1984). Effects of emotional pictorial elements in ads analyzed by means of eye movement monitoring. In T.C. Kinnear (Ed.), *NA – Advances in Consumer Research* (Vo. 11, pp. 591–6). Provo, UT: Association for Consumer Research.

Krugman, P. (1986). *International debt: Systemic risk and policy response*: William R. Cline, (Institute for International Economics, Washington, 1984) pp. xix+317. *Journal of International Economics*, 20(3–4), 389–91.

Lauterborn, B. (1990). New marketing litany: Four P's passe, C-words take over. *Advertising Age*, 41, 26.

Lavidge, R.J., & Steiner, G.A. (1961). A model for predictive measures of advertising effectiveness. *Journal of Marketing* (October), 59–62.

Lucas, D.B. (1960). "The ABC's of ARF's PARM." *Journal of Marketing*, 25(1), 9–20.

Marwick, A. (2010). There's a beautiful girl under all of this: Performing hegemonic femininity in reality television, *Critical Studies in Media Communication*, 27(3), 251–66.

McCarthy, E.J. (1960). *Basic Marketing, A Managerial Approach*. Homewood, IL: Richard D. Irwin.

McClelland, D.C. (1961). *The Achieving Society*. New York: The Free Press.

Namasivayam, N., Ganesan, S., & Rajendran, S. (2006). Socioeconomic factors influencing the decision in taking life insurance policies. In *Insurance Chronicle* (pp. 65–70), The Icfai University Press.

Ogilvy, D. (1963). *Confessions of an Advertising Man*. New York: Atheneum.

Olson, M.A., & Fazio, R.H. (2006). Reducing automatically-activated racial prejudice through implicit evaluative conditioning. *Personality and Social Psychology Bulletin*, 32, 421–33.

Pavlik, J., & McIntosh, S. (2004). *Converging Media: An Introduction to Mass Communication*. Boston, MA: Pearson Allyn & Bacon.

Pieters, R., & Wedel, M. (2004). Attention capture and transfer in advertising: Brand, pictorial, and text-size effects. *Journal of Marketing*, 68 (April), 36–50.

Rossiter, J.R., & Percy, L. (1997). *Advertising Communications and Promotion Management* (2nd ed.). New York: McGraw-Hill.

Rothbart, M.K., Ziaie, H., & O'Boyle, C.G. (1992). Self-regulation and emotion in infancy. In N. Eisenberg & R.A. Fabes (Eds.), *Emotion and Its Regulation in Early Development: New Directions for Child Development*, No. 55: The Jossey-Bass education series (pp. 7–23). San Francisco, CA: Jossey-Bass.

Schumpeter, J.A. (2008). *The Theory of Economic Development: An Inquiry into Profits, Capital, Credit, Interest and the Business Cycle* (Translated from the German by R. Opie). New Brunswick, NJ and London: Transaction Publishers.

Scott, W.D. (1903). *The Theory of Advertising*. Boston, MA: Small, Maynard & Co.

Sheth, J.N. (1976). Buyer–seller interaction: A conceptual framework. In B.B. Anderson (Eds.), *NA – Advances in Consumer Behaviour* (Vol. 3, ACR Proceedings, pp. 382–6). Cincinnati, OH: Association for Consumer Research.

Tidd, J., & Bessant, J.R. (2013). *Managing Innovation: Integrating Technological, Market and Organizational Change* (5th ed.). Hoboken, NJ: Wiley.

Treisman A. (1960). Contextual cues in selective listening. *Quarterly Journal of Experimental Psychology*, 12, 242–8.

Treisman, A. (1964). Selective attention in man. *British Medical Bulletin*, 20, 12–16.

Walster, G.W. (1975). The Walster, et al. (1973) equity formula: A correction. *Representative Research in Social Psychology*, 6, 65–7.

Wilson, T.D., Lindsey, S., & Schooler, T.Y. (2000). A model of dual attitudes. *Psychological Review*, 107(1), 101–26.

7

MEDIA MESSAGES

Learning objectives

After reading this chapter, you will be able to understand:

- The relevance of media messages to individual and society
- The rhetorical perspective of media messages
- The cultural perspective of media messages
- The psychoanalytic perspective of media messages
- The feminist perspective of media messages
- The queer perspective of media messages
- Critical evaluation of media messages
- Indian perspective of media messages

7.1 Introduction

With so many technology options available to people, creating a brand in society requires adequate positioning of media messages. Media messages are constructed to bring particular kinds of effects on the audience. All media messages are composed with a purpose drawing on the audience's expectations and exemptions. There are many who and what questions that need to be analyzed to evaluate media messages, such as: Who created the message? Who is the target audience? What is the product? What are all direct and indirect messages? What is excluded from the message to understand them properly? Media are forms of communication in the newspapers, photographs, signs, movies, television. All these contain stories of one kind or another created by authors. Different types of media messages appeal to people's minds and they interpret it by making sense of it. Deconstructing a media message can help us understand the originator of media content, their purpose, values and biases and for whom this media content has been constructed.

There are two broad formats for the delivery of media messages. The traditional media includes broadcast and print formats, and new media includes digital formats of social media and image formats. These have their strengths and weaknesses.

The spread of media messages reinforces certain types of values that have the power to persuade people and influence behavior. People have a certain degree of dignity of credibility and associations linked to media messages, expressed through writing or visual presentations.

Selective use of media-related information has also led to cyber balkanization. This means the way media consumers filter the incoming information.

7.1.1 Text without context

How are news articles for music and videos shared upon digital media reshaping the political, social and cultural landscape and affecting lives by creating a sense of subjectivity? The emergence of several media platforms allows the consumers to adopt migratory behavior of media usage of going anywhere in search of information, communication and entertainment. Media messages and their content can affect the socio-cultural aspect of life in a society.

7.1.2 Medium and audience

Media messages through the processes of priming and other psychological factors influence the audience's beliefs, attitudes and behaviors. Behavioral effects of disinhibition that legitimize the use of violent behavior through exposure, imitation through learning from others and desensitization in which continuous exposure leads indifference to violent scenes are cultivated through media messages. Media messages also influence public behavior through its modes of presentation, such as sensationalism in which favored aspects are presented in a selective manner, distorting the real picture.

Media messages through reciprocal transactions with audiences functioning as mediators between information producers and information receivers. Audiences learn and cultivate their opinions about political, social and economic realities through the use of media messages. With so many people dependent on information from mass media sources, media messages hold the power to perpetuate the delivery of realistic or manipulated information to its users. The ownership of media messages being limited to few people also reduces the possibility of media pluralism, and many important aspects of social reality are excluded by the dominant media power.

The idea of freedom of speech is compromised if sources of opinion formation and dissemination of information are not allowed to the citizens in a democratic system. One of the fundamental features of democracy is the government by the people, but this essential ideal cannot flourish if media messages manipulate the electorate by withholding information and ignoring criticism. The accountability of governance can be ensured only when citizens' voices are free, and this is possible with the spread of messages to them through media. Freedom of speech and free discussion promote more equitable social interaction.

The proliferation of media messages through contemporary media technologies and the internet have created a steady flow of transnational images that connect audiences worldwide. Globalization and homogenization of culture have become important concepts shaped by media messages. Mass media messages involve complex relationships between large sets of interacting variables, and media effects are different due to the complexity of interacting key variables. Societal structures, political stability or instability, economic situation, individuals' choice of media and awareness level of the consumers are some of the variables that determine the effect of media messages. The potential for media messages to achieve a broad range of cognitive, affective and behavioral effects increases when media messages serve as a unique and central source of information. Charles H. Cooley (1909) long ago used the term "enlargement" to refer to the idea about people's knowledge and belief systems expanding because they learn about other people, places and things from mass media. Altman and Taylor (1973) talked about the "breadth" dimension of belief structure, which refers to the number of categories in a belief system and how many beliefs are found in each category. The vast amount of information disseminated through media platforms has certainly enlarged the people's beliefs about everything, including fashion, food, health and entertainment. Mass media messages also have an impact on the value systems of the people.

Fear, anxiety and happiness messages are also inculcated through prolonged exposure to media messages in emotion-laden programs of mass media. Klapp (1972) has proposed that in societies in which mass media play central communication roles, the nature of media information has a substantial effect on people's morale and the degree of alienation. Merton (2002 [1946]) examined how a radio marathon featuring a well-known singer of that era (Kate Smith) activated large numbers of people to buy war bonds.

7.1.3 Media messages and its meanings

In the complex marketplace of the contemporary era, the lines between marketing and public relations are blurring at a rapid pace. With most branded entities jumping blindly into the social media space, the types of messages being sent and the brand portrayal are becoming increasingly important for consumers. Media messages supplied through different media platforms are strongly related to communication principles and practices rather than the mere use of technology.

Metaphors play an important role in the construction of social, cultural and political reality. Metaphors are used by media messages to communicate or transform complex ideas into simple or familiar ones by presenting only one perspective and blocking other viewpoints. Metaphors can be used in different forms to create positive or negative images through the use of language. The principle of symbolization highlights that the messages attach particular meanings that become objects of orientation for people to elicit specific feelings and actions. The role of emotions in messages can activate emotional awareness among users and have a significant impact on the behavior of people. The nature and impact of mass media messages are difficult to decode as they constitute and integrate into cultural forms.

7.1.4 Symbolic interactionism

The symbolic interactionist approach to mass media stresses social interaction and social context in understanding the social impact of new information technology (Maines & Couch, 1988; Surratt, 2001).

Media messages produce meanings through a process of symbolic interaction between one actor and another, such as between TV viewers and the programs on television. Media messages are not monologic but dialogic, trilogic and multilogic, that influence everyday life, social interactions and functioning of social institutions. The blurring of boundaries between communication modes and communication formats leads to the circulation of media messages. These formats become important in their own right, shaping the rhetoric frames including power and ideology. So many institutions of relevance with the continuous flow of messages such as religion, sports, politics and family are transformed into media-mediated reality institutions. The ecology of communication operates with the help of rules and logic of media technology-generated communication experiences. As Carey and others note, the extension of electronics into everyday life, or what they term the "electrical sublime" (Carey, 1989, p. 123), did not produce the utopia sought and predicted by many, but it had consequences for adding machinery, format and logic for getting things done, for communicating. In this age, one's competence is often judged by communicative performance, but this performance increasingly involves the direct or indirect manipulation done by information technology and communication forums.

Broadcasting which was aimed at reaching the masses has turned into "narrowcasting" to a specific and targeted audience with an aim to market products and services. The emphasis of media messages has shifted from welfare and news to entertainment, with media messages to a large extent being dominated by the elements of drama, conflict and even violence. Public space is a communication space created through mass media, and with the emergence of e-audience, communicating skills have become an extension of technological persona. Television and social media have become more important because of the visual nature of the information being transmitted as well as its capacity to transcend temporal and cultural boundaries. A key part of the communication order is to give the audience what the message "procedures" believe they will accept and find entertaining (Barrow, 1990). According to Snow (1983), one formula that has been used for this is following "idea norms". The collapsing of symbolic boundaries has produced a hybrid array of messages and views of social reality that has been delineated as post journalism news media (Altheide & Snow, 1991).

7.1.5 Technology and media

The new technological formats have affected human perception and blurred the boundaries of public and private self through messages on social media platforms.

Problem frame is used by media messages to satisfy the entertainment aspect of news and helps in the commodification of news in the form of fear. Several strategies are adopted by the producers of news to help people identify and interact with the message. Problem frame is presented in a story form with an emphasis on cultural resonance and highlighting of local items.

7.1.6 Explicit and implicit messages

Several possible mismatches can happen in speakers' intended messages and recording of the messages by the receivers and their interpretation. The process of interpretation is not a straight line of decoding but an outcome of a complex process of the hearer's interpretation influenced by a variety of factors such as expectations, knowledge, interest, beliefs and the communication style.

Contextual factors also play a role in the match or mismatch across intention, reception and interpretation of messages. There is also a possible range of continuum that exists in the utterances and reception of explicit and implicit messages. Bach (1998) analyzed the process of standardization according to which an utterance goes beyond the literal meaning and yet can be explained without special conventions.

Sometimes speakers do not communicate explicitly, demanding extra efforts in understanding and also risking the breakdown of successful communication. Sometimes explicit meanings get replaced by implicit meanings owing to media pressure imposed on the readings of the text. For example, in the film *In Your Dreams* (O. Parker, BBC2, 14 December 1997) one can easily feel the conflict between the explicit and implicit aspects of the same utterance and related social pressure imposed upon these readings.

7.1.7 Media messages and value predispositions

Cognitive psychologists have found that people are "cognitive misers" who predominantly use heuristic cues such as value predispositions and information shortcuts provided by mass media to form judgments and reach decisions about emerging science and technology. According to this perspective, knowledge levels are not a major determinant of public attitudes. Heuristic processing occurs when individuals employ the principle of least effort by using simple decision rules to make a judgment about an issue (Chaiken et al., 1989).

People often use knowledge and values while forming attitudes about certain objects, events and ideas. Their trust in something being considered as "scientific" has a strong relationship with their attitudes. The media messages frames the act as "thought organizers" and used as heuristics to form a judgment about the topics about which people have very limited knowledge.

Idealized images portrayed by media create a social value which creates pressure to strive for achieving the ideal image. The social worth of a person is also affected negatively by continuous exposure to idealized images, and their desire for interpersonal social interaction is also reduced. Media images and messages contain intended and unintended effects that are indirectly conveyed through advertisements. Media messages highlight health-related fears to advertise health products, which are very effective in stimulating self-relevant emotions and promoting them to buy the product to secure self-protection. Product integrations involve brands being highlighted through TV serial programs or stories in the films. Affective classical conditioning takes place when the pairing of good feelings is associated with the brands.

The perception of the audience can be achieved through product integrations and product placements in the form of entertainment. When consumers realize that a given communication is an attempt to persuade, they process the messages differently as compared to when no specific recognition is decoded. As compared to the adults, the young children perceive the advertised messages without precisely discriminating the intent and reality of advertising messages.

Media messages inevitably persuade as well as entertain through meanings and meanings cannot be neutral as they always convey a point of view. Media messages can be analyzed through various perspectives and important among them are rhetorical, cultural, psychoanalytic, feminist and queer perspectives.

7.2 Rhetorical analysis

Media messages are conveyed in a range of guises and make meaning through a variety of means in a media-saturated environment. The texts and subtexts of media are contextualized to offer different meanings. It is very difficult to decipher what media texts mean to the receivers of media messages, and at the best, they derive generalized comprehension.

Rhetoric refers to the ancient art of oratory through construction and manipulation of language by the creator of a text for affective purposes. The rhetorical analysis attempts to understand media texts and their meanings as constructed with the use of styles, techniques and conventions in any medium. The purpose of construction is to elicit attention, aid cognition and secure emotional, psychological and behavioral responses from them.

Lloyd Bitzer (1968) has identified the three constituent parts of rhetorical situation, namely exigence (problem existing in the world), audience and constraints (ideological make-up of persons and events). The key elements of rhetorical efforts are the struggle to create chosen audiences and the struggle to infuse the selected situation or facts with meaning. The concern in the rhetorical approach is not whether the situation on the rhetor is "dominant" but the extent in each case, to which the rhetor can discover and control indeterminate matter, using his art of topics to make sense of what would otherwise remain simply absurd.

7.2.1 Rhetorical media tools and techniques

- *Verbal rhetoric*: verbal rhetoric refers to the written or spoken vocabulary used in media communication. Different styles of words are chosen by media channels and newspapers to draw affective responses from the audience. Each broadcasting medium chooses particular rhetorical devices to have an increased influence on its audience. Sometimes the use of words are plain and simple, sometimes populist and on other occasions sensational or providing more importance to pictures than to words.

- *Alliteration*: alliteration is the repetition of starting letters of words in a sentence effectively creating a kind of rhythm. Two classic examples are "she sells seashells by the sea-shore" and "Black bug bit a big black dear". It makes the news item or name of a company or brand more catchy and easy to memorize and some common examples are PayPal, Bed Bath & Beyond and Coca-Cola. Alliteration creates a musical element in the text which becomes more attractive and appealing.

- *Rhymes allusion*: allusions make direct or indirect references to other ideas, places, people or texts which can generate affective responses. An allusion occurs when a person or author makes an indirect reference in speech text or song to an event on another figure. Take for example, "His wife was his Achilles' heel"; this is a mythological allusion and a clear reference to Achilles from *The Iliad* by Homer. His only point of weakness was in his heel. Another example is, "He met his waterloo as soon as he ventured outside the safe zone". Waterloo simply means to be crushed and defeated. It has become a common reference to the Battle of Waterloo in 1815, in which Napoleon Bonaparte's troops were crushed by Coalition European forces which also forced him to go into exile.

- *Euphemism*: euphemism refers to the substitution of more acceptable terms for those that might offend some people. This can also be described as used in place of offensive language which is mild, indirect or vague term. For example, "ethnic cleansing" is more suitable than "genocide".

- *Metaphor*: a metaphor is a phrase used to describe something as it was something else. Writers use metaphors to add color and weight to what they are trying to express. For example, if you say this person has a "sea of knowledge", you are using a metaphor to express how knowledgeable the person is. "Knowledge" and "Sea" are not literally related, but both are figuratively related because they are vast things difficult to measure. Another example: "all religions, arts and science are branches of the same tree" (Albert Einstein).

- *Metonym*: a metonym is a figure of speech in which a thing or concept is not called by its name but by the name of something intimately associated with that thing or concept. For example, "Soon the corrupt politician will be in the big house" (the big house refers to jail), or "the pen is mightier than the sword" ("pen" refers to written words and "sword" to military force).

- *Ellipses*: an ellipse (plural: ellipses) is a series of dots that usually indicate an intentional omission of a word or sentence from a text without altering its original meaning. In rhetoric, an ellipsis is the omission of one or more words from a sentence. For example: "So ... what happened?"
- *Cliché*: a cliché refers to an expression that loses its novelty or meaning because of overuse. For example, "alive and kicking" is a doublet cliché. Both words in the context mean much the same thing.
- *Presentational rhetoric*: presentational rhetoric, or how messages are presented such as accents, volume, emphasis, pace and pauses also affect the nature of the response to media messages by the audience. The term used by the media presenter relating to the language of everyday speech has greater impact as compared to the use of formal languages.

Television presenters should care about non-verbal aspects along with verbal aspects of delivery which contribute to the effectiveness of messages. Presentational rhetoric allows for the way through which sound can be used to create space, distance and ambience.

Most films and TV programs employ Foley operators to create sounds to support the images we see in order to accentuate "realism" and "verisimilitude" (Yewdall, 2007). Media messages and words are amplified and obscured to create a variety of positive effects on the audience.

Drawings, collages and animations are used to create particular rhetorical effects in the messages through photography. The pointing of the camera and rhetorical organization of shots can create an effect of a connection in space and time, contributing to affective response.

7.2.2 Analytic tools

Semiology literally means the study of "signs" and is considered useful in studying media communication. Three prominent thinkers conceptualized signs as important means to convey shared meanings in communication: Ferdinand de Saussure (1857–1913), Charles Sanders Peirce (1835–1914) and Roland Barthes (1915–80). Saussure defined his unique approach to linguistic semiology as "a science which studies the role of signs as part of social life. It would investigate the nature of signs and the laws governing them".

According to Saussure, linguistic signs comprised a combination of signifier and signified. The signifier or sound image refers to the material form of a sign perceived by the senses, such as the word "Dog" listened by a listener. The signifier is a mental concept elicited by the signifier, in this case the idea of "Dogness". Saussure further described that signs are arbitrary, and no certain relationship between signifier and signified exists. Saussure also talked about langue and parole which means the linguistic system and individual speech acts or utterances, respectively. Saussure suggested that the signs signify by the virtue of their distinctiveness from other signs, which may not be universal but social.

Peirce called his program semiotic (semiotke), which is "the quasi necessary, or formal, doctrine of signs". Peirce talked about the triadic relation between sign (representamen) object and the interpretant also classified signs into three categories of icons, indices and symbols. According to Peirce, iconic signs operate on the logic of similarity or likeness, and examples are diagrams, maps and images. Indexical signs are linked by the association to the objects they represent and described that "anything which focuses the attention is an index"; for example, the "rap on the door" as it draws our attention to someone's arrival. Symbols are the third category of signs which Peirce argued, "All words, sentences, looks and other conventional signs are symbols".

Barthes famously introduced the distinction between denotation and connotation in *Elements of Semiology* (1967). Barthes described denotation as first-order signification purely denotative (image of the signifier) and second-order signification which operates at the level of myth. For example, while "Dog" may evoke similar mental images throughout different cultures (denotative meanings), the connotative meaning of dog can vary greatly from culture to culture (such as pet family member or non-vegetarian food). Our conceptualizations of the world are guided strongly by language which also acts as a constitutive way to its understanding.

Saussure suggested that when words which are millions in number combined according to rules of grammar acquire significance and communicate effective meanings. Smiley faces, for example, are an example of an iconic relationship that describes the physical similarity between a sign and its object.

Different signs combined in different ways have their effects on the connotations of texts resulting in different readings and interpretations of signs. Umberto Eco (1979) described the relations of signs and their code when combined with many signs produces different meanings, and modes of preferred and aberrant readings can be adopted by the receiver. In preferred reading, similar codes exist between creator and receiver, whereas in aberrant reading code is used in production but the text is read using another.

Therefore, different readings that might be made of a text are the result of various aberrant readings made possible by the use of diverse codes. Media languages are guided by rhetorical techniques used to direct and anchor meaning.

7.2.3 Text and rhetorical structures

A text is a set of signs related to each other insofar as their meanings contribute to the same set of effects or functions. There are a variety of combinations of pattern signs that can exist in media texts being produced by media platforms of the internet, video games and television. Certain rhetorical structures are preferred in many media which includes clusters, form, genre and narrative.

Clusters: one of the basic rhetorical structures in texts is the cluster, or the way individual signs are related to one another. Kenneth Burke's theory of dramatism

(1952) and his concepts of purification cycle and methods of identification have been extensively used to analyze speech communication. Dramatism is mainly concerned with speakers' motives or scenes according to which action is determined. For example, "according to the Marxist Calculus – Workers everywhere share the same social motives since they all have the 'factory situation' in common" (Burke, 1952, p. 45) The factory situation serves as a terministic screen behind which laborers achieve identification (Burke, 1973). These five factors of act, scene, agent, agency and purpose are known as pentad, which can help identify the underlying motives on causes for a particular speaker. The purpose of public addresses is to remove guilt through redemption which is possible when the individual engages either in mortification or victimage. Victimage is the process through which the speaker diverts responsibility for the polluting act by implicating a third party, the scapegoat (Cragan & Shields, 1998). New rhetoric strategies focus more on identification and partially unconscious factors in an appeal to persuade the audience. Linguistic drama uses the clustering of terms to influence the attitude of its audience. Burke defined clusters as "what goes with what" and agents as "what is vs. what". Even war-like activities can obtain support with the deliberate depiction of enemy characterized in an evil and tyrannical way and presenting them as a conflict of good versus evil. Cluster terms may include images or direct verbal reference to highlight or modify god and devil terms.

Form: another important rhetorical structure in texts is in the form, which is arousing and leads to the fulfillment of desires. According to K. Burke (1969), "A work has form in so far as one part of it leads a reader to anticipate another part, [and] to be gratified by the sequence". "The arrows of our desires", Burke writes, "are turned in a certain direction and the plot follows the direction of the arrows". Burke described four general varieties of form: progressive form, repetitive form, conventional form and minor forms. Each serial or program progresses in the television dramas through providing clues and achieving the final goal in stages.

7.2.4 Visual rhetoric images

Visual rhetoric makes use of semiotics and attempts to describe signs within a contextual perspective. Visual objects are analyzed with the help of literal components, purpose of image and evaluation of its effect on the audience. Visual images play a vital role in its spread to a large audience with the availability of social media platforms. Some of the images go "viral", attracting the attention of millions owing to versatility and novelty factors. Advertisers can associate their products with the images to attract larger attention and provide the consumer tendency to link the product with the presented image.

Genre: genre (from the French *genre*, meaning kind) is a kind or class of messages (written, spoken, digital, artistic) that has distinctive stylistic criteria developed through conventions. Popular TV genres are soap operas, crime, talk shows, comedy and variety of entertainment programs. Various types of genres are used in popular culture in this electronic age, and dividing cultural products by genres has increased the number of consumers in a specific genre. Genre theorists have also used the terms for analyzing as "genre systems", "genre ecologies" which emphasizes genres as types or actions rather than types or forms of text. Though all the genres are not well received by the audiences, a few among them receive good responses from the audience through symbolic inducements.

Narrative: Gerard Genette (1930–2018) described that narrative can be divided into three levels: story, discourse and narrating. Events in a story should be described chronologically to have better effects. It is also important to establish a link between the happening of an event and its narration, which is known as discourse time and narrative time. The perspective of the narrator known as focalization can acquire internal or external focus. Temporal relations, mood and voice play an important role in the persuasion of audiences. The narrator can transport audiences to the past through flashbacks (analepses) or into the future through flash-forwards (prolepses) through effective use of narrative temporality.

How many times an event is narrated by the narrator and the voice plays a crucial role in the identification of the story by audiences. In some of the television shows, the story is told from the perspective of the narrator, and gradually viewers start identifying to see the world from the narrator's perspective.

Affect and aesthetics: the elements of music such as melody, harmony and rhythm can have a strong influence on people's affects. Affect consists of immediate modes of sensual responsiveness to the world, characterized by an accompanying imaginative dimension. Media aesthetics grew out of contributions from important theorists such as media philosophy (Fredorich Kitler) media ecology (Marshall McLuhan), medium theory (Joshua Meyrowitz), mediology (Regis Debray), critical theory (Walter Benjamin) new media (Mark Hansen) and visual culture (W.J.T. Mitchell). Media aesthetics emphasizes the importance of understanding media technologies, aesthetics (sense perception) and mediation. A high level of technological mediation redirects human attention to material and physical practices which ultimately shape the way people process sensory data and therefore serve as the basis of human meaning-making.

The role of technology to produce meanings in the media texts can be modified with differential use of color, lighting, editing, sound and framing to produce emotions. Films such as *Batman Begins* (2005) and *The Dark Knight* (2008) used darkness to create a general sense of malaise. Empathy and feelings may be crucial to our aesthetic experiences and our experiences of art.

The high emotional contagion leads to greater physiological arousal which contributes to a feeling of being moved. Other important aspects of personality and contextual factors also influence the differences in the response pattern of aesthetic experiences. More empathizing art can lead to profound and deeper aesthetic experiences which can greatly influenced by media presentation techniques.

7.2.5 Rhetorical analysis: a critical evaluation

Rhetoric is a technique used to bring desired influence on the audience through the use of styles, oratory, techniques to elicit attention, cognition and behavioral responses from them. The texts and subtexts are used by media channels to draw affective responses from the audience. Various techniques of metaphor, ellipses and clichés are used to aid impact to what is being conveyed. Analytical tools of semiology, clusters, forms, genre and narrative are applied to identify persuasive techniques used to appeal to the audience. Aesthetic elements of music mediated through technology are also widely applied to provide meaning to media texts. Rhetoric is an often-repeated technique used by media and other people involved in the process of persuading mass opinion.

THINK BOX

- Think of some ways in which the political parties use media in order to evoke emotions of people.
- Identify any five websites that you use most frequently and try to find out their focus area.

7.3 Cultural analysis

Mass media messages often contribute to the development of new cultural techniques. Media texts, hypertexts, visual texts and images combined with technological strategies have brought micro- and macro-level changes in the behavior and culture of the people. Media technologies are far from just technologies, and the mediating role of media through interactive tools shapes our perceptions, attitudes and behavior, creating its own culture. McLuhan (1964) observed that "we shape our tools and thereafter our tools shape us". McLuhan described media as prostheses, in terms of extension of physical and mental capacities. The design of specific technologies for media interaction influences cognition created interactive functions that can significantly impact cultural practices symbolically. Cultural influences manifest into social norms, attitude towards the negotiation of daily lives, sense of self and broader orientation of behavior of the people at a given point of time. Media messages, through the process of mediation and communication, modify and transform behavioral patterns and public opinion.

Media does not necessarily bring the transformation; rather, it co-constitutes the notions and perceptions to form it as a part of mainstream culture. Through tactical approaches, media technologies circulate messages claiming it to be normal and necessary for day-to-day living and for fulfillment of the aspirations to be successful for happy living. Media messages inform the ways through which media portrayed behavior as appropriated by people through the spread.

Dynamic information dissemination involves public participation interactively, and it is argued that the objective of media is to inform the second-order effect of cultivation. Media messages, having large access to people for communicating a variety of etiquettes, claim to free the flow of communication and tend to customize them for their likings and dislikings. Culture evolves with new ideas and things added to society through inventions and discoveries which can be material or rhetoric.

7.3.1 Content analysis

Cultural analysis of media messages can be done with the help of deconstruction of pieces of media with either quantitative or qualitative methods. Media content analysis was introduced as a systematic method to study mass media by Harold Lasswell (1927) initially to study propaganda. Media content analysis is used to see how people react to media messages and analyze the ideologies in the texts and transcripts aimed at producing certain cultural patterns of behavior.

7.3.2 Mass media messages and persuasion

Media and culture have strong interlinkages as different techniques of persuasion adopted to influence the behavior of people. Video games became a prominent source of glorifying violent culture among teenagers and youth drawing inspiration from them.

On 20 April 1999 students Eric Harris and Dylan Klebold entered Columbine High School in the Denver, Colorado, area and killed 12 classmates and one faculty member before committing suicide (Lamb, 2008). Studies such as one conducted by Dr. Chris A. Anderson (Anderson & Murphy, 2003) and others point to correlations between the amount of time spent playing violent video games and increased incidence of aggression. Other researchers suggest that individuals prone to violent acts are indeed drawn to violent behavior. However, they claim that by keeping these individuals in a movie theatre or at home, violent media have contributed to a reduction in violent social acts (Goodman, 2008). It is a fact that media messages stir emotional responses from the audience, and through interaction and overuse of a particular type of emotional response, they can influence the behavior of that person. While many parents are hesitant to discuss sex with their children, the media can act like a digital peer, providing sex-related information through movies, television, internet and magazines.

Online collectivism and social networking are changing the way people think and process information, and the question of originality and imagination gets blurred. The fragmentation of data that the web produces is broken into bits and bytes with emphasis on immediacy, and the rising tide of data does not offer space for critical thinking to the users. Internet-mediated messages create a culture of speed and tendency for drowning in the data, where sensationalism and hyperbole grab people's attention. It is also a growing trend among the people to jump to a conclusion without consideration of context and source of verification to be relevant in the online debate of proving superiority.

Internet-mediated messages are also becoming useful for teaching, social activities or providing help to people and communities in distress.

THINK BOX

- How do media messages influence culture? Think of some examples from your own life where you see the influence of media on the cultural practices you follow.
- Do you think media can help in developing various cultural practices that can make human life better? If yes, how?

7.4 Psychoanalytic analysis of media messages

Structure of personality: according to Freud, the personality of a person is comprised of three major systems called Id, Ego and Superego, each of which has its unique properties and contributes to human behavior. All three systems interact together, and behavior is almost the product of an interaction among these three systems. The Id is described as consisting of everything that is inherited and considered as a reservoir of psychic energy. Freud called the Id "true psychic reality" because it represents the subjective realms of inner experiences, having no knowledge of objective reality. The Id operates on the pleasure principle to release the tension of individual for avoiding pain and obtaining pleasure.

The *Id* operates based on two processes known as reflex actions and primary process. Reflex actions are automatic responses of an individual without any effort which is the inborn capacity of the person, and reactions of sneezing and blinking our eyes in case of the same dangers are examples of this mechanism. The primary process has a unique property of forming an image of an object that will overcome tension. For example, a person can have mental pictures of food items when hungry, and this is known as wish fulfillment.

The *Ego* operates on the basis of the reality principle and tries to achieve the needed object in reality and reduce the tension caused to a person. The ego also operates through a secondary process of making plans to achieve the objective through cognitive and higher mental processes. Ego is also known as the true executive of the personality as it guides the appropriate course of action suitable for achieving the desired objectives.

The *Superego* is the third system of personality structure, representing traditions, values and ideals of the society. The Superego represents the moral aspects and aims for perfection related to the ideals of society. The Superego consists of the internalized values that develop in response to the reward and punishment patterns adopted by parents and elders in the society which become part of the conscience of a person. The main function of the superego is to inhibit the impulses of Id which are not acceptable to societal norms and substitute moralistic goals for the realistic goal of Ego and aim for perfection.

Instincts: Freud talked about psychic energy which can be transformed into physiological energy and vice versa. Instincts act as a bridge between the energy of the body and of the personality. Freud considered that mental images of bodily needs expressed in the form of desires are called instincts. Any behavior performed without any formal training, experience or learning and regulated by innate biological factors are called instincts. For example, honeybees communicate by dancing in the direction of its food sources which are difficult to be described. Instinct is a quantum of psychic energy, or as Freud put it, "a measure of the demand made upon mind for work" (1946).

With the publication of his book *Beyond the Pleasure Principle* in 1920, Freud described two major categories of instincts: life instincts (eros), which deals with basic survival and pleasure, and death instinct (thanatos) such as aggressions and self-harm.

Development of personality: according to Freud, personality is formed through conflicts among the three main structures of Id, Ego and Superego in response to the sources of tension, arising due to physiological growth, frustrations, conflicts and threats. Identification and displacement are the two main methods adopted by individuals to resolve conflicts and threats. A child strongly identifies with the parents as they hold an omnipotent force during the early years of childhood. It is important to highlight that most of the identification takes place unconsciously.

Displacement: when an original object-choice of instinct is not achieved owing to certain external limitations, a new object choice is formed as a substitute which is similar to the original object choice.

> Interests, attachments and all other forms of acquired motives endure because they are to some degree frustrating as well as satisfying. They persist because they fail to yield complete satisfaction. Every compromise is at the same time a renunciation. A person gives up something that he really wants but can't have, and accepts something second or third best that he can have.
>
> (Hall, 1954/1979, p. 104)

Freud pointed out that the development of civilization was made possible by the inhibition of primitive object choices and the diversion of instinctual energy into socially acceptable and culturally creative channels. A displacement that is transformed into higher cultural manifestation is called sublimation. Freud observed in this connection that Leonardo da Vinci's interest in painting Madonna was a sublimated expression of a longing tor intimacy with his mother, from whom he had been separated at a tender age (Freud, 1910).

7.4.1 Defense mechanisms

To get relief from excessive anxiety, ego adopts mechanisms to deny or distort reality and it operates unconsciously. The principal defenses are repression, projection, reaction formation, fixation and regression (Anna Freud, 1946).

Repression: it occurs when a person fails to achieve the desired goal and undue pressure is created in conscious memory which may find expression in a disguised form.

Projection: it is a process of substituting a lesser threat for a greater threat, and sources of anxiety are attributed to the happenings of the external world rather than to the individual's own internal mechanisms.

Reaction formation: in this defense mechanism, producing impulse is replaced by its opposite; for example, hate is replaced by love.

Fixation and regression: each developmental stage has a set of characteristics that a person exhibits, but when this progress of transition from one stage to another does not take place, fixation is said to have occurred.

In the defense mechanism of regression, the person retreats to earlier stages of development due to difficulties to cope with the challenges of the current stage. For example, a child who has difficulty adjusting on the first day of school may indulge in infantile behavior of weeping.

7.4.2 Stages of development

Freud described dynamically differentiated stages of development during the first few years before adolescence which is extremely crucial and decisive for the formation of personality in the future course of life. Each stage during the first five years is defined and the basis of the relation of a particular body zone.

The Oral stage: this stage lasts till the first year of childhood, and the principal source pleasure is derived from the mouth. The oral activity provides through acts of biting and chewing, and disturbances in these activities may result in oral complexes at later stages of development.

The Anal stage: during this stage, anal zone activities are a principal source of pleasure, and difficulty in expulsion of feces creates discomfort, leading to development of complexes during later stages. The method of toilet training used by children and concerns shown during defecation has implications for the future character development of children. This stage lasts till the second year.

The Phallic stage: after the period of two years, the phallic stage begins in which sexual organs become the leading erogenous zones. The pleasure of masturbation and the fantasy life of the child combined with autoerotic activity set the stage for appearance of the Oedipus complex. Named after the king of Thebes, the Oedipus complex consists of sexual attachment for the parent of the opposite sex and hostile feelings for the parents of the same sex. This stage continues from three to five years of age.

The Genital stage: the earlier stages of Oral, Anal and Phallic are known as pre-genital stages, and the child goes for some quiet years of latency and then enters the final stage of maturity. During the Genital stage, the individual obtains gratification from stimulation and manipulation of his or her own body. This stage coincides with early years of adolescence during which the adolescent derives narcissistic pleasure and starts loving others for altruistic motives.

Freud's theory of psychoanalysis also suggests emphasis on early childhood memories and experiences playing a crucial role in future course of development. Freudian theory also talks about methods of free association and dream analysis. Free association is a method in which patients are required to say everything that comes into consciousness even if it may appear absurd or ridiculous. Free association does not care for any organized design; instead it encourages patients to talk about everything and anything that occurs to them without any restraint, which eventually allows the patients to talk about childhood experiences.

Dreams are also accorded due importance in Freudian theory as it is considered "guardian of sleep" and royal road to the unconscious. Symbol interpretation is an effective technique of dream analysis.

7.4.3 LaCanian psychoanalysis

LaCanian psychoanalysis began as a commentary on Freudian writings and finally developed an independent body of thought considering the human psyche to be framed within the three orders of the Imaginary, the Symbolic and the Real (RSI). LaCan's contribution initially revolved around the concepts of image, identification and unconscious fantasy. LaCan argued about the role of language through symbolism and imaginary of the Structuring. LaCan believed that the Real together with the Imaginary and Symbolic were inseparably intertwined.

LaCan considered the mirror stage as more than a moment in the life of the infant; it formed part of the permanent structure of subjectivity. LaCan called identification as alienation and alienation constitutes the imaginary order. "The use of the symbolic", LaCan argued, "is the only way for the analytic process to cross the layer of identification". The symbolic is equivalent to a linguistic dimension which is a product of culture as opposed to the imaginary order of nature. LaCan's Real is not synonymous with reality; the Real is undifferentiated bearing no gaps. Symbolic, on the other hand, is related presence, absence through the process of signification.

7.4.4 Psychoanalytic studies of media

Psychoanalytic film theory attempts to apply the principles of psychoanalysis in the films. From a Freudian perspective, films and movies are constructed in a way that allows people to indulge in unconscious repressed or morally prohibited pleasures. From a LaCanian perspective, films allow people to enjoy imaginary pleasures and language divides from our conscious mind.

Phallocentrism is a social condition mostly widespread in Western culture, where images or representations of the penis carry symbolic connotations of power and dominance. From a psychoanalyst's point of view, the male phallus is considered as a symbol of power represented through the presence of the father.

7.4.5 Apparatus theory

Developed by Jean Louis Baudry (1930–2015), this theory described the actual environment and technological machinery of cinema as activating ideological reality to its spectators. In his analysis of Plato's Cave Allegory, Baudry points out that the text of the cave may well express a desire inherent to a participatory effect deliberately produced, sought for and expressed by cinema.

The texts and apparatus of cinema through the help of technology disguise the reality, and the effects on the spectators are ideological. Baudry also describes the apparatus of the movie theatre bug: as moviegoers are not distracted by outside factors of light and noise, they are able to experience the film as it were reality. Apparatus theory suggests that cinema projects the dominant ideology of the culture-shaping attitude and behavior of the spectators. Baudry compares films for dream lived experiences and suggests that most of the individuals experience repression or loss of desires in the course of psychic development, and that film provides a medium through which they access them again. According to Baudry, the actual context of viewing a movie in a theatre reconstructs the situation necessary to the release of the "mirror stage" discovered by LaCan.

LaCan had described that child approaching its mirror image lacks the ability for motor control, and vision is predominant to understand the world. According to Baudry, the context of theatre where the audience is seated passively with the least movement and sees giant images on the screen creates visual dominance, allowing viewers to unconsciously enjoy in mirror stage feelings of wholeness and mastery while watching the film.

Christian Metz (1931–1993), a French film theorist, pioneered film semiotics, identified concepts of identification, voyeurism and fetishism and suggested that the reason the films are popular as art is due to its ability of inaccurate depiction of reality and delving into an unconscious dream state. In his book *The Imaginary Signifier: Psychoanalysis and the Cinema*, Metz (1982) characterizes the viewer's mental process through which spectators identifies as:

> I know that I am perceiving something imaginary . . . and I know that it is I Who am perceiving it. This second knowledge divides in turn: I know that I am really perceiving, that my sense organs are physically affected, that I am not fantasizing that the fourth wall of the auditorium (the screen) is really different from the other three. – In other words, the spectator identifies with himself, as a pure act of perception (as wakefulness, as alertness).

Freud identified scopophilia, or pleasure from looking, as one of the primary sexual pleasures and Metz described that through identification with the apparatus viewers participate in what he calls "The passion for perceiving" on scopophilia. In his article "Three Essays on Sexuality" (1905), Freud claimed that visual impressions remain the most frequent pathway along which libidinal excitation is aroused.

7.4.6 Voyeurism

Voyeurism comes from the psychoanalytic theory of Sigmund Freud and refers to the process of experiencing sexual pleasure by way of watching the desired object. In the 1954 film *Rear Window*, Alfred Hitchcock described voyeurism through the depiction of his lead actor named Jefferies spending his life surveying neighbors with the use of binoculars, while he is in a chair because of his broken leg. The people are secretively engaged in observing others, which may provide gratifications. Many art forms including cinema make use of activating the voyeuristic drives inherent in viewers to offer scopophilic pleasure. There is a lack of a true exhibitionistic object in the cinematic voyeur – no actual person to be watched – and thus increasing the lack between voyeur and object and adding to the possibility of scopophilic pleasure.

7.4.7 Fetishism

Fetishism is psychic structuring of an object or person as a source of pleasure. Metz has described fetishism in terms of disapproval which is considered inherent to the watching process in cinema. Metz suggested viewers of cinema struggle with the tensions and between consciously discarding the film as false and unconsciously believing the story as true converts their attention to fetish to relieve this ambivalence. "The cinema fetishist", Metz wrote "is the person who is enchanted at what the machine is capable of".

7.4.8 The male gaze

Psychoanalytic media scholars opened a new field of study known as the male gaze with the publication of Laura Mulvey's landmark piece "Visual Pleasure and Narrative Cinema" in 1975 (Mulvey, 2006). According to Mulvey, male gaze is the act of depicting women in the visual arts of cinema within a powerful phallocentric frame of reference. In her article, Mulvey argued that the film viewers are invited to participate through unconscious drive, and cinema narrative is framed on the basis of gendered ideology.

Mulvey considered identification and scopophilia with male presence and female absence a narrative in which a male character is treated as subject and a female as object of desire and the male gaze. Mulvey described that female characters were coded with "to be looked-at-ness" while the camera positioning and the male viewer represented the "bearer of the look".

Mulvey highlighted the patriarchal Hollywood system, and the male spectator derives visual pleasure from a dominant and controlling perspective. Mulvey also argued that the single celluloid frame and film's ability to construct the female Star as ultimate spectacle with the advancement of digital technology, the desire to possess and hold the elusive image led to repeated viewing and emergence of "possessive spectator".

The basic purpose of Mulvey's theory was to question the gendered conventions of Hollywood cinema through psychoanalysis. Mulvey acknowledges that there is an obvious interest in this analysis for feminists. It gets us nearer to the roots of our oppression, it brings an articulation of the problem classes, it faces us with the ultimate challenge of how to fight the unconscious structured like a language (formed critically at the moment of arrival of language) while still caught within the language of patriarchy. There is no way in which we can produce an alternative out of the blue, but we can begin to make a break by examining patriarchy with the tools it provides, of which psychoanalysis is not the only one but an important one. It is not to say that films are all about gaining scopophilic pleasure, but film taps into our psychoanalytic structures and orients people to receive unconscious pleasure across gendered and ideological lines.

7.4.9 Fantasy

Fantasy is considered as a mental representation of conscious or unconscious wish fulfillment and possibility of imagination related to desires and pleasures. For Freud, fantasy is formed due to repressed wishes and uses disguised forms for its manifestation. He considered fantasy as a form of defense mechanism such as daydreaming. For Freud, daydreaming or wishful fantasies can be transformed into reality through creative activities.

Melanie Klein, a psychoanalyst, regarded the unconscious as made up of fantasies of relations with objects. These are thought of as primary and innate and as the mental representation of instincts, the psychological equivalents in the mind of defense mechanisms.

Fantasy is also known as the habit of deluding oneself by imaginary perceptions, which arises from conscious or repressed wishes. In 1948, Susan Isaacs proposed that "the two alternative spellings fantasy and phantasy should be used to denote conscious day dreams fictions and so on and the primary content of unconscious mental processes respectively. In Freudian term German word *phantasie* (originating with Greece word, *phantasia*) has been used, but in popular modern usage "fantasy" is much more prevalent. The medium of film attempts to create fantasy with its ability to manipulate technology of time and space and special effects.

Fantasy films project human fears and desires as well as magic and wonder, allowing room for imagination and the fantasies of our imagination. The mediating factor of fantasy brought in with the help of technology allows viewers to connect with their own desires and wishes of imagination in reality through the process of spectating fantasy in media.

7.4.10 Critical analysis

The psychoanalytic perspective of media messages described the concepts of Id, Ego, Superego and instincts playing a major role in the development of a personality of an individual. Various defense mechanisms employed by the people help them manage various conflicts and tensions which operate unconsciously. Freud's and LaCan's theories deal extensively with psychoanalytic theory and its concepts. Dreams and use of symbolic concepts are applied by media messages to produce favorable consumer behavior for its products. Cinema as a powerful medium influences the attitude and behavior of the spectators through effective use of technology, creating ideological impact on the spectators.

THINK BOX

- Describe the role of psychoanalysis in cinema.
- Critically evaluate the use of male gaze in the context of Hollywood & Bollywood cinema.

7.5 Feminist analysis

Feminist message analysis undertakes to uncover the associations between male and female biology, culture, sex and gender. We live in a world that is stratified along categories of age, gender, class, caste, race and ethnicity in which privileges and disadvantages are unequally distributed associated with such categories. The production of media images and cultural constructions are patterned in a way to produce differential power meanings associated with the symbols of domination and oppression.

It was previously described that content analysis and semiotics relied upon the transmission model with a view that the media are agents of social control conveying stereotypical and ideological values about women and femininity. Feminism broadly is a stream of thought that explores and analyses the diverse ways – men and women are socially empowered or disempowered. Contrary to popular belief, contemporary feminism is not anti-male. Feminism as a movement emerged to end sexism, sexist exploitation, oppression and sex discrimination based upon a person's sex. The term "sex" refers to biological identity; anatomy, reproduction, hormones and gender to refer to the socially learned expectations associated with members of each sex. Sex is annotated as different from gender in the *Oxford English Dictionary*, where it says that sex "tends now to refer to biological differences". A definition by the World Health Organization (2011) describes socially constructed charateristics of women and men such as norms, roles and relationships of and between groups of women and men. The concept of gender includes five important elements: relational, hierarchal, historical, contextual and institutional. According to Seccombe (1986), patriarchy is a system of social structures and practices in which men dominate, oppress and exploit women. In general, the feminist scholars question the male values and gender stereotypes treated as objective truths.

7.5.1 Stereotyping in media

Stereotypes are generalizations about a group of people in which certain traits are assigned to virtually all members of the group, regardless of actual variation among the members (Aronson & Inzlicht, 2004).

People's belief that traits are fixed and or are malleable predict differences in the degree of social stereotyping according to "entity" and "incremental" perspectives, respectively. Homogeneity is considered a central feature of outgroups, an ingroup is also perceived to be homogenous which can be presence of threat, the minority status of the ingroup and other situational factors.

Self-categorization theorists (Oakes et al., 1994; Reicher, 1987; Turner et al., 1987) refer to the shift from personal to social identity as depersonalization, which means people are functioning on the basis of a different premise rather being less human. Because people often do behave in stereotyped ways, social attribution may indeed be quite accurate (Leyens & Yzerbyt, 1992; Oakes et al., 1994). The continuing power and strength of stereotypes lies in the combination of validity and distortion. The stereotypes in media that we see are strengthened with repeated public viewing, and sometimes members of socially oppressed groups start believing the stereotypes as reality and try to emulate them. Our everyday preaching and practice of stereotyped images reinforced through media are adapted to public perception, leading to gendered stereotypes.

Notions of masculinity are associated with physical prowess, and femininity is tied to passivity. Media texts also project the stereotypes of men as active bread earners of the family and women as an obvious expression of nurturing families. However, contemporary media has become more fluid in the representation of men and women, with changing social roles and in-depth analysis pointing to gender-stereotypical elements in media programming.

The association of logical, scientific and working sphere is related to men, whereas domestic activities predominant with emotions are related to women through media texts. A classic distortion of this binary logic/emotion stereotypical dualism is the association of men with mental activities and women with domestic activities, examples of which can be found on the television series *Star Trek:The Next Generation* – sexual subject/sexual object.

Stereotypical media representation of men and women tends to identify them as powerful and weak respectively. The famous French feminist Simone de Beauvoir captured the sexual subject/object binary poetically in her treatise on the oppression of women, *The Second Sex*.

> For him, she is sex – absolute sex, no less. She has defined and differentiated with reference to man and not with reference to her. She is the incidental the inessential as opposed to the essential. He is the subject, he is the Absolute, she is the other.
>
> (de Beauvoir, 1952, p. 19)

There are numerous instances of subject-object binary in various media texts from magazines to television and social media advertisements. For journalist Naomi Wolf, "the beauty myth tells a story: The quality called beauty objectively and universally exists. Women must want to embody it and men must want to possess women who embody it" (Wolf, 2002). The Disney film *Sleeping Beauty* (1959) is based on this binary distinction of sexual subject/sexual object. Some other prominent films highlighting young men pursuing women only as sexual conquest are the *American Pie* series (1999–2007), *Animal House* (1978) and *Old School* (2003). Gender-specific preferences portrayed through the lens of media influence the strengthening of stereotypes in real-life situations.

7.5.2 Effects of sexist media representation

The role of mass media in disseminating information is transformed into constructing a culture of entertainment images representing stereotypes as truths. It is a very common practice among the young and adolescents who are large consumers of entertainment media to follow body image, dieting behaviors which may have adverse effects on psychological well-being.

Advertising analyst Jean Kilbourne (2000) views eating disorders as one of the primary ways that "women cope with the difficulties in their lives and with the cultural contradictions involving food and eating". Media representation of sex reinforces the formation of attitudes and stereotypes which imposes unrealistic expectations, resulting in harmful individual self-image. It becomes very difficult to decode the reality of implications when a skewed media stereotype becomes the basis for social interaction.

7.5.3 Critical evaluation of feminist analysis

Feminist media message analysis describes the production of media images through which stereotypes about men and women are perpetuated. Male values are treated as dominant and objective truths and unrealistic categorizations are repeated to produce a false sense of normal leading to undesirable and harmful effects on the behavior of the people trying to emulate media-mediated norms of normal and desirable. The notions of masculinity and femininity are tied to the strict categories of desirable stereotypes which is, in fact, far from reality producing a subject/object classification category. Body image obsession has particularly affected the well-being of adolescents and youth which need to be critically understood from a feminist perspective.

THINK BOX

- Critically evaluate the role of media in producing gender binaries.
- Critically evaluate Gender stereotypes and its psycho-social effects on well-being.

7.6 Queer perspectives

Italian feminist and film theorist Teresa de Lauretis coined the term "queer theory" for a conference she organized at the University of California, Santa Cruz, in 1990. Queer theory is an interdisciplinary perspective focusing on human sexuality understanding beyond the binary of heterosexuality/homosexuality. Queer theory considers sexuality as fluid and has been associated with bisexual, lesbian, gay and gender ambiguity. Homosexuality or heterosexuality is a cultural construction that functions as heuristic, but the dynamic nature of sexual activities may allow different sexual orientations depending upon the processes of socialization. The social construction of norms including that of sexuality is a result of interaction, labeling and claims-making in a given cultural context. The evolution of queer theory began with the consideration of "queer epistemology" that opposes sexual identity categories such as gay and lesbians.

Feminist scholar Adrianne Rich (1986) refers to the constructed institution of heterosexuality as "compulsive" in the sense that people (women in particular) are coerced into identifying with the social definitions and norms of heterosexuality from birth. The process of presenting heterosexuality as a normally sought after and coherent category was achieved through stigmatizing homosexuality as abnormal, also called sexual othering. In the dominant discourse of the ideal family, husband, wife and two children are most prescribed though a joint family; family with a pet and single parent is also a possibility. Queer theory analysis also highlights the point in which media paints a picture of heterosexuality as normal and other forms of sexuality as deviant or "other" (Gay, Lesbian, Transgender and Bisexual).

Queer theorists critique, analyze texts and challenge the notions of culture and ideology portraying heterosexuality as a dominant norm and others as deviant.

Queer theory also questions the over-simplistic independent entities of biology and culture as, highlighting the importance of intersex traits and intersex individuals.

7.6.1 Stereotypes used in queerness

Natural/deviant: in the presentation by media in magazines, television and films, only a few feature non-heterosexual characters in primary roles. Hollywood has also depicted homosexuality as an indicator of deviance and criminality. Contemporary films that associated queerness to deviance include *The Silence of the Lambs* (1991) and *Basic Instinct* (1992).

Monogamous/promiscuous: there is also a tendency to link heterosexuality to monogamy and homosexuality to promiscuity, and this association is also highlighted as a support for the credibility of romantic relations by the mass media. Queer theorists emphasize to eradicate the gender roles as related to sexual classification and understanding of masculinity and femininity along with fixed parameters. Sexual minorities rarely get representation by media, and diverse sexual orientation is not visible due to its underrepresentation.

Queerness and invisibility: The works of Foucault and Judith Butler indicate that sexuality can be understood through the process of discursive construction by the use of the "invisibility" metaphor. Three of Michel Foucault's works – *Madness and Civilization* (1961), *The Birth of the Clinic* (1963) and *Discipline and Punish* (1975) – focus on concepts of "madness", "healing" or "justice", not as objective facts but rather as discourses structured around concepts which allow them to appear normal and justified. Foucault considers sexuality as an innate biological quality, a product of discursive practices made possible through negotiations of power to give it a coherent meaning. Judith Butler in her work *Gender Trouble: Feminism and the Subversion of Identity* (1999) discussed the role of language and discourse. She argued that a coherent identity category exists because people believe it. She claims, "I found myself increasingly engaged as a graduate student and young faculty member as countless feminist frameworks seemed either to elide or pathologies the challenge to gender normativity posed by Queer practices." Butler begins *Gender Trouble* by highlighting her arguments against mainstream feminism. Feminist critique, she writes "ought to understand how the category of 'women', the subject of feminism, is produced and restrained by the very structure of power through which emancipation is sought."

It is important to highlight that placing women in a coherent category creates a coherent category of subjects via a network of power. According to Butler, the cultural value created around gender influences the production of "sex" in our culture. Butler further described that understanding of "sex" as "biologically fixed" is a mythical product of our social construction of gender. In the process of discourse construction, factors of meanings, symbols, words and laws operate in a combined fashion to give way to gender identity.

There are disruptions in the conceptualization of gender which include gender, sex, practice and desire and the notion of performance itself. Butler prescribed gender performativity as enumerating a vast continuum of combination available rather than treating gender as a constant conception of one's identity.

7.6.2 Critical evaluation of queer perspectives

The queer perspective analyzes the role of media in creating binary of heterosexual as normal and homosexual as faulty which is, in fact, a cultural construct creation. The tendency of media-produced messages of projecting heterosexuality as dominant and desirable has led to the creation of a deviant minority for the people with diverse sexual orientations. Queer theorists consider this binary of a classification a created category highlighting the fluid nature of sexual orientations. The discourses that are structured to maintain such categories of gender normality are a product of a constructed process. Queer perspective takes into account the contributions of Foucault, Butler and others to highlight a new approach to understanding and analyzing diverse sexual orientations and paying due regard to intersex orientation as well. Lesbians, Gay Homosexuals are portrayed as a stigma by the powerful mass media messages which neither is scientific nor does justice to the emergence of a diversity of human behaviors.

THINK BOX

- Critically examine and reflect the queer identity.
- Do you think, queer perspectives have been understood properly by people in general? Justify your response.

7.7 Critical evaluation

The present chapter on media messages and different perspectives of media messages has offered an analysis of major theoretical perspectives. Media messages are not a simple cause-and-effect proposition in a mathematical fashion, and a deeper understanding is required to know about the content's manifest and desired objectives. Broadcast, print media and nowadays social media have become powerful techniques to influence the public opinion both at micro-level and macro-level behavioral changes. Various psychological techniques of priming, exposure to messages' selective attention, fear, anxiety, learning and imitation are employed to bring desirable changes in the behavior of the people. Belief systems and values are also determined and shaped through media messages. Advertisement organizations spend millions to catch the attention of their products by consumers. It becomes difficult to decide as to which product is necessary in reality or whether it is merely the impact of advertisement that people are drawn to such products.

Various techniques of media messages analysis much as rhetoric analysis, cultural analysis, feminist analysis, psychoanalytic analysis and queer analysis have been highlighted in this chapter to understand the dynamics of media mediated messages. Each perspective tends to read and decode the media messages from its vantage point and all these techniques are complementary. There are other forms of analysis of media messages such as organizational analysis, pragmatic analysis that is carried out to decode media messages. Other techniques of reception analysis and erotic analysis are used to understand the impact and effect of media messages.

7.8 Indian perspective

It is important to understand the growing influence of mass media messages and the Indian perspective. The impact which Bollywood cinema has produced among the masses of Indian society has had a powerful impact on the attitude and behavior of the people. The dominance of violence as a means to acquire success has also percolated among the behaviors of adolescents and youth. With the rise of social media and new media, citizen participation has increased the accountability of stakeholders in governance. The reporting of facts in an impartial manner and the long-cherished ideal of responsible journalism is always questioned on the grounds of sensationalism, publicity stunts and excessive commercialization. It is difficult to get a truthful comprehensive and representative picture of the diversity of the constituent groups representing society at large. The representation of women and marginals is accorded less space from the lens of mass media, and what newsmakers promote as timely, relevant and of greater social importance has a sizeable gap between the ideal and manifest news. Profit acts as a powerful motive for various media channels. The use of public relations consultants and media managers have grown significantly in the Indian context. A serious and critical analysis of media messages is required to understand the reality and the projected picture of reality through media messages.

7.9 Summary

Contemporary media reflects convergence and mobility de-massification of media, producing endless images of love, violence, family and politics and constructing a potential space of our social world. Mediated messages play a significant socializing force both individually and collectively. Media messages determine and influence what we learn and how we learn. Media corporations at the world level comprise the first tier of corporate media giants at the world level also called Big Five include Time Warner, Disney, Viacom, News Corporation and Bertelsmann. Other big players of media corporations include General Electric, Sony, Vivendi, and Clear Channel. The media industry as a whole is concentrated in the hands of few through a pattern of conglomeration. The multinational character of these media organizations and its global network is driven by a profit motive. Media and advertisement are closely related to each other and audiences are a target for advertisers. The financial approach to maximizing profits is done through niche marketing or narrowcasting, allowing media corporations to reach untapped markets.

The ownership pattern of a few controlling a large share of media ownership reduces the diversity and decline of democratic ideals. The stated objectives of egalitarianism, the free and open exchange of ideas, are severely limited by those who own and control media. Though recent advancements of social media provided access for ordinary citizens to share their ideas and opinions. Media messages of rhetorics encourage audiences to inhabit certain moods and used as a means of persuasion for certain actions. Theorists like Saussure described semiology highlighting the role of signs in social life. The way individual signs are associated or clustered in a text works as rhetoric. Form is the sequence of events that lead to satisfaction of desires. The role of genre, narrative, affect and aesthetics are used to create an impact in rhetorical analysis.

Another approach to analyze media messages is cultural analysis. Culture suggests that we see the world in a particular manner based upon culturally embedded knowledge. Ideologies of certain kinds are propagated with the help of myths, Doxa and hegemony. Hegemony is the process by which one ideology subverts other competing ideologies. The process of "othering" is also adopted through media representation treating the marginalized group as subordinate.

The psychoanalytic perspective of media messages analyzes the role of unconscious processes in bringing repressed desires to conscious realms. The concepts phallocentrism, apparatus theory and the male gaze have been used to analyze the media messages from a psychoanalytic perspective.

The feminist perspective of media messages attempts to highlight the misleading and simplified representation of women through stereotypical methods. A queer perspective is an interdisciplinary approach that challenges the socially constructed systems of meaning related to human sexuality. The entire spectrum of human sexuality is misinterpreted by media messages through a process called sexual othering.

Queer symbolizes a rejection of status quo traditional definitions of sexual relations which restricts the diversity of ways sexual relations are manifested. The term queer is now used as an umbrella term to refer to individual sexualities that do not fit into traditional understanding of sexuality.

The variety of media messages can influence audience behavior in many ways. It is important to recognize the various media messages to understand how mass media portrayals create meanings for consumers. The powerful role of media in the negotiation of meanings of a text can help us discover the multiple dimensions manifest and hidden involved in its functioning.

Key points

- Media messages, through the processes of priming and other psychological factors, influence the audience's beliefs, attitudes and behaviors.
- Metaphors are used in different forms to create positive or negative images through the use of language.
- The symbolic interactionism approach to mass media emphasizes social interaction and social context in understanding the social impact of new information technology.
- Rhetoric refers to the ancient art of oratory through construction and manipulation of language by the creator of a text for affective purposes.
- One of the basic rhetorical structures in texts is the cluster or the way individual signs are related to one another.
- The elements of music such as melody, harmony and rhythm can have a strong influence on people's affects.
- Content analysis is a research method to study mass media effects.
- Defense mechanisms are used by people to get relief from excessive anxiety; the ego adopts mechanisms to deny or distort reality, and it operates unconsciously.
- Voyeurism refers to the process of experiencing sexual pleasure by way of watching the desired object.
- Male gaze is the act of depicting women in the visual arts of cinema within a powerful phallocentric frame of reference.

Key terms

metaphor, rhetoric, metonym, cliché, genre, defense mechanisms, fantasy, fetishism, male gaze, queerness

References

Altheide, D.L., & Snow, R.P. (1991). *Media Worlds in the Postjournalism Era*. Hawthorne, NY: Aldine de Gruyter.

Altman, I., & Taylor, D. (1973). *Social Penetration: The Development of Interpersonal Relationships*. New York: Holt, Rinehart and Winston.

Anderson, C.A., & Murphy, C.R. (2003). Violent video games and aggressive behavior in young women. *Aggressive Behavior*, 29(5), 423–9.

Aronson, J., & Inzlicht, M. (2004). The ups and downs of attributional ambiguity: Stereotype vulnerability and the academic self-knowledge of African-American students. *Psychological Science*, 15, 829–36.

Bach, K. (1998). Standardization revisited. In A. Kasher (Ed.), *Pragmatics: Critical Concepts* (Vol. 4, pp. 712–25). London: Routledge.

Barrow, J. (1990). Teacher education: Theory and practice. *British Journal of Educational Studies*, 38(4), 308–18.

Barthes, R. (1967). *Elements of Semiology* (A. Lavers & C. Smith, Trans.). New York: Hill and Wang.

Baudry, L., & Cohen, M. (Eds.). (2004). *Film Theory and Criticism* (6th ed.). New York: Oxford University Press.

Beauvoir, S. de. (1952). *The Second Sex* (H.M. Parsley, Trans.). New York: Alfred A. Knopf.

Bitzer, L. (1968). The rhetorical situation. *Philosophy and Rhetoric*, 1(1).

Burke, K. (1941). *The Philosophy of Literary Form*. Baton Rouge: Louisiana State University Press.

Burke, K. (1952). A dramatistic view of the origins of language: Part one. *Quarterly Journal of Speech*, 38, 251–64.

Burke, K. (1969). *A Rhetoric of Motives*. Berkeley, CA: University of California Press. (Originally published 1950)

Burke, K. (1973). *The Philosophy of Literary Form: Studies in Symbolic Action* (3rd ed.). Berkeley, CA: University of California Press.

Butler, J. (1999). *Gender Trouble: Feminism and the Subversion of Identity*. New York: Routledge.

Carey, J.W. (1989). *A Cultural Approach to Communication: Communication as Culture*. Winchester, MA: Unwin Hyman.

Chaiken, S., Liberman, A., & Eagly, A.H. (1989). Heuristic and systematic information processing within and beyond the persuasion context. In J.S. Uleman & J.A. Bargh (Eds.), *Unintended Thought* (pp. 212–52). New York: Guilford.

Cooley, C.H. (1909). *Social Organization: A Study of the Larger Mind*. New York: Charles Scribner's Sons.

Cragan, J.F., & Shields, D.C. (1995). *Symbolic Theories in Applied Communication Research: Bormann, Burke, and Fisher*. Cresskill, NJ: Hampton Press.

Cragan, J.F., & Shields, D.C. (1998). *Understanding Communication Theory the Communicative Forces for Human Action*. Boston, MA: Allyn and Bacon.

Eco, U. (1979). *A Theory of Semiotics*. Bloomington, IN: Indiana University Press.

Foucault, M. (1961). *Madness and Civilization*. London: Routledge.

Foucault, M. (1963). *The Birth of the Clinic* (A.M. Sheridan, Trans.). Routledge Classics. 2003. London: Routledge.

Foucault, M. (1975). *Discipline and Punish*. London: Penguin.

Freud, A. (1946). *The Psychoanalytic Treatment of Children*. London: Imago.

Freud, S. (1905). Three essays on the theory of sexuality. In *The Standard Edition of the Complete Psychological Works of Sigmund Freud*. London: Hogarth.

Freud, S. (1910). Five lectures on psycho-analysis. In *S.E.* (Vol. 11, pp. 1–56). London: Hogarth.

Goodman, P. (2008, 7 January). Violent films may cut real crime, study finds. *New York Times*. Retrieved 11 October 2020 from http://www.nytimes.com/2008/01/07/technology/07iht-violence.4.9058958.html

Hall, C.S. (1954/1979). *A Primer on Freudian Psychology*. New York: Penguin.

Kilbourne, J.. (2000). *Can't Buy My Love: How Advertising Changes the Way We Think and Feel*. New York: Simon & Schuster.

Klapp, O. (1972). *Currents of Unrest*. New York: Holt, Rinehart and Winston.

Lamb, G. (2008). Columbine high school. *The New York Times*.

Lasswell, H. (1927). *Propaganda Techniques in the World War*. New York: Knopf.

Leyens, J.-P., & Yzerbyt, V.Y. (1992). The ingroup overexclusion effect: Impact of valence and confirmation on stereotypical information search. *European Journal of Social Psychology*, 22, 549–69.

Maines, D.R., & Couch, C.J. (1988). *Communication and Social Structure*. Springfield, IL: C.C. Thomas.

McLuhan, M. (1964). *Understanding Media*. New York: McGraw Hill.

Merton, R.K. (2002 [1946]). *Mass Persuasion: The Social Psychology of a War Bond Drive*. New York: Harper & Bros.

Metz, C. (1982) *The Imaginary Signifier: Psychoanalysis and the Cinema* (C. Briton, A. Williams, B. Brewster & A. Guzzetti, Trans.), pp. 48–49. Bloomington, IN: Indiana University Press.

Mulvey, L. (2006). Visual pleasure and narrative cinema. In M.G. Durham & D.M. Kellner (Eds.), *Media and Cultural Studies: Key Works*. Oxford, UK: Blackwell.

Oakes, P.J., Haslam, S.A., & Turner, J.C. (1994). *Stereotyping and Social Reality*. Oxford, UK: Blackwell.

Reicher, S.D. (1987). Crowd behaviour as social action. In J.C. Turner, M.A. Hogg, P.J. Oakes, S.D. Reicher, & M.S. Wetherell (Eds.), *Rediscovering the Social Group: A Self-Categorisation Theory* (pp. 171–202). Oxford, UK: Basil Blackwell.

Rich, A. (1986). *Blood, Bread, and Poetry: Selected Prose, 1979–1985*. New York: Norton.

Seccombe, W. (1986), Patriarchy stabilized: The construction of the male breadwinner wage norm in nineteenth-century Britain. *Social History*, 11, 54.

Snow, R.P. (1983). *Creating Media Culture*. Beverly Hills, CA: Sage.

Surratt, C.B. (2001). *The Internet and Social Change*. Jefferson, NC: McFarland.

Turner, J.C., Hogg, M.A., Oakes, P.J., Reicher, S.D., & Wetherell, M.S. (1987). *Rediscovering the Social Group: A Self-Categorization Theory*. Oxford and New York: Basil Blackwell.

Wolf, N. (2002). *The Beauty Myth: How Images of Beauty Are Used against Women*. New York: William Morrow and Company.

World Health Organization. (2011). *Gender Mainstreaming for Health Managers: A Practical Approach*. Geneva: WHO.

Yewdall, D.L. (2007). *Practical Art of Motion Picture Sound* (pp. 403–39). Burlington, MA: Focal Press.

8

MEDIA EFFECTS

Learning objectives

After reading this chapter, you will be able to understand:

- The concept of media effects
- Media effects on identity
- Media effects on interpersonal interaction
- Media effects on women
- Media effects on violence
- Critical evaluation and Indian perspective

8.1 Media effects

Media messages produced by various media platforms has short-term and long-term consequences on the thinking, behavior and interpersonal relations, including a wide spectrum of activities. It is a time where our geographical boundaries have been narrowed with advancements in technology, and people all over the world are far more connected than they were during previous times. As a concept, placelessness was introduced by Edward Relph in *Place and Placelessness* (1976) and indicates a growing existential (in a Heideggerian sense) hollowness when it comes to the connection between human individuals and the places they are in contact with (physically or mediated). A combination of an established consumer society, increased mobility and technological development within mass media and information technologies is blamed for a rapidly accelerating homogenization of society's places (Relph, 1976, p. 90). An inauthentic attitude towards places is transmitted through several processes or, perhaps more accurately, "media" which directly or indirectly encourages "placelessness", that is, weakening of the identity of places to the point where they look and feel alike and offer the same possibilities for experience. There, media includes mass communication, mass culture, big business, a powerful central authority and the economic system which embraces all these (Relph, 1976).

Media sources transmit information and ideas through newspaper, radio, television and digital technologies which reduce the possibilities of face-to-face interaction. It also allows freedom for its users to easily leave their geographical territories. For Robert Sack (1992), television uproots and juxtaposes one

FIGURE 8.1 Smartphone addiction.
Source: Hassan, M. (n.d.). Needpix. https://www.needpix.com/photo/1729399/addiction-smartphone-addict-addicted-arm-blue-bound-brochure-browsing

context after another far more than other media, and this obscures the real historical and geographical depth of place and weakens its relation in space and time to other places and events. Different contexts flash past by mere changing of channels, each offering a string of programs in different settings. Television exerts a powerful impact on its viewers, affecting their attitude, behavior, thinking and imagination and influencing the patterns of thinking in which they receive and process the transmitted information. Meyrowitz (1985) described that everything appears so quickly on media platforms that it hardly provides time and space for realistic and authentic understanding to occur. Media has changed the logic of the social order by restructuring the relationship between physical place and social place by altering how we transmit and receive social information.

Modern information technologies have blurred the distinction between the near and far, present and future, real and unreal; and the appearance of moving images has resulted in complex and all-pervasive effects affecting our sociocultural and psychological aspects of life.

The influence of mass media has an effect on different generations of people using it. This includes a change in beliefs, attitudes, emotional and behavioral orientations, cultural, political and day-to-day functioning of individuals and society.

Early media effects research often focused on the power of propaganda (Lasswell, 1927). American political scientist and Communication theorist Harold Lasswell, in his 1948 article "The Structure and Function of Communication in Society", wrote: "Who said What, in which channel, to Whom and with What effect?"

FIGURE 8.2 Media impact.
Source: Flicks, M. (2017). Pxhere. https://pxhere.com/en/photo/400602

Lasswell describes the role of the source of the message, the content of the message, the medium through which it is transmitted, the recipients of such messages and the effect of messages on the recipients are included as the main focus of his model of analyzing media effects.

8.1.1 Gerbner's cultivation theory

According to the cultivation theory proposed by George Gerbner, prolonged exposure of viewers on television as a medium of socialization cultivates perceptions of reality. He argued that television as a mass medium of socializing people helps in standardizing roles and behaviors of the people, and he compared the power of television with that of religion. Gerbner also highlighted that high use of television viewing results into an expression of violence and crime by the viewers as the programs on television have a high content of violent scenes.

Based on a survey, Gerbner (1969) categorized television viewers into three categories of light viewers (less than 2 hours a day), medium viewers (2–4 hours a day) and heavy viewers (more than 4 hours a day) which also contributed to the behavior pattern adopted by the people in real-life situations. While news agencies boast their allegiance to report factual, timely news, in reality, they rely heavily on sensational coverage of crime and violence.

The primary concepts related to cultivation theory include mainstreaming, resonance, mean-world, index-dramatic violence, frequency learning and heavy viewers. The culture propagated by television is so predominant that it constitutes the mainstream culture and worldview created by television culture, and it resonates in the minds of the people, leading to intensified cultivation patterns.

Mean world index means that people with long-term exposure and consumption of television programs cultivate the image of a mean and insecure world. The concept of dramatic violence highlights the use of violence as part of the plot of TV programs indicating a relationship between fear and entertainment.

Gerbner described frequency learning as the frequencies with which events are presented on television, making people think they are common aspects of reality. The heavy viewing category is described as those who watch several hours of television a day. It is generally assumed that heavy television viewing results in a consistent worldview and understanding of social reality presented on television. According to Gerbner's research, the more time spent "living" in the world of television the more likely people are to report perceptions of social reality which can be traced to television's most persistent representations of life and society.

8.1.2 Hovland's theory

Carl Iver Hovland (1912–61), a psychologist at Yale University. developed the Social Judgment theory of attitude change. Hovland talked about the sleeper effect related to attitude change, arguing that messages presented by untrustworthy sources do not result in attitude change of the audience, but after a few weeks, the association with the issue in the minds of the audience vanishes and positive attitude change starts taking place. Hovland argued that if he was able to recognize the attitude an individual has towards a trigger, he would able to predict the behavior and actions of an individual over time. Hovland also described the importance of interpersonal communication in persuasion.

8.1.3 Katz and Lazarsfeld

Katz and Lazarsfeld's *Personal Influence* (1955) is considered an influential work about "limited" media effects. This theory ascribed the impact of media effects on the inferencing capacity of community opinion leaders who explain and diffuse media content to others. Media effects were considered to be effective through the source of human agency which is also moderated by intervening variables of pre-existing opinions, selectivity on the part of the audience and interpersonal relations. Katz and Lazarsfeld's theory is based upon a two-step flow model of communication which claimed that the impact of media was limited by key influencers within social networks. Katz (2006) commented that the research agenda supplanted the "powerful media" and "mass–persuasion" concerns associated with early radio, with the enduring research question of what people do with the media. This was a diversion of early media effects theory in which the audience was considered selective and reception happened in the context of mediating social groups and networks. The "powerful media" effects paradigm proposed by Katz suggested that the audience was related to simultaneous and unmediated reception.

The social constructivism approach related to the media's role in constructing meaning and corresponding social realities. Third-person effect theory argued about attribution theory, suggesting people are more likely to offer situational factors for television's effect on themselves while offering dispositional reasons for other members of an audience.

8.1.4 Agenda-setting theory

This theory was initially proposed by McCombs and Donald Shaw (1972). It argued about the media's ability to influence audiences by imposing what they *should* think instead of what they *do* think. The origin of agenda-setting theory can be traced to the work of Lippmann (1922) who argues that mass media is a principal connection between events in the world and the images in the minds of the public.

Rogers and Dearing (1988) identified three types of agenda-setting:

1. Public agenda setting
2. Media agenda setting
3. Policy agenda setting

Agenda setting is determined by the factor of accessibility. The more prominently news media covers an issue or event, the more that particular issue becomes accessible in the audience's memories. Agenda setting is a process that refers to the effect of media agenda on society and it involves a certain degree of reciprocity between mass media and society.

Framing: Entman (2007) described framing as the process of culling a few elements of perceived reality and assembling a narrative that highlights connections among them to promote a particular interpretation. The concept of framing proposed that media's reporting with a favorable slant can lead to a particular type of ideology and thinking in society.

8.1.5 Features of media effects theories

In the past few years, the size of the media audience and its consumption has reached phenomenal proportions. With the advent of the internet, media use pattern has become individualized with a personalized character. Castells (2007) suggests that an increase in individualization and personalization of media use has enabled a form of communication that is called mass self-communication. Mass self-communication shares with mass communication the notions that messages are transmitted to potentially large audiences, and that self-selected media users select media content to serve their own needs, regardless of whether those needs match the intent of the generator of the content (McQuail, 2010). However, mass communication research focuses mainly on media reception processes, while mass self-communication puts emphasis on reception and generation (Castells, 2007). Some theories emphasized unidirectional focus on media use and certain outcomes. Other theories suggested more attention to the interaction between media factors (media use, media processing) and non-media factors (e.g. personality, social and cultural context). Broadly, media effect theories are organized along with five global features.

Selectivity paradigm: according to this perspective, out of available media resources, people selectively attend some of the messages, and only those messages they select have the potential to influence them (Klapper, 1960; Knobloch-Westerwick, 2015; Rubin, 2009). It also allowed researchers to conclude that the power of media to change attitudes or behavior is limited. The selectivity paradigm is explained through users and gratifications, and selective exposure theory argues that individual selection of media messages is guided by various psychosocial needs and desires. According to Valkenburg and Peter (2013), three factors influence selective media use: dispositional, developmental and social context factors.

Dispositional factors: dispositional factors such as temperament, personality, gender, beliefs, moods and motivation are linked to media watching behaviors. There is ample evidence for the mechanism that individuals seek congenial information (Hart et al., 2009). Cognitive dissonance reduction is not as consistent a cause of selective exposure as it was previously assumed to be (Donsbach, 2009; Hart et al., 2009; S.M. Smith et al., 2007). Several more recent theories have proposed plausible explanations for people's information, occasional attitude, inconsistent selective exposure to information and entertainment.

Developmental factors: As for development, research has shown that individuals typically prefer media content that is only moderately discrepant from their age-related comprehension schemata and experiences (e.g. Valkenburg & Cantor, 2001). Developmental factors of media usage are more pronounced during childhood as they are more avid users, but it also extends to adults. In comparison to younger adults, middle and older adults more strongly prefer non-arousing, meaningful and uplifting media content, whereas younger adults more strongly prefer arousing, violent and frightening media (Mares et al., 2008; Mares & Sun, 2010; Mares & Woodard, 2006).

Social context factors: micro-level and macro-level social factors involving parental behavior, schools and broader cultural realities play an important role in the media usage pattern of children and adolescents. People have a strong need to identify with group norms and to bolster their self-esteem by comparing their social identity to the norms and attitudes of relevant out-groups (Tajfel & Turner, 1979).

Social identity factors can be maintained through identification with those of the same age and in the same interest groups. Adolescents often watch drama to learn social lessons about how people like themselves flirt or start and end relationships, or which type of humor is appropriate (Valkenburg, 2014). Social identity theory perspectives suggest social identity gratifications for the media users.

8.1.6 Media properties

The type of media, such as audio, visual or audiovisual, and its content features produce differential effects on its users.

Marshal McLuhan (1964) described the differential impact of modalities through his means of the aphorism "the medium is the message". In the new millennium, due to advances in technology research, interest in the differential effects of media modalities have shifted. Several media theories also predict the role of content properties in the enhancement of media effects on its users. Bandura's (2009) social cognitive theory postulates that media depictions of rewarded behavior and attractive media characters enhance the likelihood of media effects. Priming theory (Berkowitz & Powers, 1979) predicts, and justified violence (i.e. violence portrayed as morally correct) enhances, the likelihood of aggressive outcomes. Transportation theory (Green & Brock, 2000; Green et al., 2004) and the Extended Elaboration Likelihood model (Slater & Rouner, 2002) propose that media messages embedded in engaging narratives lead to increased media effects, and the Elaboration Likelihood Model (Petty & Cacioppo, 1986) predicts that argument strength and/or the attractiveness and credibility of the source can enhance persuasive effects.

Despite such theories, content properties as a decisive factor for media effects is yet to be postulated as a convincing model. However, its role can't be discounted in media effects studies. In addition to content, the role of structural aspects also results in creating desirable media effects. Our attentional processes are also guided by certain stimulus properties resulting into preferred attention to certain stimulus objects.

8.1.7 Indirect media effects

Media is not only to be studied and understood from immediate aspects viewpoints; the role of indirect aspects is equally important. The indirect effect model takes into account the influence of media use in terms of independent, dependent and mediating variables paradigm. Thus, if its indirect effect does not receive proper attention, the relationship between two variables of concern may not be fully considered.

Anderson and Bushman's (2002) General Aggression model predicts indirect effects of exposure to media violence on aggression through three response states: cognition, emotion and arousal. Experiments based on Zillmann's (1996) Excitation–Transfer Model have demonstrated that residual arousal that results for any media-induced sexual excitement can intensify positive (e.g. altruistic) feelings, and negative feelings and behavior (e.g. anger, aggressive behavior).

Indirect effects of media usage are also aimed at promoting certain behavioral patterns, attitudes and beliefs which can be exploited for economic and political objectives.

In political and health communication, it has repeatedly been found that the effects of media use on political behavior are mediated by certain beliefs and attitudes.

8.1.7.1 Media effects are conditional

Media effects are not applicable in the same manner, and a variety of factors like age, gender, class, personality factors and individual differences also play an important role in generating media effects. Media message presentation, style, emotional aspects and cognitive factors also determine the impact of media effects. Past experiences of an individual, belief systems and cultural aspects also contribute to the variation in the impact of media effects.

8.1.7.2 Media effects are transactional

Another set of theorists advocate the reciprocal characteristics of media usage and its effects. The producers and receivers of media messages can influence each other owing to intrapersonal, cognitive and affective systems that impact on such transactions.

8.1.8 Networked communication effects

Walther's (1992) social information processing theory, Daft and Lengel's (1986) media richness theory and Walther's (1996) hyperpersonal communication model are some of the important theories related to computer-mediated communication. With the phenomenal rise of social media platforms like Twitter (2006), Facebook (2006), WhatsApp (2009) and Instagram (2010), online communication has enlarged the range of communication activities. The tendency of mass self-communication and mass self-disclosure has also increased in recent years. Pingree (2007) referred to the phenomenon that our own beliefs and our behavior exert influence on ourselves as an expression effect.

It is important to highlight the complex nature of media use and its effects. Some methods prescribe direct media effects, others prescribe indirect media effects. The context, content and structural properties play an important part in our understanding of the uses and effects of media and communication technology. The factors of personality disposition, individual differences, cognitive aspects, emotional aspects and context variables also influence the dynamics of media usage and its effects. There has been a growing trend in the personalization of media use with the advent of internet-mediated mass communication technology platforms.

THINK BOX

- Do you agree with the dispositional perspective of media effects?
- How far is the agenda setting theory of media relevant in present context?

8.2 Media effects on identity

Identity is defined as a "core sense of self" (Jones & McEwen, 2000) or understanding of one's self in relation to one's past and potential future (Brickhouse & Potter, 2001) and an internal self-constructed dynamic organization of drives, abilities, beliefs, and individual history (Marcia, 1980, p. 159) that explain and predict behaviors (Marcia, 1994). Identity is a dynamic process, and it changes as individuals encounter and react to events, circumstances and elements in their social environment. Identity is both individually constructed (Erikson, 1968) and socially imposed (Marcia, 1994). Identity is multidimensional, involving multiple intersecting social identities. Identity operates within specific contexts and structures.

Social identity theory suggests that individuals define their own identities concerning social groups, and such identifications protect and upgrade self-identity. Issues of self and identity are primarily understood at the level of the personal self. In social identity theory, the impact of social context and social groups has been highlighted in the way people perceive themselves and others as a basis for explaining intergroup behavior. Social identity theory suggests that social structure factors, such as perceived group status differences, perceived legitimacy and the permeable ability to move from one group to another, can predict Intergroup behavior.

Social identity theory is based upon constituents of social categorization, social identification and social comparison. Many studies have shown that increasing or decreasing the salience of group categorization produces concomitant changes in intergroup bias, but salience and identification are not isomorphic. From a social identity theory approach, cognitive motivational processes affect and are affected by group, intergroup and societal processes to influence people and think about themselves in the ways that are typical characteristics of the group determined by social context.

Social identity theory also suggests (Tajfel & Turner, 1979) that all social entities including the self can be seen as members of social groups, and social groups play a crucial role in the identity of individuals. The self-categorization theory describes the process of shifting to see the self in terms of membership in a salient group with which one also identifies (Turner et al., 1987). Self-categorization causes people to think of themselves as having the characteristics associated with group membership, a process called self-stereotyping, which leads group members to perceive themselves as interchangeable exemplars of a group rather than as unique individuals (E.R. Smith & Henry, 1996; Turner et al., 1987).

When group membership is salient, people's attributes, attitudes and behaviors converge toward those that are typical characteristics of their groups, which is classic evidence of self-categorization (Haslam et al., 1999; Hogg & Turner, 1987; Spears, Doosje & Ellemers, 1997) which also provides evidence of the group nature of such phenomena.

The term intergroup emotion, coined by Mackie, Devos and Smith (2000) and intergroup emotion theory (Mackie et al., 2000) describe systematically the uniquely group-level nature of categorization, identification and appraisal antecedents of intergroup emotions as well as their consequences for intergroup relations.

Individuals' feelings are strongly influenced based on membership in a group and resultant collective emotions might be activated via self-stereotyping and self-categorization. Individual emotions acquire different emotional experiences by being members of a group, and intergroup emotions are quite different from individual emotions.

8.2.1 Social identity and media

When categorized into groups, people are "depersonalized" or seen as embodying a relevant group prototype (Hogg et al., 1995). Ingroup and outgroup comparison and highlighting of distinctiveness are accentuated through social media platforms communication. Research suggests that exposure to positive media images can improve majority group members' attitudes about minority outgroup (e.g. Schiappa et al., 2005) along a variety of outcomes ranging from general support and positive judgments to sympathy regarding issues of discrimination (Bodenhausen et al., 1995).

Other studies also suggest that to a degree, favorable intergroup outcomes based on media exposure are contingent upon the extent to which the media depictions of race/ethnicity (even when positive) accommodate majority group norms and attitudes (Coover, 2001; Mastro et al., 2005).

It has been observed through media messages researches on the audience that it has the potential to prime viewers' perceptions from different groups and also helps in the formation of group norms and status of group members. The need for quality depictions of one's ingroup appears to be so important that audiences may actively reject and select media content to manage social identity needs. Other researches also suggest that the effective use of celebrity endorsers underscores how these individuals serve as a symbolic reference group one wishes to aspire to become.

8.2.2 Science, identity and media

Adolescents' and youth's gender-stereotyped perceptions are also guided by STEM (Science, Technology, Engineering and Mathematics) representation of public image through portrayal of masculine characteristics, and this negatively affects girls' participation, identification and interest in STEM. Media images conveyed through television programs portrayed STEM professionals largely dominated by men. The role and status of women in science have been underrepresented or represented in a distorted manner. Media portrayals of scientists on primetime television programs have presented women scientists' work in a co-opted or devalued status.

Media images of scientists, technologists, engineers and mathematicians on television and in films are cultural constructions that convey assumptions about gender and STEM (Steinke, 2005). Mass media messages serve as a symbol of power and constitute a significant source of cultural production. Researches also indicate television characters and popular media forms influence youth's work-related values and aspirations.

Social contexts, social norms and roles along with cultural traditions and media portrayals influence as contextual cues for STEM identity formation. Social learning theory describes how children learn to imitate behaviors from others in their environments through the process of "Identificatory learning" (Bandura et al., 1963, p. 533). Gender schemas, just like other schemas, help children and adolescents understand experiences and make decisions that influence their perceptions, beliefs and behavior. Research suggests that portrayals of characters on television programs can shape and maintain gender schemas, particularly when children identify with those characters (Miller & Reeves, 1976).

Oyserman's (2015) identity-based motivation theory describes both how and when people's current and active identities motivate their behavior based on the ways in which contextual cues actively shape identity in a particular context. According to identity-based motivation theory:

- Contextual cues trigger identities that are dynamically constructed and determine which personal and social identities are perceived as most accessible in that moment;
- Accessible identities influence action readiness based on perceived necessity and relevance; and
- Activated, accessible identities influence behavior depending on perceptions of difficulty. (Oyserman, 2014, 2015)

The premise of identity-based motivation theory is that "thinking is influenced by the context in which it occurs" (Oyserman, 2015 p. 2). Research has shown that female role models can have a positive impact, in particular an adolescent girl's attitude toward science (Evans et al., 1995) and their stereotyped perception of STEM professionals (Hughes et al., 2013).

STEM identity varies in its effect due to factors of media characteristics, differences in perceptions by girls including its accessibility and other contextual factors. Gender-stereotyped images certainly affect STEM identity achievement portrayed through gender-stereotyped media images. In the Indian context also the participation and enrollment of female students, even in the best technology institutes like the Indian Institute of Technology, is very low. The gender ratio is roughly 1 in every 10 admissions despite girls doing better than boys at the higher secondary level. As part of a cure for this, the Ministry of Human Resource Development directed all 23 IITs to ensure that at least 14% of their seats in the 2018 batch go to women. The government aimed to improve the gender ratio at the engineering colleges to at least 20%, or one woman in every five students, by 2020.

Mass media's use of images, words and characters to communicate to audiences perpetuates certain ideas, ideologies and norms. Identity formation through mass media platforms including digital media has implications for processes of identity formation during adolescence and adulthood. Adolescents and youth use social networking sites to interact, articulate their views and become a regular consumer to perform various types of self-expression activities. Identity formation takes place through the processes of exploration and commitment and creating a self-image for the large audiences of friends.

Personal agency in the form of self-expression among peers is pronounced within social media environments such as chat rooms blogs and bulletin boards. Much of what is done on these social media websites can be called "social grooming": maintaining a friendship, keeping track of what contacts in the network are doing via their public posts, what they are talking about and who they are interacting with, staying abreast of social events and trends and managing one's own reputation to the network (Tufekci, 2008).

Millennial youth engage in a variety of ways to explore identity through learning and nurturing interests with like-minded individuals on social media platforms. The self-worth of persons is enhanced through attention to self on social media platforms and social validation and peer approval. When youth post status updates or upload photographs from their latest social event, they are communicating to the entire network of known others who likely have multiple beliefs, opinions or hold various roles of authority in their lives, a phenomenon known as context collapse (Marwick & Boyd, 2011).

The self-satisfaction and self-worth of a person are closely related to the social approval of others. The social media network pattern has implications for self-worth perceptions. Identity negotiations on social media networks is a complex process of learning to integrate multiple aspects of one's self with others which involve a variety of people including friends, strangers, teachers, parents and many others. Digital self-expressions allow publicly identifiable and searchable records of one's identities.

In the age of media commercialization and globalization, identity aspects are being influenced by the usage pattern of social media activities. The blurring of boundaries between local and global also poses difficulties of establishing values and norms essential for identity formation.

THINK BOX

- How do media influence the perceptions of a person regarding his/her own self-identity?
- What methods can you suggest to overcome STEM identity in Indian technical education institutions?

8.3 Media effects on women

The socialization of gender roles is the process through which children learn about the social expectations, attitudes and behaviors associated with boys and girls. Gender is one of the earliest social categories which children learn from parents, schools, teachers, peers and other agencies of socialization.

Socialization is the process of internalizing the norms and ideals of the society through which cultural continuity is achieved. Socialization at the early stages sets the stage for the future course of development influenced by the societal consensus considered as appropriate and normal. The role of family, friends, peer group and workplace reinforces the values appropriate to each gender.

8.3.1 Gender socialization by family

Families play an extremely crucial role in treating males and females differently right from birth stages. Languages and behaviors adopted in the course of inter-action with boys and girls shape future behavior patterns and define boundaries. Homophily is linked to a social process where children learn network connections with the same sex rather than cross-sex.

The differential set of traits and characteristics are promoted by parents in the family and internalized by the children as life scripts in which they are promoted and encouraged to self-segregate into homogenous groups. From a Doing Gender perspective, roles and tasks in the society are practiced in a gendered way. The interaction patterns associated with gendered ways of doing are also strengthened by an institutional arrangement that legitimizes this division of fundamental nature in the society.

The self is comprised of multiple identities which are broadly categorized under personal identities, role identities and group identities. Personal identities are related to the meaning that allows a person to realize a sense of individuality. Role identities are acquired while performing a particular type of role, such as teacher, student or doctor. Group identity is a form of identity through which people identify them-selves as members of the group with whom they relate, affiliate and belong. Media plays a key role in constructing an identity of dominant masculinity. Gramsci's ideas have proved a powerful tool for understanding representations of gender in the media allowing to go beyond the study of single images to examine patterns and themes in representations.

8.3.2 Gender socialization by language

Gender socialization in the family starts at the early stages of life through treating the newborns differently, and language used is specific to gender identity, such as caring and affection to describe girls and bravery, adventurism to describe boys' identity. The use of language specific to gender is appropriated and internalized by girls and boys respectively, which works as a boundary to defining the acceptable norms of behavior by males and females. The psychoanalytic theory of Sigmund Freud relies on important concepts of internal conflict and the unconscious part of ourselves which we are not aware and described that gender is not an innate capacity but rather based on acquired characteristics. The early socialization from both mothers and fathers supports and strengthens masculine characteristics for the boys and feminine characteristics for the girls, which also form the basis for future social interaction.

Identity theory suggests that gendered identity construction perpetuates the separate identity factor which is acquired through cultural influences of family and society. The factor of identity formation is acquired through the processes of ascription, identification and resemblance with the parents which may comprise irrational and stereotypical gender expectations.

8.3.3 Role identity and social identity

Role identity is defined as the role (or character) people perform while being members of social groups. Turner et al. (1994) has also described that people define and differentiate themselves on the basis of group membership, and they enact normative roles in the direction of ingroup expectations.

The postulates of social identity theory are that perspective self-esteem and self-efficacy are affected by role identity for the sake of approval of relevant others, and that people perform such roles according to category prescriptions. Media exposure of ingroup and outgroup identity support the stereotyped perceptions and beliefs.

This categorization-based role performance is also reinforced by the fact of observing others of the same category sharing similar perceptions and the behavioral consequences for individual members to act in unison. The postulates of social identity theory focus more on shared common outcomes for group members. Social identity theory emphasizes intergroup properties more, whereas Identity theory focuses more on intra-group properties. Media plays an important role in creating ingroup favoritism and outgroup derogation.

Situational aspects have the potential to activate group identity factors in typical situations. Categorization processes are relatively stable and referred by specific terminology and sets of behaviors in terms of category and its roles. Group categorization of people through mass media increases the perception that group members are similar to one another.

Cognitive representation of a role describes the norms and association of the self with a role as represented by the Identity Standard. The activation of social identity results in depersonalization (Turner, 1984, 1985) which is the process of seeing the self in terms of the social category embodied in the prototype. Self-verification is the process through which people behave to maintain one's situational identity close to the norms and standard of the prototype.

Depersonalization and verification together involve increased feelings of shared membership, self-esteem, self-efficacy and increased emotional attachment to the members of an in-group. People tend to act in ways being more masculine or feminine to maintain gender identities. Gender also acts as a status category, signaling one's position and power in the social structure, and this identity reminds them to behave in expected ways. It is extremely relevant to understand this identity (who one is) and role (what one does) are central to one's identity formation whose outcomes influence a range of cognitive, behavioral and emotional consequences in real-life group situations.

The meanings associated with categorized role identities are shared and idiosyncratic in nature which has a strong correspondence with the role behavior. For example, the role of a mother is associated with the behavioral role of caring and nurturing, and the role of a father is associated with the power and decision-making, through the processes of socialization. Perception of gendered ways of experiencing positive and negative emotions is transmitted and perpetuated through media platforms, and these identity expectations are internalized through repeated portrayals.

8.3.4 Occupational roles

These identity prescriptions and stereotypes are also applied to the world of work. It is a dominant stereotype presented by media to highlight male characters having a job outside the home as compared to female characters. Jobs are also described as traditionally male occupations such as surgeons, military and politicians, and traditionally female occupations such as teachings and secretarial work.

A longitudinal study of sixth to eighth graders conducted by Morgan (1982) found among girls that television viewing predicted stereotypical responses over time to an index that induced measures as "women are happiest at home raising children" and "men are born with more ambition than women", even after controlling for a number of additional variables.

8.3.5 Domestic and relational roles

Media-related gender perceptions from advertising to various programs and television may influence people's attitudes regarding which type of work is the domain of males and females. Even in the Indian context, a large majority of males are associated with doing agrarian work, and domestic work is considered the responsibility of females as a part of the dominant stereotype existing in Indian society. The work of nursing and school teaching is also considered as professions related to females and the job of politics and sports are considered predominantly male activities, leading to much fewer females participating in the fields of politics and sports.

In relationship matters also, lots of restrictions are imposed upon females in terms of interaction and adversarial attitudes about romantic relationships. Many stigmas are attached to females having sex with male partners before marriage which are not applied to the male counterparts. Similarly, major economic decisions of the family are mostly in the hands of male members, considered as the head of the family.

Appearance and body image-related attitudes are also highly influenced by media messages, leading to negative body image experiences by the adolescent girls. Thinness appearance is highlighted as an ideal type, leading to dieting as an attempt to control body weight. One of the most common ways through which media affect the perceptions of beauty is the idea that "thin is beautiful", which adversely affects adolescents' self-esteem. Many researchers highlight mass media objectification of women as sex objects to increase their products, sales and services.

Media can't be considered as the sole factor affecting women, and other mediating factors of societal values, education, culture and political decision-making do play an important role in the ways how women perceive themselves and perceived by others in a society.

THINK BOX

- Critically evaluate the portrayal of women in Indian Media.
- Do you think media can create problems for women by fostering certain attitudes and beliefs? Justify your answer.

8.4 Media and violence

Baker and Ball (1969) stated, "Exposure to mass media portrayals of violence over a long period socializes audience into norms, attitudes and values for violence contained in those portrayals" (p. 376). Many government-supported studies were conducted in the United States to ascertain the effects of media on violence and undesirable effects in terms of emotional desensitization to violence. Albert Bandura in 1984 argued that audiences acquire lasting attitudes, emotional reactions and behavioral proclivities towards persons, places or things that have been associated with modeled emotional experiences. Bandura's theory was criticized (e.g. Gauntlett, 1995) on the ground that in the Bobo doll experiment, children followed model behavior witnessed in the video, implying that the same behavior that will be imitated by children in actual situations can't be generalized.

Social cognitive theory is considered an influential approach, which suggests that aggression may be activated by learning and priming aggressive scripts. The moral panic theory proposed by David Gauntlett (2007) published online article media studies that described the shortcoming of traditional media studies of not looking at the blurring of boundaries between audiences and producers.

The studies of mass media and violence analyze the impact of the relationship between themes of violence in media sources with real-world aggression and violence. The studies related to media exposure and violence are not related in a cause-and-effect model, and it is a result of a more complex process of mediating variables. A large number of researchers suggest the hypothesis that media violence portrayal causes desensitization and a climate of fear. However, other theorists suggest media violence can contribute to aggressive behavior, but viewing violent films and television does not make children aggressive in a spontaneous way, and it is a gradual outcome of socio-cultural factors. Studies conducted in laboratory situations and studies related to a limited number of field experiments can't form the basis of generalization for media effects on violence. Some studies on video games link to aggressive behavior while other studies indicate no strong links between playing violent video games and aggression in adolescents. In some researches, playing video games has been associated with clear cognitive benefits in certain situations.

Aggression is a complex behavior caused by multiple factors, some of them known and some still unknown, while some researchers consider the studies highlighting media violence and effect on behavior as a publication bias to simplify a complex process. Media effects theory of violence has been described under the headings of social learning theory, social cognitive theory, the catalyst model and other theories.

8.4.1 Social learning theory

Social learning theory suggests that learning can occur through observation and imitation of others Julian B. Rotter (1954) described the holistic interaction between the individual and the social environment as reinforcers of learning new behaviors. Rotter's theory highlighted the contribution of subjective expectancy and value of reinforcement as an indicator of the likelihood of a behavior.

Observational learning may or may not involve imitation. For example, you may see a person crossing the red-light signal and be caught by traffic police, and thus you may avoid doing so to avoid punishment. In this case, you learned from your observation, but you did not imitate what you observed. Bandura (1986) highlighted that observational learning occurs independent of reinforcement, but other factors of attentional processes, retentional processes, behavioral production processes and motivational processes influence the processes of observational learning.

Bandura believed that perceived self-efficacy and intrinsic reinforcement tends to be maintained more effectively if it has been externally reinforced by others. Self-efficacy beliefs predict effective behavioral functioning. According to

Bandura, radical shifts in moral behaviors can be performed through the use of several mechanisms to dissociate representative acts from self-sanctions. This may include moral justification, euphemistic labeling, advantageous comparison, displacement and diffusion of responsibility, distortion of consequences, dehumanization and attribution of blame. Euphemistic labeling is used to describe the reprehensible acts respectably. Bandura also suggested that television programs showing violence portrayed as permissible, successful by superheroes can act as a model behavior that can encourage viewers to follow violent behavior patterns.

8.4.2 Social cognitive theory

Bandura in his recent writings (1999, 2000, 2001, 2002) emphasized the importance of human agency or agents of human experience and activities guided by planning and cognitive schemas. Features of human agency are characterized by intentionality, forethought, self-reactiveness and self-reflectiveness. This theory highlights a central role to cognitive, vicarious, self-regulatory and self-reflective processes. In televised representations, many aspects of physical aggression are portrayed as acceptable solutions to overcome conflicts which gradually legitimize, glamorize and trivialize human violence factors.

Struggles and aggression as a means to overpower opponents are prized more through electronic media, which acts as a vehicle for justification for the viewer's adopting such means. On the other hand, dehumanization weakens self-restraints against cruel and aggressive acts, and humanization fosters compassionate forms of behavior. The disengagement mechanisms are used in various television programs to exploit aggression by use of brutality for commercial advantages. The social construction of reality through the lens of mass media cultivates images in the society to be adopted as norms through the symbolic social promotion of behavior.

8.4.3 Catalyst model

The catalyst model proposed by Ferguson et al. (2008) suggests that genesis of violence is media is a weak contributor of violence and that other factors such as genetic, family and peers are more powerful contributors to crime and violence. The process of violence is also influenced by child's temperament, personality aspects and motivational aspects. Baron and Richardson (1994) define aggressive behavior as behavior not necessarily physically injurious nor illegal, but intended to cause physical harm and humiliation to another organism that wishes to avoid the harm. Violent behavior is defined as "typically restricted to acts" which are intended to cause serious physical harm. Short-term environmental factors such as financial troubles, relationship troubles and legal troubles can act as motivation for crime.

8.4.4 Excitation transfer theory

Zillmann and Bryant's (1974) excitation transfer model described that arousal by a media stimulus may be erroneously attributed to arousal created by different stimulus and it can increase the feelings of aggression. Zillmann (1988) also suggested that once activated, arousal which may have disappeared may extend the feeling of aggression through transfer of arousal under similar conditions.

This particular model of transfer of arousal to aggression works on the mechanism of priming theory through lowering the threshold for using them.

8.4.5 Social interaction theory

Aggression is an act in which a person intends or threatens to harm another person. According to Tedeschi's (1970) coercive power theory, harm-doing to others is adopted as a technique to influence others. Aggression is also considered as punishment, which implies that harmful act is done in response to some offensive behavior. Offensive behavior may result due to non-compliance of norms and orders.

The following are factors that can contribute to violence and related activities:

Aggressive conditions: according to this approach, aggressive cognitions and semantic activation lead to subsequent aggressive behavior. Accessibility of aggressive thoughts are acquired through certain conditions facilitating the activation of aggressive behaviors. For example, if a person is always playing with guns and other arms, it is possible that associations related to guns such as shots, crime and war may produce accessibility of aggressive thoughts.

Aggressive emotions: Arriaga et al. (2006) used the State Hostility scale (SHS; Anderson, Deuser & DeNeve, 1995) to describe the participant's current aggressive feelings. After engaging in violent games, the stimulus resulting from such games may increase aggressive dispositions to some degree.

Physiological arousal: in our day-to-day activities, there are many physiological arousals which vary along with our encounter with different activities. High level of arousal for prolonged time periods is often associated with health risks and aggressive behaviors. With level of changing arousal, other physiological measurements such as heart rate, blood pressure and galvanic skin response also increase.

8.4.6 Desensitization effect

Excess exposure to media violence may result in an emotional desensitization effect which is a diminished feeling of empathy and concern toward the victims of violent acts. Repeated exposure to violent media messages reduces the impact of responses through a process of habituation undermining the feelings of concern and sympathy that may have occurred in case of actual violence. Social media has become a platform for sharing videos of intolerance and hate in some situations. The result of large-scale violence viewing is that people start accepting it as an ordinary part of life activities, which ultimately desensitizes them of the true consequences of violence.

The GAM model (General Aggression Model; Anderson, Gentile & Buckley, 2007) described that repeated exposure to media violence can lead to aggressive beliefs and attitudes and desensitization to violence acts.

8.4.7 Media violence and its effect on children

Jeff Lewis's book *Media Culture and Human Violence* (Lewis, 2015) challenges the conventional approaches to media violence at research. The link between media and violence is not simplistic; rather, it is also guided by forms of "violence thinking" embedded in social hierarchies which helps us shape our beliefs through politics and cultural discourses. The new culture of kids sharing information with peers and becoming too immersed in the virtual reality of cyber-culture is also resulting in addictive or obsessive dangers posed by new media. Domination of the children's toy market has led to the corporate construction of childhood which represents a dangerous colonization of children, indoctrinating them with the values of consumerism and instilling an illusory sense of empowerment.

Bandura talked about modeling of aggressive behaviors by children watching violence on media. It is difficult for children differentiating the imaginary world from real-world events. A large number of children spend long hours using television and video games which constitute violent messages. Some of the researches in this area suggest that strong exposure to media violence by the children contributes to aggressive beliefs, attitudes and behaviors which can result in depression, desensitization to violence, nightmares and sleep disturbances. Children learn through media by imitating, observing and implementing media messages in real-life situations as they can't easily discriminate between fantasy and reality. Interactive media such as video games and internet through violent media content increases the probability of aggressive thinking and behavior varying with moderating factors of societal and parental guidance.

Research by psychologists L. Rowell Huesmann and others (2003) described that long hours of television viewing by children results in aggressive behavior patterns during adulthood. Anderson and Dill (2000) in their review suggested that exposure to violent video games increases aggressive tendency and decreases empathy and prosocial behavior tendencies. Schemas and normative beliefs of aggression as acceptable modes of script for solving social problems are adopted by children through observation of violent media messages. The observation of violence as a means for solving problems activates the thinking for aggressive behaviors and is adopted as a desirable and useful method. The correlation between childhood exposure to media violence and childhood aggression is highly replicable even across researchers who disagree about the reasons.

There are a variety of parenting factors, such as parents' intellectual ability, parents' aggression and other socio-cultural context factors, that strongly determine the child's exposure to media violence and the child's subsequent aggressive behavior. Media violence factors affect children in varying degrees influenced by psychological principles of observational learning, habituation, desensitization and excitation transfer which can be moderated in its effect by other factors.

8.4.8 Media violence effects on youth

Research on violent media messages reveals a likely increase in the aggressive behavior of children and youth. Several studies indicate a short-term and long-term relation between media violence and aggressive behavior with widespread accessibility to various media forms such as television, movies and the internet.

Some studies relate to violent effects of media on aggressive thinking, beliefs, attitudes and behavior. Other studies focus on multiple factors in addition to media violence affecting aggressive behavior and highlight the developmental perspective of media violence. It is suggested that children with aggressive tendencies are more prone to developing as violent adolescents and violent youth.

The total time spent on media activities, the content of media usage and other social context factors influence the degrees of variation in violent media effects. A study by Donnerstein and Berkowitz (1981) highlighted the role of the combined effect of violent portrayals with sexual stimulation and the resultant impact of assaulting behavior of males towards females.

In other studies, Huesmann and Guerra (1997) noted that youth believing in violence as the acceptable norm and justifying this tendency increases violent tendencies. Nisbet and Cohen (1996) argued that the factor of retaliation was treated as honorable and as a contributory factor of violent tendency among the youth. The culture of using violent words in daily interaction also contributes to the process of a violent tendency among youth. A high proportion of television programs and movies contain violence, leading to violent behavior patterns among youth through excessive exposure to violent messages and music videos.

Several studies evaluated the impact of media violence on the attitude and behavior of youth, but results of these studies differ substantially, and more cross-sectional and longitudinal studies are required to arrive at an authentic conclusion. A greater number of interdisciplinary researches involving psychology, communication, sociology and other disciplines are required for a refined and better understanding of the consequences of exposure to media violence on youth.

It is generally agreed among media researchers that violence is certainly transferred to the viewers through observational learning, cognitive processing and schemas acquired through the consumption of violent media messages. Beliefs, attitudes

and perception of violent media messages are also guided and varies from the interpretation, knowledge and situational dimensions of the recipients of media messages. Individual differences in terms of personality traits and intellectual awareness
also vary the effect of media violence on children and youth. Social environment,
situational variables and cultural factors with strong sanctions against violence play
the moderating effects role in media violence and its impact on youth behavior.
Few studies have also highlighted the role of parental aggressiveness, coldness and
viewing habits increase or decrease the effects of media exposure on violence.

Parental restrictions to access of violent media and interventions adopted during
media interaction of children can also differentiate the degrees of impact related
to violent media-message effects. Studies also indicate gender variation and intergenerational variation, which is also well researched by the producers regarding
children's preferences for different genres.

THINK BOX

- What can be the role of media in encouraging or discouraging violence among masses?
- Is social media responsible for increased violence in society?

8.5 Critical evaluation and Indian perspective

Several studies conducted in the past few decades highlight the role of media violence on all sections of people, particularly violent effects on children and youth.
Media effects have far reaching consequences on people's attitudes and behavior.
Media messages also affect self-identity and social identity through its complex
interplay in interpersonal situations.

The harmful effects of media in creating desensitization to violent activities are
widely acknowledged by the researchers of mass media. Media script does play a
role in the formation of depersonalization. Much of the contemporary media content is dominated by the prevalence of violent content in its continuous flow of
information, entertainment and news programs. Media violence messages through
repeated exposure produces aggressive scripts and interpersonal schema which
influences aggression-supporting beliefs and attitudes about appropriate social
behavior. It would be immature to attribute every aspect to violent media messages
alone, and a detailed analysis incorporating the importance of several other factors
needs to be conducted.

The challenge for media researchers in exploring the inter-disciplinary perspective is to arrive at a convincing understanding of media and violence. Media
violence effects have also percolated to Indian society, affecting children and

numerous youth. A large number of children and youth spend significantly long hours receiving media messages through the proliferation of news and media, including video games, music videos and social media. Violent media messages are entering the home without any filtration, inviting the active participation of very young children with the least parental supervision. A large number of parents from weaker economic status hardly pay any attention to their children's use of media violence messages. How to be better consumers of media messages needs to taught more scientifically. The educational backwardness of Indian citizens also contributes to the problem of violent media behavior patterns due to a lack of knowledge. Media-related rumors also contribute to the emergence of false notions leading to violent reactions by the ignorant masses. Sometimes people also fall prey to unverified religious discrimination messages, leading to large-scale violence in India. It is therefore necessary to improve the level of media literacy and awareness in our country to overcome the negative effects of media messages for all sections of people in society. Several instances are reported by newspapers of violence related to media rumors in different parts of the country.

THINK BOX

- Has the media replaced the role of society in the socializing process? How?
- What should be the role of media in promoting social and cultural values?

8.6 Summary

Mass media has had a profound impact on societies and their culture. In the contemporary period, it plays a crucial role in influencing people's minds irrespective of geographical boundaries. The main function of media in a society is to provide news and information to the masses, which even comprises the elements of entertainment and education. Mass media occupies a large proportion of our time and has the powerful potential to influence the attitudes and behavior of the people. Its influence has increased dramatically over the years, significantly changing beliefs, attitudes, emotional, physiological and behavioral states.

There are empirical methods to measure long-term and short-term media effects. Early media-effects theory focused on the use of propaganda techniques to unite people. Limited media effects theory (Katz & Lazarsfeld, 1955) differed with all-powerful media effects and focused upon the idiosyncratic nature of media effects on individuals and audiences. Media effects theory also argues about indirect media effects, stating that people are affected by the interpersonal ability of their leaders. Gerbner proposed cultivation theory, arguing that media cultivate a collective consciousness and suggested that television helps as a means of socializing people.

Agenda-setting theory examined media's power to decide the thinking of its users. The agenda setting of the audiences is influenced by the factor of accessibility. Exposure to mass media violence messages has emotional effects on the audience, leading to the development of violent attitudes. Aggression scripts are initiated by people watching violent media. Some theorists also argue that the link between media and violence is not direct and other meditational factors of the socio-cultural environment also contribute to its impact.

Media messages which are selected by audiences can influence their behaviors. Personality factors, temperament, moods and motivation are conditional, which means media messages will have different types of effects on the people varying due to age, gender, class and educational backgrounds.

Media also impacts the identity of persons. Social media has the potential to create ingroup and outgroup perceptions through selective depictions of characteristics portrayed in the media. Media also plays a crucial role in STEM Identity (Science, Technology, Engineering and Mathematics) creation in the society. Certain stereotypes and prejudices are portrayed through mass media, creating a gender-specific identity. Mass media through its role of socialization creates categories that are reinforced at family and social levels. Media's effect on children and their aggressive behavior has been an area of intense research among media scholars. Violent media content increased the possibility of aggressive behavior for children watching them through imitation and observation. The observation of violence as a means for solving problem-solving is adopted by children as they can't easily differentiate reality and imaginary situations.

The effects of mass media on socialization are influencing the micro and macro environment. Whether it is written, televised or socially communicated, it is playing the most significant force in shaping an individual's beliefs and culture. Micro-level effects of media are conditional and transactional, mostly focused on short-term effects. Macro-level effects create influence and socio-political and economic aspects. In this new era of internet-mediated society, social media have begun to play a crucial role in forming public opinion about a wide range of issues. The issues of media and violence, as well as false news, are being debated among scholars of media psychology. Mass communication through the extensive circulation of information can persuade people and affect public opinion. How humans adjust and adapt these new modes of communication will determine its advantages and disadvantages. A high level of media literacy and broader conceptualization of its effects can maximize the rewards of new technology to people in a society.

Key points

- Cultivation theory proposes that prolonged exposure of viewers on television as a medium of socialization cultivates perceptions of reality.
- The mean world index means that people with long-term exposure and consumption of TV programs cultivate the image of a mean and insecure world.
- Mass media is a principal source of connection between events in the world and the images in the minds of public.
- The concepts proposed that media's reporting with a favorable slant lead to a particular type of ideology and thinking in society.
- Increase in individualization and personalization of media use has enabled a form of communication known as mass self-communication.
- Media images of scientists, technologists, engineers and mathematicians has led to the emergence of STEM identity.
- Identity-based motivation theory suggests that thinking is influenced by the context in which it occurs.
- Media also plays a crucial role in gender socialization.
- Exposure to media violence over a long period of time may result in increased aggression among viewers, especially children.
- Schemas and scripts portrayed through media are easily imitated.

Key terms

placelessness, framing, general aggression model, hyperpersonal communication, ingroup and outgroup, depersonalization, dehumanization, euphemistic labeling, excitation transfer, schema

References

Anderson, C.A., & Bushman, B.J. (2002). Human aggression. *Annual Review of Psychology*, 53, 27–51.

Anderson, C.A., Deuser, W.E., & DeNeve, K.M. (1995). Hot temperatures, hostile affect, hostile cognition, and arousal: Tests of a general model of affective aggression. *Personality and Social Psychology Bulletin*, 21, 434–48.

Anderson, C.A., & Dill, K.E. (2000). Video games and aggressive thoughts, feelings, and behavior in the laboratory and in life. *Journal of Personality and Social Psychology*, 78, 772–90.

Anderson, C.A., Gentile, D.A., & Buckley, K.E. (2007). *Violent Video Game Effects on Children and Adolescents: Theory, Research, and Public Policy*. Oxford, UK: Oxford University Press.

Arriaga, P., Esteves, F., Carneiro, P., & Monteiro, M.B. (2006). Violent computer games and their effects on state hostility and physiological arousal. *Aggressive Behavior*, 32, 358–71.

Baker, R.K., & Ball, S.J. (1969). *Mass Media and Violence: A Staff Report to the National Commission on the Causes and Prevention of Violence*. Washington, DC: United States Government Printing Office.

Bandura, A. (1986). *Social Foundations of Thought and Action: A Social Cognitive Theory*. Englewood Cliffs, NJ: Prentice-Hall.

Bandura, A. (1999). A social cognitive theory of personality. In L. Pervin & O. John (Eds.), *Handbook of Personality* (2nd ed., pp. 154–96). New York: Guilford.

Bandura, A. (2000). Exercise of human agency through collective efficacy. *Current Directions in Psychological Science*, 9, 75–78.

Bandura, A. (2001). Social cognitive theory: An agentic perspective. *Annual Review of Psychology*, 52, 1–26. Palo Alto, CA: Annual Reviews, Inc.

Bandura, A. (2002). Growing primacy of human agency in adaptation and change in the electronic era. *European Psychologist*, 7, 2–16.

Bandura, A. (2009). Social cognitive theory of mass communication. In J. Bryant & M.B. Oliver (Eds.), *Media Effects: Advances in Theory and Research* (pp. 94–124). New York: Routledge.

Bandura, A., Ross, D., & Ross, S.A. (1963). Imitation of film-mediated aggressive models. *Journal of Abnormal and Social Psychology*, 66(1), 3.

Baron, R.A., & Richardson, D.R. (1994). *Human Aggression* (2nd ed.). New York: Plenum.

Berkowitz, L., & Powers, P.C. (1979). Effects of timing and justification of witnessed aggression on the observers punitiveness. *Journal of Research in Personality*, 13, 71–80.

Bodenhausen, G.V., Schwarz, N., Bless, H., & Wänke, M. (1995). Effects of atypical exemplars on racial beliefs: Enlightened racism or generalized appraisals? *Journal of Experimental Social Psychology*, 31, 48–63.

Brickhouse, N., & Potter, J.T. (2001). Young women's scientific identity formation in an urban context. *Journal of Research in Science Teaching*, 38, 965–80.

Castells, M. (2007). Communication, power and counter-power in the network society. *International Journal of Communication*, 1, 238–66.

Coover, G. (2001). Television and social identity: Race representation as "white" accommodation. *Journal of Broadcasting and Electronic Media*, 45, 413–31.

Daft, R.L., & Lengel, R.H. (1986). Organizational information requirements, media richness and structural design. *Management Science*, 32, 554–71.

Donnerstein, E., & Berkowitz, L. (1981). Victim reactions in aggressive erotic films as a factor in violence against women. *Journal of Personality and Social Psychology*, 41, 710–24.

Donsbach, W. 2009. Cognitive dissonance theory – Roller coaster career: How communication research adapted the theory of cognitive dissonance. In T. Hartmann (Ed.), *Media Choice: A Theoretical and Empirical Overview* (pp. 128–49). New York: Routledge.

Entman, R.M. (2007). Framing bias: Media in the distribution of power. *Journal of Communication*, 57(1), 163–73.

Erikson, E.H. (1968). *Identity: Youth and Crisis*. New York: Norton.

Evans, M.A., Whigham, M., & Wang, M.C. (1995). The effect of a role model project upon the attitudes of ninth-grade science students. *Journal of Research in Science Teaching*, 32(2), 195–204.

Ferguson, C.J., Rueda, S.M., Cruz, A.M., Ferguson, D.E., Fritz, S., & Smith, S.M. (2008). Violent video games and aggression: Causal relationship or byproduct of family violence and intrinsic violence motivation? *Criminal Justice and Behavior*, 35, 311–32.

Gauntlett, D. (1995). *Moving Experiences: Understanding Television's Influences and Effects*. London: John Libbey.

Gauntlett, D. (2007). *Creative Explorations: New Approaches to Identities and Audiences*. London: Routledge.

Gerbner, G. (1969). Toward "cultural indicators": The analysis of mass mediated message systems. *A V Communication Review*, 17(2), 137–48.

Green, M.C., & Brock, T.C. (2000). The role of transportation in the persuasiveness of public narratives. *Journal of Personality and Social Psychology*, 79, 701–21.

Green, M.C., Brock, T.C., & Kaufman, G.E. (2004). Understanding media enjoyment: The role of transportation into narrative worlds. *Communication Theory*, 14, 311–27.

Hart, W., Albarracin, D., Eagly, A.H., Brechan, I., Lindberg, M.J., & Merrill, L. (2009). Feeling validated versus being correct: A meta-analysis of selective exposure to information. *Psychological Bulletin*, 135, 555–88.

Haslam, S.A., Oakes, P.J., Reynolds, K.J., & Turner, J.C. (1999). Social identity salience and the emergence of stereotype consensus. *Personality and Social Psychology Bulletin*, 25, 809–18.

Hogg, M.A., Terry, D.J., & White, K.M. (1995). A tale of two theories: A critical comparison of identity theory with social identity theory. *Social Psychology Quarterly*, 58, 255–69. doi:10.2307/2787127

Hogg, M.A., & Turner, J.C. (1987). Social identity and conformity: A theory of referent informational influence. In W. Doise & S. Moscovici (Eds.), *Current Issues in European Social Psychology* (Vol. 2, pp. 139–82). Cambridge, UK: Cambridge University Press.

Huesmann, L.R., & Guerra, N.G. (1997). Children's normative beliefs about aggression and aggressive behavior. *Journal of Personality and Social Psychology*, 72, 408–19.

Huesmann, L. R., Moise-Titus, J., Podolski, C. and Eron, L.D. (2003). Longitudinal relations between children's exposure to television violence and their aggressive and violent behaviour in young adulthood. *Developmental Psychology*, 39, 201–21.

Hughes, R.M., Nzekwe, B., & Molyneaux, K.J. (2013). The single sex debate for girls in science: A comparison between two informal science programs on middle school students' STEM identity formation. *Research in Science Education*, 43, 1979–2007.

Jones, S.R., & McEwen, M.K. (2000). A conceptual model of multiple dimensions of identity. *Journal of College Student Development*, 41, 405–14.

Katz, E., & Lazarsfeld, P.F. (1955). *Personal Influence*. New York: Free Press.

Katz, J.E. (2006). *Magic in the Air: Mobile Communication and the Transformation of Social Life*. New Brunswick, NJ: Transaction Publishers.

Klapper, J.T. (1960). *The Effects of Mass Communication*. Glencoe, IL: Free Press.

Knobloch-Westerwick, S. (2015). *Choice and Preference in Media Use*. New York: Routledge.

Lasswell, H. (1948). The structure and function of communication in society. In L. Bryson (Ed.), *The Communication of Ideas*. New York: Harper and Brothers.

Lasswell, H.D. (1927). *Propaganda Technique in the World War* (p. 261). Cambridge, MA: MIT Press.

Lewis, J. (2015). *Media, Culture and Human Violence: From Savage Lovers to Violent Complexity*. London: Rowman and Littlefield.

Lippmann, W. (1922) *Public Opinion*. New York: Macmillan.

Mackie, D.M., Devos, T., & Smith, E.R. (2000). Intergroup emotions: Explaining offensive action tendencies in an intergroup context. *Journal of Personality and Social Psychology*, 79(4), 602–16.

Marcia, J.E. (1980). *Handbook of Adolescent Psychology*. New York: Wiley & Sons.

Marcia, J.E. (1994). The empirical study of ego identity. In H.A. Bosma, T.G. Graafsma, H.D. Grotevan, & D.J.D. Levita (Eds.), *Identity and Development: An Interdisciplinary Approach* (4th ed.). Belmont, CA: Wadsworth.

Mares, M.-L., Oliver, M.B., & Cantor, J. (2008). Age differences in adults' emotional motivations for exposure to films. *Media Psychology*, 11, 488–511.

Mares, M.-L., & Sun, Y. (2010). The multiple meanings of age for television content preferences. *Human Communication Research*, 36(3), 372–96.

Mares, M.-L., & Woodard, E.H. (2006). In search of the older audience: Adult age differences in television viewing. *Journal of Broadcasting and Electronic Media*, 50(4), 595–614.

Marwick, A.E., & Boyd, D.M. (2011). I tweet honestly, I tweet passionately: Twitter users, context collapse, and the imagined audience. *New Media & Society*, 13(1), 114–33. doi:10.1177/146144481036531

Mastro, D., Tamborini, R., & Hullett, C. (2005). Linking media to prototype activation and subsequent celebrity attraction: An application of self-categorization theory. *Communication Research*, 32, 323–48.

McCombs, M.E., & Shaw, D.L. (1972).The agenda-setting function of mass media. *The Public Opinion Quarterly*, 36(2), 176–87.

McQuail, D. (2010). *McQuail's Mass Communication Theory*. London: Sage.

Meyrowitz, J. (1985). *No Sense of Place: The Impact of Electronic Media on Social Behavior*. New York: Oxford University Press.

Miller, M.M., & Reeves, B. (1976). Dramatic TV content and children's sex-role stereotypes. *Journal of Broadcasting*, 20, 35–50.

Morgan, M. (1982). Television and adolescents' sex-role stereotypes: A longitudinal study. *Journal of Personality and Social Psychology*, 43, 947–55.

Oyserman, D. (2014). Identity-based motivation: Core processes and intervention examples. In S. Karabenick & T.C. Urdan (Eds.), *Motivational Interventions: Advances in Motivation and Achievement* (Vol. 18, pp. 213–42). Bingley, UK: Emerald Group Publishing Ltd.

Oyserman, D. (2015). Identity-based motivation. In R. Scott & S. Kosslyn (Eds.), *Emerging Trends in the Behavioral and Social Sciences: An Interdisciplinary, Searchable, and Linkable Resource* (p. 2). doi:10.1002/9781118900772.etrds0171

Petty, R.E., & Cacioppo, J.T. (1986). *Communication and Persuasion: Central and Peripheral Routes to Attitude Change*. New York: Springer Verlag.

Pingree, R.J. (2007). How messages affect their senders: A more general model of message effects and implications for deliberation. *Communication Theory*, 17, 439–61.

Relph, E. (1976). *Place and Placelessness*. London: Pion.

Rogers, E.M., & Dearing, J.W. (1988). Agenda-setting research: Where has it been, where is it going. *Communication Yearbook*, 11, 555–94.

Rotter, J.B. (1954). *Social Learning and Clinical Psychology*. New York: Prentice-Hall.

Rubin, A. (2009). Uses-and-gratifications perspective on media effects. In J. Bryant & M.B. Oliver (Eds.), *Media Effects: Advances in Theory and Research* (pp. 165–84). New York: Routledge.

Sack, R.D. (1992). *Place, Modernity, and the Consumer's World: A Relational Framework for Geographic Analysis*. Baltimore, MD: Johns Hopkins University Press.

Schiappa, E., Gregg, P.B., & Hewes, D.E. (2005). Can one TV show make a difference? *Will & Grace* and the parasocial contact hypothesis. *Journal of Homosexuality*, 51(4), 15–37.

Slater, M.D., & Rouner, D. (2002) Entertainment-education and elaboration likelihood: Understanding the processing of narrative persuasion. *Communication Theory*, 12, 173–91.

Smith, E.R., & Henry, S. (1996). An in-group becomes part of the self: Response time evidence. *Personality and Social Psychology Bulletin*, 22, 635–42.

Smith, S.M., Fabrigar, L.R., Powell, D.M., & Estrada, M.-J. (2007). The role of information-processing capacity and goals in attitude-congruent selective exposure effects. *Personality and Social Psychology Bulletin*, 33, 948–60.

Spears, R., Doosje, B., & Ellemers, N. (1997). Self-stereotyping in the face of threats to group status and distinctiveness: The role of group identification. *Personality and Social Psychology Bulletin*, 23(5), 538–53.

Steinke, J. (2005). Cultural representations of gender and science: Portrayals of female scientists and engineers in popular films. *Science Communication*, 27(1), 27–63.

Tajfel, H., & Turner, J.C. (1979). An integrative theory of intergroup conflict. In W.G. Austin & S. Worchel (Eds.), *The Social Psychology of Intergroup Relations* (pp. 33–48). Monterey, CA: Brooks/Cole.

Tedeschi, J.T. (1970). Threats and promises. In P. Swingle (Ed.), *The Structure of Conflict*. New York: Academic Press.

Tufekci, Z. (2008). Can you see me now? Audience and disclosure regulation in online social network sites. *Bulletin of Science, Technology and Society*, 28(1), 20–36.

Turner, J.C. (1984). Social identification and psychological group formation. In H. Tajfel (Ed.) *The Social Dimension: European Developments in Social Psychology* (pp. 518–38) Cambridge: Cambridge University Press.

Turner, J.C. (1985). Social categorization and the self-concept: A social cognitive theory of group behavior. In E.J. Lawler (Ed.), *Advances in Group Processes: Theory and Research* (Vol. 2, pp. 77–122). Greenwich, CT: JAI Press.

Turner, J.C., Hogg, M.A., Oakes, P.J., Reicher, S.D., & Wetherell, M.S. (1987). *Rediscovering the Social Group: A Self-Categorization Theory*. Oxford: Basil Blackwell.

Turner, J.C., Oakes, P.J., Haslam, S.A., & McGarty, C. (1994). Self and collective: Cognition and social context. *Personality and Social Psychology Bulletin*, 20, 454–63.

Valkenburg, P.M. (2014). *Schermgaande jeugd [Youth and Screens]*. Amsterdam: Prometheus.

Valkenburg, P.M., & Cantor, J. (2001). The development of a child into a consumer. *Journal of Applied Development Psychology*, 22, 61–72.

Valkenburg, P.M., & Peter, J. (2013). The differential susceptibility to media effects model. *Journal of Communication*, 63(2), 221–43.

Walther, J.B. (1992). Interpersonal effects in computer-mediated interaction: A relational perspective. *Communication Research*, 19, 52–90.

Walther, J.B. (1996). Computer-mediated communication: Impersonal, interpersonal, and hyperpersonal interaction. *Communication Research*, 23, 3–43.

Zillman, D., & Bryant, J. (1974). Effect of residual excitation on the emotional response to provocation and delayed aggressive behavior. *Journal of Personality and Social Psychology*, 30, 782–91.

Zillmann, D. (1988). Mood management through communication choices. *American Behavioral Scientist*, 31, 327–40.

Zillmann, D. (1996). Sequential dependencies in emotional experience and behavior. In R.D. Kavanaugh, B. Zimmerberg, & S. Fein (Eds.), *Emotion: Interdisciplinary Perspectives* (pp. 243–72). Mahwah, NJ: Erlbaum.

9

CRITICAL ISSUES IN MEDIA PSYCHOLOGY

Learning objectives

After reading this chapter, you will be able to understand:

- Critical issues related to mass media
- Media psychology's role in citizenship
- Media psychology's role in pedagogy
- Meanings and myths created by moving images
- The concept of digital altruism
- Critical evaluation and Indian perspective of media psychology

9.1 Introduction

The realm of mass media encompasses a wide range of political, economic, ideological and cultural issues of society. A large number of factors are associated with the formation of public opinion on wide-ranging issues, such as environment, education, climate change, gender relations, government policies, democratic ethos and cultural habits, that are determined and influenced to a large extent by the mass media.

The needs of consumers, and all their expectations to fulfill daily life activities, are produced, controlled and disciplined by media messages. Our conceptions and perceptions of family life, social interchanges, perceptions of happiness in life, career choice, art, lifestyles, sexual orientations and business aspirations are heavily reinforced through symbolic interactions of messages emanating from the lens of media. The commodification of culture through advertisement activities creates fantasies in the minds of people constituting a major part of people's consciousness. Mass media through its overarching presence has the ability to engage audiences to produce popular imagination.

Managing the consent of a large number of people through repetitive portrayal leads to the emergence of mass culture through dramatic presentation of messages relating to human anxieties, fears and emotions. Our values, standard norms of living, work identity and gender identity are manipulated, repaired and manufactured by the lens of media.

Citizens' participation in democracy has increased with the rise of participatory media which includes community media blogs and YouTube channels in which citizens are participants in the creating process. The nature and dynamics of public discourse have been transformed into a conversation among people which is more open-ended. The interactive mode of media has helped to evolve journalism from lecture mode to conversation. This participatory media has also transformed the nature of the audience to participants.

The term "citizen media", coined by Clemencia Rodríguez (2011), typically refers to private people who produce media content despite not being journalists. Typical commercial corporate media giants have experienced a decline in recent years, with the advent of citizen-produced media high in terms of status and public credibility.

9.1.1 Alternative media

The concept of alternative media highlights and advocates the concerns of people who are not accorded due attention from the mainstream media through representing the interests of marginalized groups. Jurgen Habermas described that freedom in a democracy is expressed in the form of private autonomy and public autonomy. Habermas expressed that ideas and opinions of the people generate public discourse, and all political legitimacy comes from the communicative power of citizens. Rich communication of everyday life through public argumentation helps to produce norms. Habermas (1970) described the public sphere as explained through contextual immediacy permitting flexible consideration of a wide variety of ideas and strong public sphere procedurally regulated through communicative power. Habermas used the metaphors "sluices", "transformers" and "sensors" in the lifeworld to describe how inconsistent themes of diffuse public opinion can be translated into binding laws through parliamentary decision-making.

Guided by emotions and empathy through ritual and repetition, the core vocabulary of media messages tries to addresses the inner life feelings acting as a therapeutic voice. Alternative media also provides a platform for collective voice and action. Mainstream media portrayal ignores the voice of local groups such as environmental groups, human rights groups and civil rights groups.

Participatory culture promoted by alternative media allows citizens to play an active role in collecting, reporting, analyzing and disseminating news and information. By allowing citizens' participation, alternative media contributes to the empowering of a civic attitude and allows citizens to move from literacy to participation.

Sponsorship and advertisement considerations are negligible or least in alternative media, and the possibility for grassroots representation is increased. Local participation of indigenous groups creates opportunities for the empowerment of specific groups that are ignored or overlooked by the traditional mainstream media. Subaltern groups are the groups ranked inferior socially who get a voice within hegemonic political discourses, allowing them space to challenge subaltern status through direct participation. Through active participation, subaltern groups reshape their identities and social status, enacting their citizenship-producing power and letting their voice be heard. Social media platforms of blogs, Facebook, Twitter, Instagram and others used for spreading news and information allow ordinary citizens to bypass the gatekeepers of traditional mainstream media and share the information and perspective these citizens deem important. Internet information sharing is different from the top-down approach; it allows the users space for mobilization through the cultivation of interpersonal works and provides a voice towards social change.

9.2 Digital media citizenship

Digital media citizenship refers to the responsible use of technology by anyone who uses computers, internet or digital devices to engage with society on any level. Citizen journalism is based upon citizens' active participation in collection, dissemination, reporting and analysis of news by the general public by means of internet.

In this age of digitalization of social life, cultural life and the terms of citizenship are undergoing wide changes. The boundary between private and public is blurring, with increasing activities on the public space of social media platforms. Digital media citizenship also deals with digital relationships, activities and personal goals. Digital citizenship also has responsibility to supervise cyberbullying activities, emotional and mental aspects of internet communication and etiquettes to be followed by users, known as "Netiquette". By disrupting the established ways of mainstream media communication, citizenship in cyberspace is dynamically related and impacts upon the action and understanding of political agency. Digital citizenry promotes the opportunities for equal socio-economic participation through lowering the barriers to entry as a citizen in society. Digital Citizen participants deliberate and debate online which provides a better opportunity for engagement, mobilization and social inclusion.

There are some core principles of respect, education and protection in the promotion of digital citizenship. The problem of a digital divide emerges with uneven distribution in the access, use and impact of digital technologies between any number of distinct groups. The digital divide is differentiated on the grounds of age, wealth, access and type of technology; also, the factors of digital skills and media literacy affect the process of the internet divide. There are digital divides based on worldwide broadband availability across countries on the globe with people living in nations with limited access as disadvantaged groups. Digital media platforms also function as a vehicle for the plurality of viewpoints and multiplicity of voices allowing citizens to participate, offer criticism and become informed citizens. It encourages the free flow of discussions on a wide range of topics and catalyzes open and well-informed dialogue.

FIGURE 9.1 Early digital exposure.
Source: Mamchenkov, L. (2007). What Is That? Retrieved from https://www.flickr.com/photos/mamchenkov/371926413/

Citizen journalism, also known as public journalism, guerrilla journalism or street journalism, has become an alternative mode of news gathering and reporting with its relation to the political and public sphere. There are several good examples of citizen journalism reporting on major world events such as the 2013 protests in Turkey, the 2010 earthquake in Haiti and the Syrian civil war. This poses a huge challenge to the professional and institutionalized practices of mainstream media.

Citizen journalism acts as a critical voice reporting the events from the grass-roots level and less influenced by the logic of economics. This form of citizen journalism varies from classical journalism where information does not remain the sole prerogative of the journalists. Instead, citizens without much professional training perform the role of journalists with information based on primary sources. Terms such as hyperlocal journalism, actualizing citizens and liquid citizenship are also used to describe the interactions and experiences that individuals face to become citizen journalists. The position of being always on the receiving end as an audience has now been reinvented, and it has changed the journalistic spectrum of citizen reporting and analysis, making the profession of journalism as a distributed community

9.2.1 Journalistic transformation

The transformation of the journalistic profession from traditional journalism to citizen journalism has also led to innovations in journalism rewarding novel efforts to involve citizens. Traditional news outlets have submerged into technology convergence, with major media institutions combining print, video and social media in their reporting process.

The information-production process and its dissemination to the masses, once the professional authority of the journalists, has been altered with the entry of citizen journalists. Earlier journalists exercised the collective power of interpretive community and were united through their collective interpretation of the key events which ultimately influenced constructions of reality. But these conceived authorities of institutional power of press expertise, knowledge and exclusive access to information now have informal players in the form of bloggers and other social media journalists, also known as citizen journalists. Apart from the mainstream media, the capacity of cyber-news room has grown in importance and transparency, and citizen journalism has become a major contributor for construing facts and perspectives on a diverse range of issues, events and ideas surrounding our socio-political environment.

If journalists from mainstream media are reporting certain events, citizen journalists also write on the same issues with professional etiquette and their stories are also listened by the people as truths. Though citizen journalism has not gained the same authority, they are certainly becoming a part of the news production community. In 1999 Peter Merholz coined the term "Blog" to describe the action of publishing one's personal thoughts, commentary, essays and links online. This entry of blogs has certainly influenced and lowered the barriers to entry as a journalist, which has raised significant concerns about the practice and image of the journalistic profession.

Developments in the field of technology are continuing to transform journalism with the growing popularity of social and digital media. Though there are many dark areas of standards of accuracy, credibility and transparency which can't be strictly enforced, it is clear that traditional values of journalism require more professionalism than before.

THINK BOX

- Describe critically the concept of digital media citizenship.
- Is citizen journalism the future of journalism?

9.3 Media psychology and pedagogy

Pedagogy is often described as the approach to teaching and learning. It refers to the processes of learning and teaching and the study of how knowledge and skills are imparted in an educational context. The beginning of pedagogy philosophy is attributed to Johann Friedrich (1776–1841) who highlighted the five steps of preparation, presentation, association, generalization and application crucial for the teaching process. Critical pedagogy is aimed at the transmission of norms, values and beliefs which can have cognitive, emotional and environmental impacts in the development of a worldview.

9.3.1 Pedagogical differences of media

The epistemological positions and goals of learning guide the design of teaching and selection of appropriate media as different media have the variable potential for learning outcomes. Important considerations that should be taken into account while deciding what media to use include content, structure and skills. Olson and Bruner (1974) claim that learning involves two distinct aspects: acquiring knowledge of facts, principles, ideas, concepts, events, relationships, rules and laws; and using or working on that knowledge to develop skills.

Mass media also differs in the extent to which they can represent various kinds of content as they vary in symbols systems (text, sound images) used to encode information (Salomon, 1979). The differences between media are determined in the way they combine symbol systems. The ideas and concepts understood by people are often the result of the integration of content acquired from various media sources. The impact of media in their ability to handle concrete or abstract knowledge also differs a lot with the media design differences

The pedagogical affordances (perceived possibility of an object in relation to its environment) of a medium depend on the subjective interpretation of the user rather than the presentation of the concepts. The advantages of pedagogical practices to be effective require an understanding of the needs of the students, the nature of their subject area and pedagogical features of the medium. Mass media choices have multiplied in recent years, and multiple mediated instructional methods have enriched instructional environments. The fundamental problem – a problem of ideological hues – is who chooses the contents of a syllabus for the students.

E-learning allows opportunity for connecting with people residing in remote corners. The main benefit of this digital resource is its greater flexibility of access, reproduction and manipulation. Task analysis, accounting and computing power is the advantage of digital tools. Online platforms can provide vast amounts of information in a very short span of time. They operate on the principle of rule-based learning like producing products in factories. For example, algorithmic approaches involve the application of given procedures and rules in a defined ways to find a solution.

Salmon's (2004) incredibly popular e-learning model prescribes five stages: access and motivation, online socialization, information exchange, knowledge construction and development. Digital natives are used to receiving information really fast. They like to parallel process and to multitask. They prefer random access and thrive on instant gratification. They prefer games to serious work.

Digital consumerism encourages proliferation of e-learning to a large number of students considering them as consumers. The large number of e-learning corporations invade people's privacy, manipulating politics and creating false needs in the society. Digital consumerism is used to influence consumer behavior, leading to the destruction of psychic and collective individuation. E-learning advertising attempts to equate the social with the material by utilizing images and slogans of philanthropy. In fact advertising images falsely propagate that the control lies with the consumer when they actually disempower and objectify the consumer. The power of technology helps in monopolization of mental space and creates a huge market.

E-learning materials also lead to quantification and homogenization. E-course books being prepared by the government will lead to a state of monopoly on education contents as no government can be politically neutral. The fundamental problem – a problem of political nature and colored by ideological hues – is who chooses the content and on whose behalf the choosers' teaching will be performed – in favor of whom, against whom, in favor of what, against what.

What is the role of education in the programmatic organization of content? Neither justice nor learning is promoted by the e-learning model because educators insist on packaging instructions with certification. Certification constitutes a form of market manipulation and is plausible only to the schooled mind. Once people have the idea schooled into them of mechanical transfer of knowledge, they tend to accept all kinds of rankings. There is a scale for the development of nations, another for intelligence of babies, even progress toward peace can be calculated according to body count. In a schooled world, the road to happiness is being paved with the consumer index. The latest is the example of colleges and university rankings. This tendency of e-learning material production looks like any other modern staple. It is a bundle of planned meanings, a package of values, a commodity whose balanced appeal makes it marketable to a large number of students to justify the cost of production. Consumer pupils are taught to make the desires conform to marketable values. Hence, colleges and institutions of eminence with high rankings talk of pay packages they provide to their students, not the quality and social contribution of such individuals.

Commitments to unlimited quantitative increase vitiates the possibility of organic development. A world of ever-rising demands is not just evil – it can be spoken of only as Hell. A whole society is initiated into the myth of unending consumption.

Daniel Bell argues that our epoch is characterized by extreme disjunction between cultural and social structures, the one being devoted to apocalyptic attitudes the other to technocratic decision-making. The growing risk of health caused by excessive use of electronic devices is posing health threats to the user. Intense staring at screens for long leads to tiredness and difficulty in sleep patterns.

Furthermore, online classes often restrain students from getting the appropriate stimulation required for holistic development. In such a scenario, their social and emotional development might get affected due to lack of exposure to real classroom teaching learning experiences. The students might experience lack of emotional bonding with fellow students, and the teachers also cannot provide adequate social and emotional support. This can result in increased problems related to the mental health of students. There is high probability of psychological issues like anxiety, stress and depression due to increased social isolation and decreased connectivity with the real world. The increased dependence on the virtual world, which somehow is also getting promoted by the current settings of online classes, is also causing more stress by increasing the learning burden on students, especially those with special needs and those from the marginalized sections of the society with fewer opportunities for access to resources for e-learning.

The whole range of extracurricular activities, an integral aspect of multiple intelligence, is also ignored by online learning. The current global market for e-learning has reached approximately US$107 billion and Indian online learning business was US$2 billion in 2016 and was expected to reach US$6 billion by 2020 (White paper on digital learning www.technopark.com, 2016). Educomp, Vedantu, My Private Tutor, NIIT, Meritnation, Byju's are some of the leading players of digital education in India. E-learning can cause social isolation, and prevention of cheating during online assessment is complicated.

9.3.1.1 Classroom teaching

In the area of literacy, reading of the world is more necessary than reading of the word provided by the progressive teachers in the classroom. In the classroom situation, learning is contingent to emergent reality, and students take responsibility for their learning. Piaget and Vygotsky highlighted the learners search for meaning is acquired through active and personal experimentation. Role learning, reflection, interaction and social contexts are key constituents of classroom model as most of the learning are situated in contexts.

Barab and Duffy (2000) highlighted the importance of context-dependent learning in which efforts are made to make the learning activity authentic to social context. According to Bandura's vicarious learning approach, a great deal of learning is situated which can be understood at the social-anthropological level, in which the need to learn is desired in the form of participation in a wider community through joint engagement. Another important aspect places high value on the identification with learner groups. Associative, constructive and situative learning theories provided focus on the importance of presence of other people, emphasizing the value of collaboration. The intrinsic advantage of classroom teaching involve inculcation of morality, values, social roles, ideological orientation and identity. Classroom teachers are committed to a wide range of facilitative skills of negotiating with diversity in collaborative context.

Learning is not mechanically printed letters but a space or opportunity to be performed, emerging from the interactions of teachers and students as a form of artistry. That is why we have dozens of societies in colleges ranging from debate, cultural, dramatic, dance and sports, to name a few. Learning also is not a procedural rule-based learning. Rather, it requires learners exposure and participation to events or incidents of real-life situations. Students learn to respect gender sensitivity through co-existence of boys and girls in the classrooms. They also learn team spirit and participate in social issues through fieldwork by visiting marginalized areas and NGOs. They become good leaders in the society through leadership skills they learn acting as member and heads of such societies. Many students enumerating their life journey describe participation in college societies as a turning point of success in their lives.

Kolb's learning cycle, probably one of the best-known experiential models (Kolb, 1984), presented an action-based learning-by-doing approach. He prescribed a four-stage cycle comprising of experience reflection, abstraction and experimentation.

College/university students staying in hostels and playing in playgrounds are engaged in authentic learnings of exploration and enquiry and have opportunities for social and political discourse. They also learn mediating capacity in case of intergroup rivalry among student groups, particularly at the time of union elations. Needless to say, with the lack of face-to-face communication so many students do not share their problems with their parents, particularly their relationships. Good teachers play a supportive role to overcome emotional turbulence very essential for growth and development of personality. College friends become lifelong friends, a great moral support for a person's lifetime. Alumni networks also help juniors of the colleges, promoting prosocial behavior and altruism aspects.

Technology cannot inculcate ethical practices required for shaping the all-round qualities of youth considered as bedrock for the future of a nation.

The education system, curriculum and disciplinary practices textbook selection are not neutral spaces, and decisions regarding these processes are deliberated and determined by the political system. Bloom's taxonomy of educational objectives was a product of a series of conferences from 1949 to 1953, the first *Handbook of Cognitive Domain* was published in 1956, the *Handbook of Affective Domain* was published in 1964 and a revised taxonomy for the cognitive domain was published in 2001. Bloom's taxonomy of educational system highlighted the importance of cognitive and emotional aspects necessary for the future development of students.

A large number of our population is without a critical understanding of how society functions, not because they are inherently incapable of it, but on account of precarious teaching-learning contexts which they are provided. Progressive pedagogy methods must focus upon the factors through which students' curiosity is nurtured and they become investigators in the ongoing quest for the revelation of the "why" of things and facts of the world.

Pedagogy practices expose the subjects to the objects to be taught, which is mediated through digital techniques. The role of students in choosing the content, a necessary and democratic way of dealing with the content, is largely missing from the popular concepts of education mediated through the digital landscape. Mass education provided through internet-enabled techniques does not permit much of the diversity necessary for critical awareness. Training and transfer of knowledge provided through technological support do not provide us with our understanding as ourselves as historical, political, social and cultural beings. A critical understanding of the technology-related knowledge transfer is required to know about its language, its dialectical relationship with thought and the world without either demonizing it or divinizing it.

The technology-dominated education system has created a dominant class – its class culture, its class semantics, its syntax, its dreams and natures which produce popular knowledge and popular culture restricting the growth of cultural pluralism. Effective pedagogical practices should have the ability to create multiculturality, not as a simple juxtaposition of cultures but a pluralism consisting of the realization of freedom, fearlessness of being different and involving the co-existence of different cultures.

In the pedagogical practice of digital technology, reality and fantasy distinctions are blurred as expressions of reality may be distorted due to mechanistic presentations. Dominant elites who have control over the media try to conform to the masses of their objectives. Through manipulation of priorities, dominant elites can lead people in a false perception of priorities for achieving populist desires.

9.3.2 Digital impact on language

With the advent of digital pedagogy, the tradition of written culture has undergone serious changes. Written culture depends strongly upon specific conventions of vocabulary and grammar with due care paid to spellings. However, this culture is being challenged in several ways, which involves a general shift towards linguistic informality. The written theories and philosophies encouraged readers to argue, reflect and critique other people's thoughts which also challenged received truths. The digital practices of anytime and anywhere have set the stage for modern life on the clock obsessed with time and speed. Flooding of messages in the digital and internet mode with a vast magnitude of written material at our fingertips but how to craft it to the best use needs careful attention. In the words of Norwegian sociologist Thomas Eriksen:

> If [email] more or less entirely replaced the old-fashioned letter, the culture as a whole will end up with a deficit, it will have lost in quality whatever it has gained in quantity.
>
> (Eriksen, 2001)

9.3.3 Media literacy education

Media, through its various networks of newspapers, television and the internet, produces a socio-cultural and academic function of enhancing communication. Media literacy skills can help students create and interpret media content to their advantage. It also helps students to gather various sources of information and develop a readiness to express one's views and attitudes through interaction with the media. It can help students take independent and informed decisions about themselves and learn about the world around them.

FIGURE 9.2 Media literacy sources.
Source: Retrieved 21 June 2020 from https://pixabay.com/vectors/media-literacy-technology-4168719/

Media and information play a central role in shaping perceptions, beliefs and attitudes of the youth. Media also helps to dismantle stereotypes through counter-experiences available from different forms of media. Digital games are not only an entertainment activity but it has also educational and psychological benefits for the users. Children learn patience and problem-solving skills where digital games work as enablers of learning.

Media education promotes cooperation and collaboration among large number of users and learning from the experiences of large sections of people across the globe. The e-library provides students with scope for consultation to a large number of books and materials, reducing the sole dependence on teachers. A variety of media content is available for teaching and learning, and its choice should be determined by the teaching philosophy and skills that need to be developed in learners.

9.3.4 Digital research and online interviewing

In the verbal and face-to-face interview, data collection takes too much time, and transcribing the data is a lengthy exercise. It is also difficult for the interviewer to take samples from distant geographical regions and from different countries. In the method of online interviews, the interviewer gets in touch with the participant in a chatroom and asks questions relevant to the research topic.

Sometimes online interviews are also conducted by sending questions through email, and the participant's response is received after some duration of time limits. It is also important in online interviews to have rapport formation before starting the actual process of interview. In the internet-mediated interviews, other basic factors of conducting good research such as the purpose of the interview, knowledge of the participants, and the external context of the research should be explained well in advance.

Although non-verbal and para-linguistic components of communication are missing in this mode, this is a widely used technique by researchers all over the world.

9.3.5 Cyber ethnography

Cyber ethnography is the online research method for the study of communities and cultures through internet-mediated interaction. Ethnography (software) was developed by US sociologist John Seidel and launched in 1985 by Qualis Research Associates for storing, retrieving and organizing data.

Ethnography is the study and systematic recording of human cultures. It is a detailed and in-depth description of a group, community or culture. Ethnography is also referred to as "thick description", a term coined by anthropologist Clifford Geertz (1966). Ethnographers try to develop an understanding of culture through "Emic", or insider point of view, and "Etic", or external social scientific perspective of reality.

Bronislaw Malinowski (1922) is considered a founding father of ethnographic fieldwork, which is considered as a reflexive process of knowing about social, cultural, historical aspects of a culture or community. Ethnographers look for exploring meanings of symbols which also evokes powerful feelings and thoughts. For example, the swastika is considered a condensed expression of the Nazi movement. Methods and techniques used by ethnographers include interviewing, participant observation, equipment (tape recorder, computer), analysis and report writing.

Ethnographers conduct the study by exploring daily life activities of the people in normal settings and attempt to discern life cycles and cultural themes. Ethnomethodology developed during the 1960s with Harold Garfinkel's studies of the "taken for granted" assumptions used by the people. Ethnomethodology studies are conducted either through observations or indirectly by audio-video recordings.

Cyber ethnography is also known as Netnography which is the application of ethnographic methods to online fieldwork research conducted by sociologists, psychologists, anthropologists and other researchers. Most of the activities performed online are studied by cyber ethnographers and expressed in the form of signs and texts. Cyber ethnographers also participate online to understand the meaning of behavior in a culture or community. Virtual ethnography can't replicate the ethnography in letter and spirit, owing to certain differences of intense engagement, spatial and temporal differences, but web page interaction is also an extension of lived realities. Markham (2004) suggests that the internet can also be considered as a milieu or culture in which people develop specific forms of communication and specific identities.

Kendall (1998) has suggested that online participants' sense of self is reflected after observing their online activities for significant periods. Virtual communities are social aggregations that emerge from the Net when enough people carry on those public dimensions long enough, with sufficient human feeling to form webs of personal relationships in cyberspace (Rheingold, 1993, p. 5).

Virtual ethnography can't be a true substitute for ethnography as so many important aspects studied and observed in reality situations can't be recorded in it. To develop a comprehensive ethnography of the virtual, it will be desirable to record the real-life activities through some links beyond computer and internet use.

Virtual ethnography can provide some clues regarding linguistic and interactive patterns. There are also issues related to ethics of privacy in cyberspace and the anonymity of the participants, and these dilemmas are ill-defined.

THINK BOX

- Using examples demonstrate how media can be used to improve pedagogical practices?
- How can digital research help in the process of research?

9.4 Digital storytelling and narrating transportation

In the words of Immanuel Kant, science is organized knowledge and wisdom is organized life. The significance of storytelling is also described in lines from Muriel Rukeyser's poem "The Speed of Darkness". The universe is made of stories, not atoms. Our comprehension of the world consisting of cognitive, affective, perceptual, imaginary, existential and phenomenal experiences can be understood as being composed of stories.

Narrative inquiry is a form of qualitative research that takes the story as data for knowing and making sense of reality. Narratives incorporate everyday activities, the social context through its protagonist, the narrator, and make a coherent story. The help of constructions and reconstructions of life events, when told to others, may also influence how others see the storyteller. Various methodological studies incorporate narrative research, and important among them are socio-cultural, naturalist and literary. The socio-cultural stance looks at the cultural narratives that influence the individual experience. The naturalist stance focuses more on specific descriptions of the content of people's stories about significant issues. The literary stance is more concerned with the mode of discourse such as images, rhetorics and metaphors used by the narrator. The narrative method of data collection is considered a process of negotiated interaction and co-construction between the researcher and the participant both responsible for the emergence of the story.

FIGURE 9.3   Digital tools for narrative transportation.
Source: https://pixabay.com/photos/computer-laptop-work-place-mouse-2982270/

9.4.1 Digital storytelling

Digital storytelling employs auditory and visual methods of storytelling, which can be less inhibited and more spontaneous and can account for individual experiences. Narrative data analysis preserves the individual's voice, connecting them to events, the passage of time and individual intentions. Digital storytelling is the art of telling stories with a mix of digital media combined with graphics, video and music to provide information on a specific subject. Educators use the storytelling techniques with good use of technology such as video, a podcast or slide show to represent an idea or a concept.

During a short period, large amounts of information can be transmitted to the students. Barone (1992, p. 143) describes storytelling as an artful practice which "eschews formal theory" (of either the scientific or philosophical type) and "systematic method". Haraway (1989, p. 4) demonstrates how closely fact and fiction can be related in her description of biology as a narrative practice. Biology is the fiction appropriate to objects called organisms. Biology fashions the facts discovered from organic beings. Organisms perform for the biologist, who transforms that performance into a truth attested by disciplined experience, i.e. into a fact, the jointly accomplished deed or feat of the scientist and the organism. Both scientists and the organism are actors in a storytelling practice.

Digital science of technology-mediated communication and popular culture are intricately woven of facts and fiction. Fabricated versions of stories are presented to the people who are imagined as facts, appealing in form. Technological practices of digital media may be considered a kind of storytelling practice embedded with metaphors of progress and speculative fiction. Storytelling is a complex production with many tellers and listeners, not all of them visible or perceptible.

The art of storytelling represented through digital media masks the fictitious aspects when told synthetically. Commercial things are easily woven with educational values in an aesthetic way of stories which are well absorbed by the audiences. Through the use of digital storytelling, entertainment is interwoven with technology where users of stories participate, which gradually turns into popular culture.

Every story has combined features of reality, reflexivity, criticality and deconstruction. So many fictions are presented as facts in the form of stories through media. Television imagery can be used and reconstituted to bring desired changes in the behavior and perception of the audience.

9.4.2 Narrative transportation

The experience of a person being placed and immersed into the world of story (narrative) is called narrative transportation. Narrative transportation theory proposes inquiring about the individual's experience through narratives including three-dimensional factors of place, temporality and social context.

Herman (1995) described the narrative in the following way:

> First, the initial situation is outlined ("how everything started") then the events relevant to the narrative are selected from the whole host of experiences and presented as a coherent progression of events ("how things developed") and finally the situation at the end of the development is presented ("what become"). The persuasive experience of being transported into the world of the story is known as narrative transportation.

Narrative transportation occurs by viewers or readers feeling engrossed in the story characters and the plot which affects their affective and cognitive states by being transported into the story world and narratives. Narrative persuasion, done through mass media, is influenced by the factors of content and use of literary devices of emotional connectivity with the audience. Narrative transportation with the articulation of languages are capable of constructing reality for the audiences. People's attitudes and beliefs are modified with the effective use of narratives having profound persuasion effects. Narratologists often distinguish two important aspects of narrativity, known as content and discourse.

Narrative transportation is also influenced by the flow and immersion with the characters of the story. Identification with the characters of the story affects the process of transportation. Other psychological factors of empathy and mental imagery also help the receiver to strongly relate with the story.

FIGURE 9.4 Literary mode of narrative transportation.
Source: https://pixabay.com/photos/library-sky-birds-mystical-clouds-425730/

THINK BOX

- In your views, what does it mean to be media literate?
- Explain the different views of understanding media literacy.

9.5 Moving images: meanings and myths

Moving images takes us to places and ideas through visual displays, and sound provides shape to our imagined or perceived worlds. The moving images of cinema and other forms of visual production invite its viewers to engage cognitively and emotionally to the visual narrative. There are various degrees of affective associations that viewers occupy through these moving images. Visual moving images are more attractive when sounds, images and words are able to connect to the viewer's sentiments, affects and the imagination pervading everyday lives.

Moving images in this era of digital technology are reshaping the identities of people at individual and group levels, and our perception of the world is strongly influenced by this process. The moving image of cinematic production creates "us" and "them" in the portrayal of different cultural groups representing ethnographic impulse. Through the moving images, meanings can be altered to myths through subjectivizing objectivity, and real can be molded to unreal. The digital habit of people has seen a sharp increase in the tendency toward photography, and people have turned into image collectors.

Cinema, like every artistic medium, is also a social and economic process in which people collaborate to produce cinematic images and texts. Movies in the movie theatres and other modes of digital platforms have been used to gather people together for a viewing of commercial and artistically creative works for recreation. For Henri Bergson (1907), the concept of "[c]inematographical apparatus" "movement is reality itself", the movement through projecting apparatus of cinema intellect is represented spatially and temporally where the film functions the same as an intellect to create mechanistic reality. Gilles Deleuze (1990) described frames and continuity of images within a frame (sets, props, colors and implicit sounds) to create a world beyond the frame. He also described the concepts of shot and montage adding to the phenomena of movement which puts the cinematographic image into a relationship with the whole. He even provided a taxonomy of moving images, also known as cinesemiotic, which included perception image, affection image, action image and mental image, expanding the taxonomic concepts of Bergson and Peirce. Deleuze described the concept of cineosis, explaining that film is made up of multiple movements. Images are a dominant point of view of the whole film.

9.5.1 Authenticity in moving images

That authenticity of the same art expression depends upon identifying the original author is a measure of the degree to which an artist's work is committed to personal expression. The authenticity of expression is linked to the artist's background beliefs, ideals and traditions. In the moving images, a work of fiction is used to create verisimilitude to convince the audience that what is being presented is factual.

9.5.2 The geomorphology of the visible

Films create worlds through its territoriality distributed across the world constituting and affecting our day-to-day perceptions and understandings of the world. Our everyday geographies are influenced by our ability to explore the space around us, including domestic space and public space, and we learn to spatialize and distinguish between public and private, ours and theirs.

One of the things that cinema does is geomorphing, territorializing the everyday issues through decorative illustrations and images and creating reference points in our daily lives of connecting things from the real world to the iconic world of cinema. The world presented through moving images may be stylized, theatrical, surrealist, poetic or fantastic, and narratives used may be fictional or non-fictional drawing, mobilizing the attention of its viewers on the subjects represented by them. The affective machinery of cinema changes the landscape of the places, which adds meanings to our memory and expectations.

The science of cinema also provides a strong connection and integration to places, landscapes and regions distinct with each other through thematization and perceptual dramatization. Cinema mode of moving image representation smoothens the discrepancies of spectatorship immersed within the film through segmentation of scenes, sequence and episodes.

Cinema remakes natural from a material world, and films aim to produce two broader narratives. The first narrative is taken for a granted perspective which reassures its viewers of solutions for the problems, and the other narrative shows troubles and conflicts without offering a final resolution. But there is also a set of films whose narratives fall between these two, and a film's acceptance or rejection is also determined by the level of awareness of its viewers and cultural context.

Our ideas and beliefs are mediated and shaped by visual technologies of moving images. In this age of motion pictures and modern visuality, visual images have a profound impact on how we perceive the world. The reproduction of places and landscapes through visual media made these places more accessible and available as images which can circulate more rapidly and attract more to the perception of the masses. Photographers such as Carleton Watkins mastered this "monarch of all I survey" trope which framed elements to provide a three-dimensional effect of looking through a landscape. The use of "magisterial gaze" changes a place as an elevated position to be gazed at and admired for its sweeping beauty, hence to be possessed by its viewers.

What viewers retain through moving images is not divisible into categories of spectacle, narrative and meaning. Instead, it is the synthesized entirety in a condensed form that is retained as memorable. Moving images of cinema are a movement of thought, affect and image that is received in a combined fashion by the viewer.

Landscape aesthetics produces naturally through the effective use of technology and transforms the materials of abstraction to desirable notions of material meanings. A linear perspective is created by visuality constructed out of material, discursive and semiotic variables spread across cultural and geographical boundaries. Environmentalists all over the world use photographs and visuals as their chief tool to witness on behalf of the new scientific world news of ecology.

Cinema and moving images have a tremendous capacity to create greater voice in films through artificially created perspectives of technology.

9.5.3 Evolutionary perspective of helping

Evolutionary biologist Richard Dawkins (2006) in his classic book *The Selfish Gene*, highlighted that it is not the survival of the fittest individuals but the survival of the individual's genes as a more important aspect of helping behavior.

Hamilton's (1963, 1964) kin selection theory described that behavior can eventually become part of the common inheritance of the species. Hamilton's rule further highlighted that altruism will be more likely to evolve when the benefits to the recipient are high and the costs to the altruist are low. Kin selection provides a fundamental explanation for the high levels of altruism that are routinely observed between close kin in a vast variety of species. Cooperative genotypes can proliferate by interacting preferentially with cooperative phenotypes and r (coefficient of relatedness) can he further broadened to represent the probability that an altruism beneficiary has co-operative phenotype. Helping behaviors can be integrated at a mass level through effective use of technology.

9.6 Digital altruism

Millions of people are using digital technologies to help people in need with moral engagements and meta-cooperative efforts. The term "altruism" was first coined by August Comte and used to refer to others. The broad spectrum of digital altruism include activities of volunteerism related to charity to the poor people, health care facilities, pro-environment action programs, child care, educational upliftment of the disadvantaged and many such initiatives.

Digital altruism uses technological innovation techniques to support character strength virtues of gratitude, justice, forgiveness, hope and kindness. Creative digital altruism uses digital platform for cooperation in confronting issues that benefit humanity. World Community Grid, an IBM-sponsored philanthropic initiaive begun in November 2004, handles projects like "Fight AIDS @ Home", "Discovering Dengue Drugs" and "Help Conquer Cancer" at the global level. Other organizations such as the Bill and Melinda Gates Foundation and many websites support digital altruism activities of health care in India. Everyday portrayal of digital altruism may give rise to emergence of caring behavior among its users.

Digital altruism involves using digital technology to support the development of prosocial strengths and virtues. Every day there are numerous examples of people in India and abroad of helping others for larger social causes. Among the most common ways of collecting donations for charity are door-to-door collections, telemarketing and e-commerce based charity activities. The firefighters, policemen and ordinary citizens have done a great amount of work to help others in a variety of ways and to bring positive changes in the life of others. Such people include Daro Bilhore, who began a crusade to fill up every single pothole in Mumbai and have filled over 600 potholes, which can endanger the life of commoners.

The Roy Foundation in Bihar uses digital platform to help poor children's education and helping poor in Bihar. Several NGOs are working in the area of education, health citizens' rights, right to information, human rights, gender empowerment, women, children, persons with disabilities providing legal assistance, advocacy and capacity building.

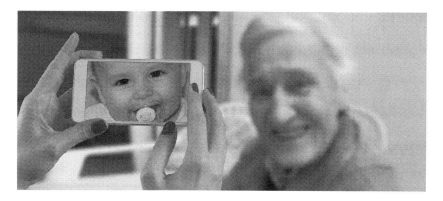

FIGURE 9.5 Displaying empathy.
Source: https://pixabay.com/photos/smartphone-face-woman-old-baby-1987212/

The Bill and Melinda Gates Foundation does a lot of philanthropy for improving people's health and well-being in India. Foundations are working to provide help for road accident victims as well as a supportive legal framework for bystanders to help the victims of road accidents. The Rockefeller Foundation has been helping scientists the world over in finding new ways to increase rice production.

There are thousands of stories when people help others and millions of stories when people do not help.

9.6.1 Reciprocal altruism

Reciprocal altruism is a behavior whereby an organism performs an altruistic action with the expectation that the other person will perform altruistic acts in return. The concept of reciprocal altruism was developed by Trivers (1971), which states that cooperation can evolve if interaction partners can engage in a mutually beneficial exchange of costly altruistic acts. Reciprocal altruism is different from mutualism, in which trusting partners benefit mutually via exchange and cooperation becomes individually adaptive.

The costly signaling theory developed by biologists Zahavi (1975, 1977) and Grafen (1990) describes that a costly trait of engagement in altruistic behavior can bring reputational benefits to the signaler and make him or her seem as a potential and more attractive to others as a social partner. Empathy plays a critical role in the process of altruism. Martin Hoffman (2000) suggests that altruism has two requirements, one affective and one cognitive.

According to C. Daniel Batson's (1991) empathy altruism hypothesis, if someone feels empathy towards another person, they will help them irrespective of the feel of what they gain from it. Neuroscience researches support the biological capacity for empathy and other factors of upbringing of offspring done cooperatively also play a critical role in the evolution of empathy.

A growing body of research indicates a positive relationship between helping others and feeling better. Helping others also reduces people's own distress and helps themselves recover from traumatic experiences.

THINK BOX

- Do you think that recent communication technologies are giving rise to new forms of altruism? Justify your answer with appropriate examples.
- What can be the possible consequences of digital altruism?

9.7 Indian perspective

With the expansion of media and social media platforms, so many marginal groups neglected by the mainstream media have been able to put forth their views at the macro level. So many social media platforms in India have become powerful voices through accurate and credible reporting of socio-political events. Several bloggers and online news platforms, with a significantly large number of followers, play important roles in influencing the political opinions of the people contributing to voting behavior in elections. People have become very much aware of their rights and in cases of deficiency or malpractices in the corridors of power, these events are highlighted in a big way, influencing the policies and decision-making of the governments. A lot of criticism of VIP culture has reduced the practice of "red tapism" and accountability of the persons highlighted through various media platforms. Some examples include the quality of midday meals, lack of facilities in railways, hospitals and airlines; they are frequently highlighted by Twitter and other social media platforms, forcing authorities to pursue corrective measures.

Absenteeism of teachers from classes, lack of medicines and timely intervention of doctors, inordinate delay in the issue of certificates, poor construction of roads and bridges, delay in the relief activity in case of natural disasters, delay in the filing of complaints at police stations and all such matters of public use are easily noticed and highlighted through social media putting pressure on the agencies to provide the remedial course of action. Use of RTI's (Right To Information) through emails, electronic tendering and e-ticketing have brought transparency to the system.

Similarly, many people holding high offices are easily captured for their misdeeds through spy cameras, and such news becoming viral necessitates disciplinary and legal action. In some of the glaring instances of injustice with growing social media complaints, the government of the day also takes suo motto cognizance and initiates corrective steps to improve the situation. Mass media narratives' presentation style also creates imaginary doubts and fears in people's minds through presentation of selective or distorted presentation of reality. In the past few years, the role of social media and fake videos circulated through social media platforms have created serious law-and-order problems in various parts of the country. Unverified news reports and doctored videos comprising elements of religious animosity are potential sources of conflict among the citizens. Banning of the internet is an effective control mechanism to stop happenings of any untoward incidents in tense situations.

Digital altruism is a new area which has revolutionized the thinking, outlook and prosocial activities of the Indian people. Several individuals and groups are providing a good deal of support to the people in need by helping them through internet connection centers of help. So many good works are being carried out in the field of organic farming, agriculture, providing food to the hungry providing legal justice to the underprivileged, and health facilities at door through effective use of digital technologies.

This growing landscape of internet and cyberspace is a complex world of possibilities and challenges, and how far it becomes advantageous to us depends upon our media literacy and our ability to harness its potential in the right direction. Just handling it, and treating this new advancement which is a reality at present and future times, in a binary of good or bad, will not be an appropriate way to approach this emergent reality. A lot of human creativity, positivity, enlargement of human potential philanthropy, peace, educational and economic upliftment can be achieved through proper use of this world of internet and digital technologies.

9.8 Summary

Mass media in the contemporary world has acquired crucial importance owing to its ability to influence socio-political, cultural and economic dimensions of society. The impact of mass media to persuade the masses can lead to changes in attitudes and expand the horizons of thought. Mass media can change the mindset and people's behavior through shifting patterns of media citizenship. The concept of alternate media provides a platform to the people who are not represented through mainstream media. Local groups and marginal groups get an opportunity to express their viewpoints through direct participation.

Digital media citizenship allows people to use the internet in order to engage in society, politics and government. Digital citizens get a primary framework to use information technology for empowerment and enlargement of democratic goals. Dynamic citizen participation through digital platforms allows possibilities for social inclusion, citizen-powered democracy and civil engagement. Social media platforms allow people to function as citizen journalists and help to lower the barriers to entry for participation as a citizen within society. Nowadays, more young people are turning to websites such as Snapchat, Instagram and YouTube. The range of activities undertaken through digital media platforms includes digital education, commerce and entertainment. Students and youth can align collectively through texting and tweeting to react on issues of social and environmental importance.

The technology can play a crucial role in achieving goals of the teaching-learning process. Cyber ethnography is an online research method for the study of communities and culture. Digital storytelling is a powerful technique to represent an idea or concept to educate the masses.

Narrative transportation helps viewers to be transported into a world of stories and narratives. Moving images are visual displays and sound which can provide shape to our perceived world. With the use of technology, cinematic production of moving images can create a world of fiction as factual and authentic.

Digital altruism has the vast potential to improve humanity from many different types of evils that we face. People can involve a large number of volunteers at no cost by raising awareness through digital media. Helping behaviors and health care programs can receive wider awareness through the effective use of digital technology. Varying types of discrimination and social evils can be easily overcome with wider awareness programs through the digital initiative. Even in India, the Right To Information (RTI) has brought greater transparency and accountability in the system.

It can be concluded that the vast network of the internet is full of possibilities, and its utilization in the right direction can become a turning point in our socio-economic and cultural improvements.

Key points

- Alternative media is a platform to highlight issues and concerns not provided due attention from mainstream media.
- Digital media citizenship refers to the responsible use of technology by anyone who uses computers, internet or digital devices to engage with society at any level.
- Communication etiquettes to be followed by internet users are known as Netiquettes.
- Citizen journalism is an alternative mode of journalism by the common citizens of news gathering and reporting in public sphere.
- Pedagogy is described as the approach to teaching and learning.
- Cyber ethnography is the online research method for the study of communities and cultures through internet-mediated interaction.
- Ethnography is the study and systematic recording of cultures.
- Digital storytelling is storytelling through auditory and visual methods.
- Narrative transportation is the individual's experience through narrative.
- Digital altruism is an act of helping others through internet-mediated platforms.

Key terms

media citizenship, citizen journalism, pedagogy, ethnography, cyber ethnography, digital story-telling, magisterial gaze, digital altruism, reciprocal altruism, bystander effect

References

Barab, S.A., & Duffy, T. (2000). From practice fields to communities of practice. In D. Jonassen & S.M. Land (Eds.), *Theoretical Foundations of Learning Environments* (pp. 25–56). Mahwah, NJ: Lawrence Erlbaum Associates, Inc.

Barone, T.E. (1992). Beyond theory and method: A case of critical storytelling. *Theory into Practice*, 31(2), 142–6.

Batson, C.D. (1991). *The Altruism Question: Toward a Social Psychological Answer*. Hillsdale, NJ: Erlbaum.

Bergson, H. (1907). *Creative Evolution* (A. Mitchell, Trans.). Paris: Presses Universitaires Françaises.

Dawkins, R. (2006). *The Selfish Gene: 30th Anniversary Edition* (3rd ed.). Oxford, UK: Oxford University Press.

Deleuze, G. (1990). *Logic of Sense* (C.V. Boundas, Ed.; M. Lester, Trans. with C. Stivale). New York: Columbia University Press. (Original French ed., 1969)

Eriksen, T.H. (2001). *Tyranny of the Moment: Fast and Slow Time in the Information Age*. London: Pluto Press.

Geertz, C. (1966). Religion as a cultural system. In M. Banton (Ed.), *Anthropological Approaches to the Study of Religion* (pp. 1–46). London: Tavistock.

Grafen, A. (1990). Biological signals as handicaps. *Journal of Theoretical Biology*, 144, 517–46.

Habermas, J. (1970). *Technology and science as ideology. In Toward a Rational Society* (J. Shapiro, Trans.). Boston, MA: Beacon Press.

Hamilton, W.D. (1963). The evolution of altruistic behavior. *The American Naturalist*, 97, 354–6.

Hamilton, W.D. (1964). The genetical evolution of social behavior. *Journal of Theoretical Biology*, 7(1), 1–52.

Haraway, D. (1989). *Primate Visions: Gender, Race, and Nature in the World of Modern Science*. New York: Routledge & Kegan Paul.

Hoffman, M.L. (2000). *Empathy and Moral Development: Implications for Caring and Justice*. Cambridge, UK: Cambridge University Press.

Kendall, L. (1998). Meaning and identity in "cyberspace": The performance of gender, class, and race online. *Symbolic Interaction*, 21(2), 129–53.

Kolb, D.A. (1984). *Experiential Learning: Experience as the Source of Learning and Development* (Vol. 1). Englewood Cliffs, NJ: Prentice-Hall.

Malinowski, B. (1922). *Argonauts of the Western Pacific*. London: Routledge & Kegan Paul, Ltd.

Markham, A. (2004). Internet communication as a tool for qualitative research. In D. Silverman (Ed.). *Qualitative Research: Theory, Method, and Practices* (2nd ed., pp. 95–124). London: Sage.

Olson, D., & Bruner, J. (1974). Learning through experience and learning through media. In D. Olson (Ed.), *Media and Symbols: The Forms of Expression, Communication, and Education* (73rd Yearbook of the NSSE). Chicago, IL: University of Chicago Press.

Rheingold, H. (1993). *The Virtual Community: Homesteading on the Electronic Frontier*. Reading, MA: Addison-Wesley.

Rodríguez, C. (2011). *Citizens' Media against Armed Conflict: Disrupting Violence in Colombia*. Minneapolis, MN: University of Minnesota Press.

Salmon, G. (2004). *E-Moderating: The Key to Teaching and Learning Online* (2nd ed.). London: Taylor & Francis.

Salomon, G. (1979). Media and symbol systems as related to cognition and learning. *Journal of Educational Psychology*, 71(2), 131–48.

Trivers, R. (1971). The evolution of reciprocal altruism. *Quarterly Journal of Biology*, 46(1), 35–57.

Zahavi, A. (1975). Mate selection – A selection for a handicap. *Journal of Theoretical Biology*, 53, 205–14.

Zahavi, A. (1977). Reliability in communication systems and the evolution of altruism. In B. Stonehouse & C.M. Perrins (Eds.), *Evolutionary Ecology* (pp. 253–9). London: Palgrave.

INDEX